MW00764165

Rum and Axes

A volume in the series
Anthropology of Contemporary Issues
Edited by Roger Sanjek

Rum and Axes

The Rise
of a Connecticut
Merchant Family,
1795–1850

JANET SISKIND

Cornell University Press Ithaca & London

Portions of Chapters 5 and 6 appeared in *Medical Anthropology Quarterly* 2:199–214, 1988, and *Dialectical Anthropology* 16:35–48, 1991.

First published 2002 by Cornell University Press

Printed in the United States of America

Library of Congress Cataloging-in-Publication Data

Siskind, Janet.

 Rum and axes : the rise of a Connecticut merchant family, 1795–1850 / Janet Siskind.

  p. cm. — (Anthropology of contemporary issues)

  Includes bibliographical references and index.

  ISBN 0-8014-3932-9 (cloth : alk. paper)

  1. Connecticut—Commerce—History. 2. Merchants—Connecticut.

 I. Title. II. Series.

 HF3161.C7 S57 2001

 381′.09746—dc21   2001002720

Cornell University Press strives to use environmentally responsible suppliers and materials to the fullest extent possible in the publishing of its books. Such materials include vegetable-based, low-VOC inks and acid-free papers that are recycled, totally chlorine-free, or partly composed of nonwood fibers. Books that bear the logo of the FSC (Forest Stewardship Council) use paper taken from forests that have been inspected and certified as meeting the highest standards for environmental and social responsibility. For further information, visit our website at www.cornellpress.cornell.edu.

Cloth printing 10 9 8 7 6 5 4 3 2 1

FOR EMILY, JAKE, AND NICOLE

Contents

Acknowledgments

I am indebted to many people who assisted me in numerous ways, ranging from friendly concern to careful criticism, as I worked on this book. Specifically, I am grateful to Ralph Klein for his enduring encouragement and critical reading of innumerable drafts. I owe Timothy Coogan a particular debt of gratitude for his guidance along the path of historical research.

Others, who read the manuscript and gave timely and generous critiques, are Charles Tilly, Robert Paynter, Jonathan Prude, and Cornell University Press's friendly editors Fran Benson and Roger Sanjek. Karen Bosc, Bettina Drew, and Ange Romeo-Hall helped to straighten out the prose, and my fellow members of the Cultural Pluralism Seminar provided intellectual stimulation as well as a supportive audience for a major chapter.

While innumerable archivists and librarians make this kind of research possible, I especially thank Alesandra Schmidt Woodhouse and Jeffrey Kaimowitz of The Watkinson Library, Trinity College; Judith Johnson and Ruth Blair at The Connecticut Historical Society; and the late Elizabeth Swaim of Wesleyan University Library, Special Collections and Archives, for their invaluable, shared expertise.

A grant from the Early American Industries Association and a Faculty Research Grant from the Research Council of Rutgers University helped to defray some of the costs of research. Rutgers University's award of a sabbatical leave gave a valuable opportunity for uninterrupted writing.

Friends have been essential to this long process of work, and I am, therefore, extremely grateful to Anne-Marie Cantwell, Françoise Dussart, Frances Rothstein, Marjorie Baron, Robin Moore, David Singer, Stephanie Griffin, Claudia Leslie, Kaarli Tasso, and Pamela Wardwell.

Rum and Axes

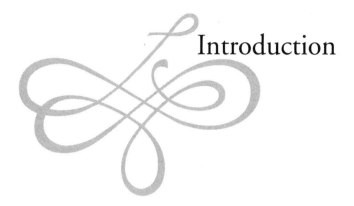

Introduction

In New England, the beginnings of capitalist industrialization initiated a new relationship between owners and workers, simultaneously engaging and divisive, which would profoundly shape American understandings of work and community. This narrative of a family, the Watkinsons and their nephews, the Collinses, in the years 1795 to 1850, presents a close-up of the process by which New England's merchants amassed the capital to become industrial entrepreneurs, organized factories and private corporations, and, as regionally emergent upper classes, took on the hegemonic task of constructing philanthropic and cultural institutions. Who they were and how their "work" in organizing and maintaining their enterprises shaped who they became provide the focus of this historical ethnography of class and culture.[1]

This postrevolutionary period was a time of turbulence, discord, and invention, though most of those who lived it continued to go about their daily activities—farming in the countryside, buying and selling in the towns, plying their trade as artisans, or moving farther west for land or to the city to find their fortunes. Slavery and Indian removals continued unabated as Jeffersonians, Federalists, and Jacksonians debated philosophies and fought for power. The rapid development of roads and canals drew an increasing number of farmers into a deeper commitment to the market, raising crops and livestock for sale rather than bartering a tiny surplus eked out from the households' subsistence needs.[2] Merchants grew in wealth and power, and many New England towns began resembling those of England with rich and poor, landed and landless, creditors and debtors.[3] Congregations seethed with the religious ferment of the Second Great Awakening.[4] Among these and other critical interrelated elements of the national scene, none were to have a greater impact on American lives and futures than the new industrial factories, still relatively few in number, spreading along the fast-running streams that provided their power.[5] It was not the technology in and of itself that presaged significant changes, but the beginnings of a new capitalist relationship between and among groups of people, a relationship of class, based upon the complex, partially oppositional connections between owners who profited and "free" workers—that is, workers free to sell their labor.

The knowledge, if not the direct experience, of capitalist relationships had traveled along with the first settlers to North America. It was only with the advent of the factories, however, that such relationships began to play a part in the lives of significant numbers of New Englanders. They brought together into a close contact of mutual dependency and unequal power people of different social strata and experience—former merchants with former farmers or artisans. They transformed the old bonds between master craftsmen and journeymen or among fellow mechanics into ones of permanent inequality. And they set up a social scene in which workers and owners, each among themselves, had the potential for both competition and cooperation. "Class" is the process of working out these multidimensional interactions, and "culture" is the process of working through the meanings and practices that shaped and were shaped by these encounters.[6] Thus, New England's merchants brought the meanings and practices they had developed through their years of trading with the West Indies to their role of industrialists. Consciously and unconsciously, they generated new meanings and practices, new cultural ways to order these experiences, as they struggled with the communities around them for new interpretations of property rights, fought bitterly with their competitors, and, above all, contended with the first generation of factory workers for control over time, wages, and skills.[7] The resultant set of definitions of responsibilities, obligations, privileges, and powers would become part of what is today in the United States assumed to be "natural."

"Natural" and "common sense" are words of challenge to any ethnographer, since the task of ethnography is to "make the familiar strange, and the strange familiar" (Comaroffs 1992, 6). Distant in time and place, nineteenth-century New Englanders were "strange" in the sense of holding different beliefs than twenty-first-century Americans about important elements of daily life, such as family, religion, health, and the meaning of success. The work of ethnography entails setting out the context within which these beliefs are understandable, if not completely familiar. The same necessity arises for cultural domains such as money, work, and property, which appear familiar and, therefore, transparently natural and rational. Here the task is to render visible their cultural construction and historical context. The archives offer a glimpse of a time when much that is currently accepted as natural was once unthinkable or fiercely contested.

The work of innumerable historians has made it possible to construct a partial picture of this period despite their many different interpretations of the past.[8] A number of excellent accounts of the early years of industrialization present the workers' side of this early nineteenth-century negotiation over meanings and practices, dispelling previous notions of a smooth American transition into capitalism.[9] Studies of the formation of other regional upper classes, such as Wallace's (1972) description of Rockdale, Delaware; Johnson's (1978) of Rochester, New York; and several of Boston, provide extremely useful comparative material—though, with the exception of Dalzell's (1987), the descriptions and analyses of Boston's elite tend to focus on their cultural institutions rather than their involvement in production.[10] The present narrative pays close attention to the work of merchants and industrialists, their everyday efforts to increase their capital. It describes how these experiences were related to the other social and cultural domains that contained their lives.[11]

The path from our past to our present seems inevitable, but in 1795 when the Watkinsons left England to settle in Connecticut, many other possibilities existed. The documents they left afford us a sense of the contingencies, the what-might-have-beens. Through their letters, especially, one can learn some of their understandings, uncertainties, hopes, and fears. The reader in our time may know what followed from their actions, but these people in their time could neither plan nor predict the outcomes. They did what seemed proper and profitable, considering their own, their families', and, at times, their communities' well-being as they perceived it. In order to communicate some of those "forming and formative processes" (Williams 1977, 128), I have tried to preserve a sense of the individuals, the various Watkinsons and Collinses who people these pages.[12] Young Samuel Watkinson Jr. describes his difficulty in understanding the new social setting of New England as he ponders where he and his family will find their proper place; his brother John urges his suppliers to quickly send down the horses as he attempts to organize a cargo for the West Indies; Samuel Collins complains daily of his suspicions of his competitors; and David Watkinson shares a profound admiration of the new Wethersfield prison.

This then is a study of a particular family over three generations, but it is most definitely not a family history. They were neither typical nor outstanding, but they spoke the language of the time and place, took part in the activities of their social network, accepted or rejected the particular discourses that engulfed them. Their writings, to friends and relatives, business associates and employees, are permeated by their class and culture, revealing the limits and potentials, the conscience and consciousness of an American upper class.

The Watkinsons emigrated from England to Connecticut in 1795. They are not counted among the wealthiest, oldest, or most famous of Connecticut's families, yet rich collections of their papers exist partly because in the 1840s and 1850s one member of the family, David Watkinson, became known as an unusually generous philanthropist whose charitable activities included taking an active role in founding two historical archives in Hartford.[13] These collections include documents relating to David himself, his parents, and several of his eleven siblings, as well as a journal kept by his wife, Olivia. In addition, an older brother, John, a successful merchant and industrialist in Middletown, left a series of account books and a letterbook containing drafts of letters.[14] David and John's nephews, Samuel Watkinson Collins and David Chittenden Collins, were founders of an important industrial endeavor, the Collins Company, which manufactured axes, adzes, and edged tools, and, prospering from 1826 to 1966, was one of the largest and most technologically advanced factories in New England in the 1830s and 1840s. They left a valuable collection of correspondence, contracts, and a memoir.[15] With the addition of bills, newspaper advertisements, city directories, and miscellaneous papers, these documents make up the raw materials from which this narrative is constructed.

From these texts a picture emerges of complex individuals. The patriarch, Samuel Watkinson Sr., robustly enjoyed his life, his family, the beauty of the Connecticut River and the rolling country around Middletown. John, the oldest son, was a careful and successful businessman, a pillar of Middletown's community. Samuel Jr. and Richard were close in age but different in temperament. Their letters, written in their early twenties, reveal Samuel to have been a serious and ambitious young man, while Richard appeared to be playful and humorous. David's letters show him to have been responsible, religious, generous, and self-important. William, who failed, revealed more of his inner life in his letters than did his successful brothers—swings from hope to despair and unexplained silences. There are no letters from Edward, the brother closest to David, who also became a wealthy and respected member of Hartford's elite, and a few from the youngest brother, Robert. In one of them, written when he was the managing director of a textile factory, he bitterly reproached David for meddling in the business.

The majority of the men's letters were business letters, some written to family members and some to associates. But several of the Watkinsons also maintained a correspondence over the years with old friends in England. These letters were more expansive, describing their new lives and discussing the differences between Old and New England. The women's letters carried on the work of creating and maintaining bonds of kinship and friendship, dependability and loyalty. They expressed the joys of family, the sorrow over a child's death, and other emotions, but far fewer of their letters remain in the archives.[16]

The archives do not include letters written by Sarah Blair Watkinson, the matriarch of the family. She came from a well-to-do Scottish family related to both merchants and gentry. She had met and married Samuel on a visit to her brother, Dr. William Blair, who had settled in Lavenham, Watkinson's village in Suffolk County, England. A letter from her sister, Grizel, written shortly before the wedding took place, dismissed the fears Sarah had expressed about her lack of experience as a housekeeper. A letter from her father at the same time advised her to express her opinions to her husband, but to defer to him in case of disagreement.[17] Sarah raised twelve children and was described by one of her neighbors as a quiet, domestic woman. Their children mentioned her in their letters, and her messages were relayed by one son to another. Although Sarah was quiet, she was a vital presence in the lives of the family, and even in their later years she and Samuel enjoyed riding their horses together through the Connecticut countryside.

A handful of letters written by the Watkinsons' daughters still exist. Among them are a few letters of motherly concern that Mary, the eldest, wrote to her grown daughter. None remain from the next two sisters, Eliza (Elizabeth) and Sarah, but there is a drawing book of Ann's, which contains skillful renderings of flowers and a dog, as well as some quietly good watercolor studies of Middletown. There are several letters from Jane to brother David, describing a trip to Jacksonville to attend the wedding of one of her sons. She wrote about a stop in New York to visit brother William and a pleasant sojourn in Cincinnati. Her letters were filled with discussions of relatives but told little of the places. David's wife, Olivia, wrote letters and a journal that show her to have been a woman of charm and grace with a serious mind and an ability to vividly describe what she saw. William's wife, Elizabeth, is known only from several sad and reproachful letters, written after he had left her.

I have quoted extensively from their letters and from those of the Collins brothers to give readers an opportunity to hear the Watkinson family's voices directly, both to get a sense of them as individuals and to listen to the language of the period without my intervention. All emphases in quotations are from the original. Presentations of self in the letters vary not only with the writer but also with the actual or imagined audience. The letters were rarely spontaneous; they allowed the writer the opportunity to rewrite, erase, or, decide not to mail them at all. Such unsent mail sometimes exists in the letterbooks, where copies of letters—generally business letters transcribed by clerks—were kept. Despite or even because of the self-consciousness of letter writers, the letters reveal culture, the shared ideals and shared perceptions believed to be acceptable to the receiver. Journals were also written for an audience, an unseen and unknown one that might have been more appreciative or more critical than a known one, so these too were shaped by cultural expectations. Even account books, seemingly merely dry, factual records, were shaped by convention into a cultural discourse that concealed as much as it revealed.

Archival research resembles archeology in that interpreting the absence of data is almost as important as interpreting what is present. The most blatant silence in the Watkinson collections is the almost total absence of references to slavery. In transplanting themselves to America, the Watkinsons seem to have easily accommodated themselves to this ubiquitous institution. Although they did not own slaves or engage in the slave trade themselves, they were acquainted with Middletown's three slavers and with families who owned slaves, and they profited from the slave production of the West Indies. In 1800 David Watkinson traveled extensively throughout the Southern states[18] but his and the family's letters include only two passing and morally unreflective references to slavery. One occurs in a letter from David to an old friend in England. "Every part of this country except some of the Slave States is enjoying unexampled prosperity. The Farmer, Merchant, Mechanic and Manufacturer, are all enjoying a fair business and good common labour is in great demand."[19] The second appears in a letter from Samuel to David Collins (quoted in chapter 5), discussing the problem of shaping axes to the careless usage of slaves.

Their British friends, however, were anything but silent on this topic. A neighbor of the Watkinsons in Middletown, Mary Russell, a visitor from

England, wrote of her father's dismay at the sight of American slavery. In an entry to her journal dated February 11, 1798, she alluded to her father's travels around the country, which included "a visit to Coll Washington who resides in Virginia on a large estate.... The universal custom of having slaves in Virginia & Maryland—my Father found very disagreeable & the cruel manner in which they were in general treated must shock the feelings of every friend to humanity whose heart is not hardened by education & a habit of regarding the Negroes in a light not superior to Beasts."[20]

Another British comment on Washington's slaves was mentioned in Olivia Watkinson's journal many years later. "The obliging Scotsman our companions name, was John a proprietor of a large glass works in Grenock he spoke of Washington with admiration, regretting a character so near perfection should have any blemish, in his opinion the only one was having Slaves on his estate, had he gave them their freedom his character would have been perfect."[21]

The Reverend Ward, another old friend from Suffolk, described to David Watkinson his daughter's response after traveling to the United States with her husband. "Mr & Mrs M[arch] were much pleased with Connecticut.... Mary says she felt at home with you but at Savannah in a foreign land. Slavery highly excited her indignation."[22] Her husband, Mr. March, was also articulate about the evils of slavery, reporting that the cholera epidemic then devastating England was believed to be God's punishment for the sin of slavery. Considering the extent of the Watkinson and Collins archives and the number of English comments, the paucity of references to slavery is a silence that speaks loudly of the cultural constraints imposed by involvement in the social networks of the mercantile trade.

Yet accident certainly determines some of what is or is not to be found in the archives, and while some silences may be interpreted, many mysteries remain. Why, for example, did William stop writing to the two brothers who had been his partners? Was there ill will or are the letters simply missing? Why are there no references to Samuel Collins's wife, Sara, when so many of the Watkinsons commented on the charm and loveliness of his brother David's wife, Clarissa? Where was Sara when Samuel asked his brother to inform her that the children's health was good but requested, "Please ascertain whether she is in Hartford and if not put the enclosed in Post Office and pay the postage for me."[23] What did Olivia mean when she described her meeting with "4 married ladies," on a trip to London, "all I believe blessed with good husbands but not with children, as for my self situated as I have been, I do not know but that I ought to consider it a blessing that I have them not"? [24]

The organization of the chapters is chronological as well as topical, and each chapter is centered around one or two members of the family. Chapter 1 traces the Watkinsons' journey in 1795, looking back to their old home in England and following them to their new one in Middletown, Connecticut. This chapter introduces Samuel Watkinson Sr. and Samuel Jr. as they scan New England's social landscape through the lenses of their previous understandings of class and learn to adjust to their new setting.

Chapter 2 contains the correspondence of Samuel Jr. and Richard, from 1796 to 1798, when they were employed as merchants' clerks in New York City. This chapter portrays their experience as up-and-coming young men in the city and of the kinship and gender relationships within their family. It provides a view of the lives of their sisters in Middletown, to whom many of the letters were addressed.

In chapter 3 the account books and business letters of John Watkinson provide a rich source for a description of the everyday concerns of a merchant trading with the West Indies during the lucrative years from 1797 to 1812. Three voyages are followed in detail, from the assembling of the cargo of Connecticut produce to the sale of the rums and sugars on their return. An analysis of John Watkinson's accounts reveals the mythical properties of bookkeeping.

Chapter 4 follows several of the brothers through the transitional period, 1812–1820, when, like many other merchants, they sought alternatives to the West Indian trade, which was drastically disrupted by the War of 1812. John turned to textile manufacturing, and a comparison of his new industrial and his old mercantile accounts documents continuities and changes.

Chapters 5 and 6 fully examine the new class relations that were being shaped by industrialization and the factory system as experienced and discussed by two entrepreneurs of the next generation, Samuel Watkinson Collins and David Chittenden Collins. Samuel's letters and memoirs covering the years 1826 to 1846 provide an extraordinary view of this complex and contentious process. His memoirs contain remembered events, copies of speeches he made to his workers, and one that they made in response.

Chapter 7 traces the rise of David Watkinson and his fellow directors of Hartford's industrial, financial, and philanthropic institutions. David's letters show both his personal commitment to religious and benevolent causes and the role they play in establishing upper-class cultural dominance. This chapter also includes the sad but enlightening moral saga of William and his family and a description by David's wife, Olivia, of their visit to Great Britain.

In the Conclusion I review the important elements of capitalist culture that developed from 1795 to 1850 in New England. Among them were the sanctification of the market, the legitimization of private corporations as autonomous institutions, the definition of work as a behavior validated only by its sale, and the social and moral separation of workplace from community.

CHAPTER I

The Voyage

In mid-April of 1795 Samuel Watkinson, his wife, Sarah, and their children arrived in London from their home in Lavenham, Suffolk County. Samuel was then fifty years old, his wife, fifty-one, and their twelve children—seven sons and five daughters—ranged in age from Robert, nine years old, to Mary, twenty-six.[1] They expected to make only a brief stay at the Bull Inn before taking passage to America on the *Minerva*. Unfortunately, ten days later, on the very evening before they were to sail, the ship caught fire while at anchor. The blaze was brought under control and their "boxes, casks, and beds" were rescued undamaged from the hold, but the *Minerva* had suffered too much water damage to be seaworthy.[2] No other ship with enough space for the large family was scheduled to sail for America, so they divided into three groups and took whatever passage became available. John, the eldest son, boarded the *Factor* at the end of April. Samuel Jr., Richard, and their sister Sarah, along with her husband, two children, and a servant, followed a month later on the *Mercury,* while the parents and the rest of the family remained in London in lodgings for two more weeks before boarding the *Eliza,* bound for Boston.[3]

THE FAMILY OF SAMUEL (B. 1745) AND SARAH BLAIR WATKINSON (B. 1744)

Mary (b. 1769)
Sarah (b. 1770)
John (b. 1772)

Samuel Jr. (b. 1773)
Elizabeth (b. 1775)
Richard (b. 1776)
David (b. 1778)
William (b. 1779)
Ann (b. 1781)
Edward (b. 1783)
Jane (b. 1785)
Robert (b. 1786)

Clearly this was a serious undertaking—costly, difficult, and even dangerous. A group of some sixty friends and acquaintances followed their example and set off for America at the same time, leaving behind property, family, and a familiar and beautiful countryside. Like the Watkinsons these were well-established families of a middling class, neither poor nor aristocratic, who felt that the new United States could provide them with the fresh air of freedom and an unlimited future that could not be found in their familiar Suffolk homeland. Like many of the earlier settlers of New England they were from the region of England called East Anglia, and like them they were members of small religious congregations known as "dissenting societies," because their beliefs and forms of worship differed from those of the established, state-supported Anglican Church. Like those earlier immigrants they were fleeing religious and political intolerance, but they were also attracted by hopes of achieving a level of social standing and respect that was closed off to them at home. These were intricately related motives that reflected the complex forces at work in late eighteenth-century England.[4] Political currents over which they had no control and in which they played only minor roles had begun to seriously affect their lives.

Over the past several decades in the urban and industrializing regions of England an increasingly wealthy and well educated middle class—many if not most of whom were Dissenters—had formed political clubs pressing for parliamentary reforms to limit the power of the landholding aristocracy. Taxed for every military adventure the government undertook and further taxed to support the Anglican Church, they sought a change in the structures of government that would allow them to play a part in political life and to gain access not only to power but also to its financial rewards. Above all they sought to separate church and state. By no means revolutionaries, they had no thought to include the lower orders in their plans. They had applauded the Americans' victorious struggle and admired the new American Constitution, which showed that a more equitable political system could be achieved without threatening property or social standing.

The startling events of the French Revolution had a tremendous impact on every level of English society: the most powerful monarch in Europe had been dethroned, the established Church dismantled, and the rights of man proclaimed. New, more radical political clubs sprang up in industrialized London, Sheffield, and Manchester; the clubs included working men, artisans, and middle-class members and demanded equal representation and universal suffrage. The governing aristocracy reacted with fear and repression. As a new war with France broke out—or was provoked—the government treated protests against the status quo as traitorous acts.

France and England had long existed in alternating states of war and peace. Rival empires for a hundred years, they competed for colonies and prizes and sought to build larger and larger fleets in a race for sea power. This jockeying for advantage had never before prevented people of each country from traveling back and forth or taking part in commerce and intellectual exchange. While this war was as much about the English merchants' investments in Holland and the two nations' prized plantations in the West Indies as previous wars had been, it was also about fear of the spreading infection of revolutionary ideas into England. The government issued a stream of propaganda, demonizing the enemy without and within.

Beginning with a proclamation against seditious writings in 1792, the British government escalated its suppression of dissent to the suspension of habeas corpus and arrests of the leaders of the radical societies in 1794. Some were jailed, some transported, a few executed, but several of the leaders escaped or were eventually released and fled to the new United States. At the government's urging a voluntary Loyalist army primarily composed of and supported by propertied aristocrats was organized to defend against the dangers of French invasion, and a secret service was established that paid spies to infiltrate suspect organizations.

The wave of propaganda and repression grew to encompass those merely sympathetic to reform. Dissenters, such as the Watkinsons, and anyone who was believed to have sided with the American colonies or the French revolutionaries were under suspicion. Riots occurred, targeting suspected traitors and supporting Church and king; the riots were alleged to be spontaneous but probably were instigated by the government. The victims were generally rich Dissenters, whose property and persons were attacked as local authorities looked on or supported and encouraged the rioters.

In Lavenham as elsewhere the climate was stormy, as indicated by several descriptions of these times by members of the Taylor family, friends and neighbors of the Watkinsons. The father, Isaac Taylor, an engraver and artist from a family of writers and printers, was a leading member of a small Dissenting congregation, along with Samuel Watkinson; two of Taylor's children, Jane and Ann, were close friends of two of the Watkinsons' daughters.[5] In her memoirs Ann Taylor Gilbert described the local tensions between the Anglican clergy and the Dissenters. "The rector and curate of our day were of the old school, free livers, yet religiously hostile to the little band of dissenters who occupied a small 'meeting-house' that nestled under the shade of some fine walnut trees, standing back from the street" (1876, 20).

An atmosphere of danger permeated daily life. "Troops of ill-disposed, disorderly people often paraded the streets with this hue-and-cry, halting, especially, at the houses of known and leading dissenters....And it was not from an ignorant populace only that danger was to be apprehended. A system of oppression and espionage was adopted, which threatened to violate the free privacies of life. No one felt safe in expressing a political opinion, even at his own table, if a servant stood behind his chair" (Gilbert, 78). The Watkinsons had good reason to fear that they might be targeted. Samuel Watkinson was known to be a leading member of the Dissenting Society. Their house was one of the best in the village, located on the main street with grounds, gardens, orchards, warehouses, and a pool (Gilbert, 26). According to Ann Taylor Gilbert, the threat of riots and the danger of political repression were what led the Watkinsons and their neighbors to emigrate.

America was the home of safety to which all who could emigrate began to cast a longing eye, and under the conviction that England would become less and less of a mother country to her children, our friend, Mr Watkinson, to the inexpressible regret and loss of the circle with which he was connected, announced his intention of transplanting his family to that land of liberty. Of Mr Watkinson's twelve children, one daughter had married a gentleman holding a farm not far from Lavenham, and not only did they consent to share the removal, but others, to the number of sixty in the neighbourhood, took advantage of the convoy, and left at the same time. (Gilbert, 79–80)

The threatening political climate provided the immediate impetus for the Watkinsons' departure, although the Taylors and other friends and relations remained behind. But additional reasons also played an important part in the decision to emigrate. Watkinson, along with many other professionals and tradesmen in Suffolk and elsewhere, had concluded that England no longer provided a future—a future defined in class terms. With capital said to be worth £30,000 (Gilbert 1876, 26), equivalent roughly to a few million dollars today, and twelve children, the Watkinsons sought a more hopeful place for both.

Watkinson was a master wool comber, a merchant manufacturer. As a "master" he supervised the purchase of raw wool, distributed it to his wool combers to clean and comb, put it out to women to spin, and managed its collection and sale. Lavenham had a history dating back to the Middle Ages of being a rich and thriving center of the wool and cloth trade. Although by the eighteenth century much of the trade had moved elsewhere, wool combing and spinning were still the center of the economy. In a town where building after building reflected the history of wool and trade, where an annual feast honored St. Blaise, the patron saint of wool combers, a master wool comber was an important person.[6]

In addition to his profits from the wool trade, Watkinson gained income through renting land to a tenant farmer, by leasing other real estate, and from investments in stock.[7] The Taylors regarded him as a man of substance and had great respect for the entire family, describing them as "well ordered almost to a proverb, and well educated too" (Gilbert, 76). Admired and respected by the Taylors, the wool merchants, and others of a middling status, the Watkinsons' social position nonetheless was below not only the aristocracy but also the local gentry. These were small landowners or, more often, tenant farmers, who rented from one of the large landowning aristocrats, hired laborers, and managed the farms as small capitalist enterprises. If they were Anglican, these small gentry might play a role as local dignitaries, while the large aristocratic landlords—Anglican, of course—from whom they rented filled important positions on the national level (Newby et al., 1978).

Even within the small meetinghouse used by the Watkinsons and other members of their Dissenting congregation, social distinctions were carefully maintained, and the seating arrangements themselves were careful statements of social position. Tradesmen, who made up the main body of the congregation, were seated in the central pews. They were people such as "the Lungleys, shopkeepers of repute and means, as most of these good folks were." They included Mr. Buck, the linen-draper; Hitchcock, the clerk; a retired flour dealer with a "snug independence"; and William Meeking Jr., the eldest son of the baker-shopkeeper, who played the bassoon to accompany the psalm. The Taylors and the Watkinsons sat here as well (Gilbert 1876, 29).

A few of the local gentry were Dissenters, and one such family sat in the "Squire's Pew." The occupants were a widow and two daughters, one married to a Mr. Hillier. Their pew was "carefully screened at both ends from the vulgar gaze." Although Gilbert ranked them "among the small gentry of the neighborhood," she noted that, "the tradespeople were as a rule better informed." The poor members of the congregation sat in the galleries, men on one side, women on the other, along with the boys and girls of the Sunday school (Gilbert, 29–30). These were probably families of wool workers whose humble, mud-floored cottages lined the side streets of Lavenham (Gilbert, 56).

Absent from the congregation, of course, were any of the large landowning aristocrats as well as those "ill-disposed, disorderly people," who threatened the Dissenters. These were local people who were "heathen" in Gilbert's view. Hard-pressed by the deepening economic troubles of the times and place, landless and jobless, they were outside the categories and understandings of the Taylors and their friends.

A scandal erupted among the congregation when the minister, whose family was in trade, presumed to propose marriage to Mr. Hillier's sister. The squire was outraged, and he and his relatives resigned from the congregation while the minister and his bride left town (Gilbert, 29). The gentry, even those who shared religious convictions, considered themselves superior to tradesmen and demanded a deference that was resented by these "better informed," well educated and respected families. Upper-class assaults on their self-esteem were as threatening to the middle-class sense of self as the physical attacks on their persons and properties.[8]

A few years before they emigrated, Sarah, one of the Watkinsons' oldest daughters, had successfully crossed the line that separated tradesman from gentry by marrying Jacob Pledger, a Suffolk farmer (Gilbert, 80). But the Watkinsons had four more daughters and seven sons for whom the future appeared to hold less promise. Their voyage to America was not only an effort to find a safe harbor but also an endeavor to find a setting that fit their ideas of what their lives and that of their children should be. Along with their capital, they carried to New England class-based perceptions of a proper way of life.

Watkinson had begun making preparations for leaving Lavenham at least a year before their actual departure. He wrote to his broker to purchase shares in the Bank of the United States in New York,[9] and arranged with his cousin Robert Watkinson and his friend William Meeking Jr. to handle his business affairs: to collect rent from his farm tenant, to sell his house, and to look after a few of his old pensioners from the wool trade. Although he turned over the Lavenham Meetinghouse records, which had been his responsibility, to Mr. Taylor,[10] he continued to contribute to the Meetinghouse from America for another ten years, and he and several members of his family corresponded with their relatives, William Meeking Jr., and other former neighbors and fellow Dissenters throughout their lives.

Samuel Watkinson Jr. wrote first about his experiences on the voyage and his perceptions of his new country. Samuel was the second son, twenty-two years of age when he left England. He wrote to Meeking on July 8, two days after he and his party had landed at Marblehead, Massachusetts. "I have the pleasure to inform you of the safe arrival of the *Brig Mercury* at Marblehead with all the passengers in good health and spirits; after a pleasant passage of 37 days, viz. July 6th. Scarcely any of us felt the sea sickness enough to be worthy of mention. As our passage was so short we had fresh provisions all the way; and could in general enjoy our meals notwithstanding the motion of the vessel, which none of us were so thoro'ly reconciled to as to wish to go to sea again."

He described their passage west on the *Mercury* with a young man's enthusiasm for a great adventure. Within the first few days of their voyage, while they were still in the English Channel, they were accosted by English privateers looking for French sympathizers. "A few hours after I wrote to you from the Downs (where we made no stay) we were haild by a shot by an English Privateer who wanted to hear news and were saluted again in the same manner on the 4th June; they made many inquiries the principal of which were respecting the French, viz. whether we had seen any of their traders and if we were not bound to France and laden with provisions." The following day they encountered a fleet of English merchants, traveling in a convoy for protection. The rest of their voyage proceeded without incident. "till we had the infinite pleasure of casting anchor on the Shore of Freedom."

They first made land at Newfoundland and on their voyage south along the coast met with a school of porpoises. "A new sight now offered itself to us of an innumerable number of Porpusses jumping out and in the water; thro the midst of which the ship passed. The captain struck several with the harpoon but could get only one on board. It was about six feet in length very round, male and about a foot thick. The inside of it was extremely like that of a hog; the flesh eats like beef, the colour of the flesh after laying upon deck a day or two, was very disagreeable and loathsome, being nearly as black as my hat from the quantity of blood left in it."

A perceptive and curious ethnographer, he noted the occupations of the natives as well as the landscape and weather.

July 1st we reached Brown's Bank where there were a great number of small fishing schooners; which in general belong to farmers on the American shore who devote their leisure days to the profitable article of fishing. . . . As we proceeded in shore (into Ipswich Bay) a pleasant prospect presented itself of the country round about Newbury a considerable seacoast town with a good river.

The shore to the SW appeared very rocky as we proceeded and in a very rough place we were gratified with the sight of a considerable and flourishing town (Cape AnTown) supported by Agriculture and Fishing and Commerce and having a good river.

They passed the towns of Beverly and Salem and finally reached the *Mercury*'s home port of Marblehead, where they were greeted by the inhabitants "with much civility hospitality and curiosity."[11]

There is no record of the eldest brother's, John Watkinson's, passage on the *Factor* beyond Samuel Jr.'s mention that it had been a pleasant eight-week passage to Philadelphia. Samuel and Sarah Watkinson and their remaining children embarked on June 16 on the *Eliza*. Sixteen-year-old William wrote to Meeking from Deal on the southwest coast of England, describing how they too encountered the war as they sailed close to France in the Straits of Dover. They had been proceeding slowly because the wind had subsided. "Before we anchored we were fired at by one of the guard ships, at about a mile distance, we heard the Ball pass by us and fall right ahead of us, upon which we hoisted our colors (being American) they did not stop at that, but fired again and again. We then brought to a little and were boarded by the ship's boat full of men, after staying a little while and looking at us etc. etc. they went off."[12] The remainder of the voyage was uneventful, but the twelve-week passage was long and trying.

They landed in Boston, where they had agreed to meet the rest of the family. John, the first arrival, had traveled to Marblehead to meet the second contingent. Sarah Pledger and her family stopped in Boston to await the last arrivals, while John, Samuel Jr., and Richard traveled southwest to the Connecticut River Valley, looking for a town to settle in and a house.

They had thought at first to stay in Hartford, where they had been offered the loan of a house, but they decided instead on Middletown. Samuel Jr. wrote about their new home to his mother as soon as he learned from the newspaper that their ship, the *Eliza,* had arrived in Boston. "This Town is extremely pleasant and healthy; the inhabitants show great attention to us and long very much to see the rest of the family here. I have engaged a house...there is no other house in this town or Hartford which, all things considered, you will like so well."[13]

In early November, almost seven months after they had left Suffolk, the family was safely reunited in Middletown. The river and gently rolling hills provided a setting for their new home that was described by one of the sons as even more charming than what they had left. The city was comparable in size to Lavenham, with approximately two thousand people living in three hundred households.[14] In comparison, New York City in 1790 had a population of 32,328; Boston, 18,038; and Philadelphia, 42,520 (Price 1974, 126).

Despite its small size, Middletown in 1795 was a complex urban site, rivaling Hartford in numbers and importance as a commercial center. Middletown's inhabitants were divided by religion, occupation, wealth, and politics into many different and crosscut communities with ties to other places and people. The Congregational church had the largest congregation, but several other denominations were also active. Foremost among these was the Episcopal church, followed by Baptists, Methodists, and one group of Strict-Congregationalists (Field 1819, 136–37).

Farming was still the most common occupation within the surrounding township, and even in the center of the city, merchants, artisans, and the Congregational minister kept livestock and vegetable gardens next to their houses (Hall 1981, 9). There were numerous merchants of varying types, large and small, retail and wholesale, including two or three slave traders, as well as artisans, ships' masters and sailors, laborers, servants, slaves, ministers, and lawyers.[15] There were "eleven stores of dry goods, twenty-two grocery stores, two hardware stores, two crockery stores, one fur store, two apothecary stores, one paper store, two book stores, two book binderies, two goldsmiths' shops, four tailor shops, three milliners' shops, one hat factory, two bakeries, three butchers' stalls, two tallow chandleries, two tanneries, three shoe stores, two saddlers' shops, four lumber yards, three cabinet shops, two chaise makers' shops, two tinners' shops, four blacksmiths' shops, two rope walks, and one sail loft" (Field 1819, 41, quoted by Hall 1981, 10).

Situated on a bend of the Connecticut River with a fine, natural harbor, the small city was and had been a commercial center for most of its existence. Beginning as a hub of local trade it had become part of a mercantile network extending to Boston, New York, Europe, Africa, China, and, above all, the West Indies. When the Federal Customs House was established there shortly after the War of Independence, Middletown began its important function of entry port for the entire Connecticut River.[16]

In Middletown, as in other New England cities, differences in wealth and status were important, visible in houses, coaches, education, and dress.[17] Historians describe late eighteenth-century New England towns as increasingly stratified, growing more and more to resemble English villages with their distinctions of wealth, education, and manners. Certain families monopolized positions of leadership, and poverty was becoming a serious problem as the numbers of indigent or unfortunate grew beyond the limited resources that each town allotted for their upkeep.[18]

The late eighteenth century was a volatile period, not only or primarily because of the Revolution, but, like the Revolution itself, because of factors that were pushing aside older social structures, while newer forms had yet to solidify into a predictable pattern of relationships. In an earlier period in Connecticut, farmers had shown deference to a social and political educated elite, "The Standing Order," composed of lawyers, landed gentry, and ministers of the established Congregational Church. These patterns had crumbled as wealth that was founded on mercantile trade drastically realigned social positions and values. Some of the old Connecticut families entered trade, and some of the old landholding families remained influential; however, the major source of the growing differences in wealth—the West Indian trade—had shaken up the certainties and continuities of the old colonial order without replacing them with a clearly defined new one.

Middletown, like every town in New England, was divided by the recent emergence of party politics. Federalists and Jeffersonians regarded each other with grave suspicion. Party aligned roughly with religion, wealth, occupation, and political affiliation, though political passions even divided some families. Federalists tended to be Congregationalists, affluent merchants, professionals, or large landholders. Among them were families who had handed down political offices for generations. Jeffersonians tended to be artisans and farmers as well as members of other religious denominations—Episcopalians, Baptists, or Methodists.

The Federalists, committed to a strong central government run by an enlightened, educated, and responsible elite, regarded the Jeffersonians with fear as radical levelers and potential revolutionaries who would seize power and property following the example of the French Jacobins. Jeffersonians supported an ideal of equality among all (white, propertied) men and saw the republic as an association of state governments that should serve as the important sites where independent men could together preserve their freedom and wisely determine the policies that should be followed. The Jeffersonians suspected the Federalists of royal ambitions and of plans to tax the farmers and planters in order to enrich the merchants and bankers. In Middletown as throughout the country feelings ran high.[19]

This was the scene that the Watkinsons entered in search of a promising site for their future. They came well prepared with letters of introduction and a sizeable capital, both of which proved invaluable in opening doors to opportunity, but they found many discrepancies between their expectations and the actualities of New England. Before traveling to the United States, Samuel Jr. had read Morse's *American Geography* and had been pleased to recognize near Norwich, Connecticut, "the plain rendered famous by the fight of the Indians under chiefs Uncas and Myantons."[20] His knowledge of the social geography of this new scene was less applicable; many of his early letters reflect his attempts to fit this new social landscape into an English social map as he carefully observed the differences between the social distinctions that he perceived in New England and those he had taken for granted in Suffolk.

In Lynn, Massachusetts, for example, he noted that, "The poor are decently drest and do not go about begging."[21] On the surface, the observation appeared simple, but it revealed his preconceptions. Why did Samuel consider these decently dressed people poor? He seemed to assume that a particular class of people existed who in England would have been working or begging, dressed in rags, yet who in North America fared differently. Their clothing was not the basis on which he made his judgment. Peering through the lens of his Suffolk-shaped categories of social status he was able to discern poor people beneath their "decent dress."

He noted that few farm laborers were available for hire and used the word "poor" when he suggested that this was due to the availability of cheap land, which ". . . invites the poor with the idea of Independence."[22] Again, his use of "poor" was clearly a class term, since someone who had land or the possibility of getting it and sufficient wherewithal to farm it was not "poor" in the sense of not having enough to eat or enough clothes to wear. In the following year he began to refine his social topology. "Merchants and persons of independent fortune, dress as well as those of the same station in England, but the inferior tradesmen and working people are far better clothed; you see here neither poverty nor rags."[23]

As he adjusted his perceptions to his new experiences, he dropped the term "poor" and substituted "common people." "The common people go remarkably well drest; it is indeed surprising to an Englishman to see quantity of Broad cloth and kersimers silks, and sattins that are worn by them. On Sunday you will scarcely see a person wearing cotton stockings (unless lately from England) almost every one, (Black or white) will have silk stockings."[24]

Unfortunately, the archives do not contain any comparable letters written by the women of the family in these early years of their emigration. But another Englishwoman, Mary Russell, who became a part of the Watkinsons' new circle of friends and acquaintances in Middletown, kept a diary that described her view of the social scene. A young woman, twenty-nine years old when she began writing in her diary in November 1797, she had arrived in Middletown with her father, two sisters, and a brother a year before. The father was engaged in the sale of lands held by a British company. The family had come from Birmingham planning to emigrate, but eventually returned to England after four and a half years in Middletown.

Mary's idea of proper behavior between members of unequal social standing was disturbed by an experience at White's Tavern when "the young woman who had waited on us & set the table etc. sat down when we did at Table to make tea for us with as much ease as if she had been one of our party."[25] This young woman may have been a daughter of the proprietor or a hired girl, possibly a farmer's daughter, working as "help," with the understanding that this was merely temporary employment. "*Help* as they call it here," wrote Russell, not only resented the word but avoided the deference associated with "servants." Russell, however, continued to use the term "servants." "We have now just got a new maid servant from Chatham in Mrs Allens place & also a black boy in Patricks & both promise to suit pretty well, tho the woman is rather too Yankyfied."[26] In this context "Yankyfied" undoubtedly meant showing a lack of deference.

In a similar vein Samuel Watkinson Sr. commented that "People here will not bear to be treated aristocratically."[27] In general, the scarcity of both female and male labor made good servants as difficult to find as farm laborers. Samuel Jr. described the reaction of some of his fellow English: "There are but few english ladies who are quite satisfied with this Country: it being difficult to find white servants that know how to conduct themselves as servants and the Blacks are much worse." He continued smugly, "But gentlemen do much better having fewer wants than the ladies or not requiring so much to be waited upon."[28] On the contrary, as discussed in chapter 2,

Samuel Jr.'s sisters found themselves occupied with the men's wants as well as with other housework.

Samuel Jr. considered himself a gentleman, and he recognized a commonality between himself and many of the people he and his family met as they traveled through New England. He described the pleasant time they had had in Cambridge, Massachusetts, where they had found "good society." In another letter his reference to "the People" clearly indicates that he is referring to those whom he considered to be of his own social status. "The People have every where shown us a great deal of politeness and attention; they are very sociable intelligent and friendly. They dress extremely well and live all in good houses, but they have no good Beer."[29] He may have hoped to impress his friend by bragging in this letter about his new home, though echoing a typical English complaint about beer. However, the significant words are "the People," and the significant assumption is that his correspondent will understand who is here included and who not.

The young men of the family had expected to take up farming in New England, with the supposition that this was the occupation of gentlemen as it was in England. However, they quickly discovered that in New England farmers did most of their own work, helped by their families but rarely or only occasionally hiring a laborer, as labor was scarce and expensive. This was not, as Samuel Jr. wrote, what the Watkinsons had in mind. "We have given up the idea of Farming excepting as an amusement or an assistant to other business. Labour being very high, there are very few improvements made on the farms to please the eye; they have therefore a slovenly appearance." He continued with a description of how a farm should be run. "A farmer who has been used to see his corn well cleaned from weeds; his ground well plowed; his pastures fine, his horses taken good care of with a choice of servants to do every thing he wishes, would find himself extremely disapointed if he expected to find the same things here."[30]

Samuel Watkinson Sr. concurred with his sons' decisions to give up the idea of farming, describing to Meeking the life of a New England farmer.

You perceive they have given up farming the high price and scarcity of labourers occasioned by the war is very discouraging and they think it would not answer much at this time to any other than a working farmer. Such men do very well. They begin with little besides credit, bring up their family to do the work of the farm and to spin and weave (few without looms in their houses in which they make cloth and linen plain and figured and Linsey Wollsey) They give their children a good plain education and clothe them well but seldom any money to spare till the farm and stock is divided at last. Their gains upon so small a business being generally spent in improving the land and buildings and increasing the stock.[31]

This was not the life for the Watkinsons, and their previous occupation in England, the wool trade, was out of the question. In Connecticut women combed and spun for their families and exchanged some of their yarn for credit at a general store. Samuel Watkinson Sr. advised Meeking to remain in Lavenham, adding, "Very little can be done in the wool trade that I can perceive at present. Wooll and spinning are too dear combing is done by women on two pitchcombs for hose yarn for family knitting."[32]

The Watkinsons turned their thoughts elsewhere. They had traveled to New England with introductions to "People," men like themselves of good families with large amounts of capital, who belonged to the Congregationalist faith. They found that these men were engaged either in manufacturing or in the mercantile trade. As they traveled from Newburyport southwest to the Connecticut River towns, Samuel Jr. and his party visited several factories. In his journal he wrote favorably of an establishment near Newburyport."The situation of the manufactures at this place...is excellent in respect to the falls as mill seats and the goodness of the navigation below them; the distance from Newburyport by water is 15 or 16 miles. The nail factory and the wool factory are both under one roof."[33]

He also visited a cotton factory near Salem, Massachusetts, and a duck cloth factory in Beverly. He tried to inspect a large cotton factory at Pawtucket, Rhode Island,[34] and a hosiery factory in Norwich, Connecticut, but the owners of these factories refused to permit him to see their machinery. He had better luck in Hartford, where the owner showed him around his duck-cloth manufacturing mill and told him that the factory paid 25 percent on his money.

Most of the men they met were well-known and successful Connecticut merchants. Foremost among them was Jeremiah Wadsworth, one of the richest men in the country, a friend of Alexander Hamilton's with a nationwide reputation. Wadsworth had been a successful merchant even before he served his country and himself by managing large quantities of money and goods as commissary general of the Continental Army and later as commissary for the French troops in America. Samuel Jr. made a note in his journal that on August 11, 1795, he took lodging at a Mr. White's in Hartford "thro the recommendation of Wadsworth" and that a few days later, he had met

"William Ely, Mr. Stow of Middletown, and Colonel Wadsworth." While less influential than Wadsworth, both Stow and Ely were respected and prosperous merchants.

In Middletown the Watkinsons were entertained by additional members of well-off merchant families. "Yesterday eve went to Capt. Wetmore's to tea and met there Jeho Star[r] and his lady."[35] The captain was both a ship's master and an investor in the West Indian trade; Jehosophat Starr was an important merchant. In many ways the Watkinsons were preadapted to this social niche of trade and "good society." Their dealings in the wool trade had involved them in a market in which the price of raw wool, the cost of labor, and the demand for spun yarn were crucial elements to be calculated. Provided with ample capital, the young Watkinsons set out to become merchants or merchants' wives.

Samuel Jr.'s "the People" and "good society" were labels for well-off families who resembled an upper class in terms of their wealth and property and their pronounced efforts to make marriages among members of families like themselves. But they lacked any sense of unity or identity of purpose, and, above all, they were neither structurally nor culturally opposed to any other group.[36] They are better described as forming several prominent social circles whose connections extended into various parts of the region. The Watkinsons became part of this network of social circles.

In Middletown the families who immediately recognized the Watkinsons as fellow members of "good society" were Congregationalists, who welcomed them into the church when they arrived in Middletown. Samuel Sr. described his first attendance there with humor.

My spirits were much hurt by the disasters previous to setting out and the length of the voyage, but thro' mercy I have surmounted them all and never had better spirits nor was more hearty than at present. But the voyage gave me so old an appearance that they seated me the first sabbath between an old Colonel near 90 and a General of 70 close by the pulpitt whether in compliment to my wisdom in emigrating or that they supposed I had really lost some of my senses thro' age I will not determine. But being neither dead nor blind I removed one seat back and seated myself with two others each about 80 one of whom soon after paid me visit and was surprised to hear I was the youngest.[37]

Middletown's Congregational church symbolized the significant ways in which the Watkinsons' new home presented a remarkable contrast to their old. In Lavenham the Anglican church stood on a hill above the village. Its soaring Gothic tower, which dominated the landscape, was visible for more than a mile into the countryside.[38] The melodic pealing of its bells across the fields had set the time by which life and death and work and prayer were to be regulated. The Watkinsons' small Dissenting Society met in a small house, which was rented at a nominal fee from one of the members and was located inconspicuously along one of the village streets. In Middletown the large, though ungainly, two-storied Congregationalist First Church of Christ stood solidly in the middle of town. Built in 1715 to replace the congregation's 1668 log church, it would be abandoned in 1799 for a fine new building, complete with tower, on Main Street (Hazen 1920).[39] So with a sea change the Watkinsons were transformed from being suspect Dissenters, potential radicals, and socially disadvantaged tradesmen to being members of the socially elect in Connecticut's state-supported, established Congregational church.

In a letter written the spring after their arrival in Middletown, Samuel Jr. narrated to a friend the story of their voyage and extolled the virtues of his new country.

> With great pleasure I remember the day on which we met; the day that saw a family unite.... We had made a happy escape from the apparent danger of civil war; from a scene of luxury and its attendant opposites Poverty and distress; from a land of taxes to support a venal court from the stigmas and abuse which we had shared in common with the friends of Liberty. We were arrived in a country of Liberty and Independence free from religious Intolerance from Poverty and from Riches where the Taxes that were collected were applied to the sole purpose of defraying the necessary expences of the Government and where the inhabitants as far we can yet judge of them are intelligent and social.[40]

Samuel Sr., writing during that same week of April 1796, to his friend Meeking, expressed similar sentiments, though his style was more restrained. "The sacrifice I made in coming here I do not repent of. The religious and civil opinions and manners of the people please me much...a country professing a finer climate *and Liberty* Civil and Religious unknown with you."[41] Although in several letters to Meeking he looked back on the wool trade and its traditions with nostalgia, it never blinded him to economic reality. The "yarn trade" was failing, and capital could earn more in the United States. "It grieves me to hear of its distresses, but it would kill me to be in it. . . . I think money is better employed here where from 8 to 16 per cent may be made without risque or trouble and provision very reasonable."[42]

At home in Middletown, Samuel Sr. played the part of an English country gentleman. His son Samuel described his father's pastoral pleasures. "I think that I never saw my Father look so well as he does at present, the climate agrees extremely well with his constitution. He keeps a horse and chaise and with Mother or some of the family rides out almost every day or goes out sailing and fishing in the Connecticut river."[43]

The Watkinsons found their social landscape as congenial as the physical setting. Mary Russell described a party at the home of Elijah Hubbard, an important member of their new circle and one of the wealthiest merchants in Middletown. "On the 22 of Feby," she noted in her diary, "we had a very pleasant Dance at Mr Elijah Hubbard there were 50 persons there besides their own family, they have the best house in Town so that the company were very well accommodated."[44]

In another entry she painted a bucolic scene of a summer picnic given by the Watkinsons, set in the hills (which she considered to be mountains) near Middletown. "We had one very pleasant excursion to the mountain. . . . Mr Watkinson's family invited the party & had a cold dinner sent— the mountain is about 6 miles from here very pleasantly situated. . . . [W]hen we arrived we found the Table all set out ready under a most beautiful Tree at the top of the mountain." It began to rain, and the gentlemen set up an awning. "We saw the rest of the party at the foot of the hill where they stayed till the shower was over but sheltered themselves in their Carriage. . . . [T]he rain was soon over & the rest of our party joined us we were then, 27 in number—Mr Saml Watkinson played on the flute & as he placed himself . . . it sounded charmingly."[45] The flute player was the senior Samuel Watkinson, and their party included several members of their social circle in Middletown—some wealthy merchants and their families, the Congregational minister, and visitors from England.

The Watkinsons had found a setting well suited to their background and to their hopes for the future. They had "bought a very convenient house in a good and central situation."[46] The capital that Samuel Watkinson had brought with him was fruitfully invested in bank shares and turnpike stocks, in manufacturing and trade, in the marriages of his daughters, and in the training and commercial ventures of his sons. While his sons embarked on careers in the West Indian trade, Samuel Sr. followed his investments, kept track of his properties in Lavenham, advised his children, and enjoyed life in Middletown. In the many letters the Watkinsons wrote back to England there were no regrets. On the contrary, the Watkinsons were confirmed in their choice over the next ten years by the increasingly difficult times of their old country and by their own success. Through correspondence and occasional visits, they maintained strong ties to friends and relatives in Suffolk, yet, paraphrasing Samuel Sr.'s words, they were truly and successfully transplanted.

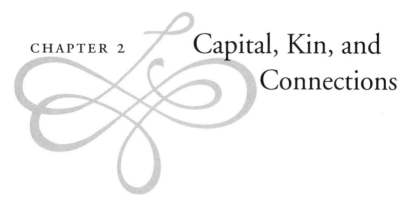

CHAPTER 2 — Capital, Kin, and Connections

The mercantile trade held out to the young Watkinsons the possibility of wealth and high social status, if not the certainties of class that they may have envisioned. Merchants were the prime movers of society in these years, but even the most casual use of the term "class" cannot contain the wide variety of entrepreneurs who were considered or who described themselves as merchants. In the larger cities the term "merchant" was generally reserved for wholesalers, distinguishing them from shopkeepers or grocers; in smaller cities, such as Hartford and Middletown, merchants combined "navigation," an export-import enterprise, with the running of a general store. In the small cities only a small number of such merchants became wealthy, and though these few and their families loomed large on the social scene many more lived modestly at the level of artisans.[1] The Watkinsons' capital and letters of introduction had brought them ready acceptance into the upper reaches of Middletown's network of mercantile families.

Families, not individuals, were the cornerstones of success in the mercantile enterprise just as they were in every other eighteenth-century endeavor.[2] Families were still the major institution for occupational training or for taking care of the sick, elderly or insane, and, in the absence of corporations or lending institutions, they were the primary source of capital and business connections.[3]

Commerce moved along personal ties—ties of friendship, kinship, and marriage. Banking facilities were still rudimentary; credit was based on personal trust so that accepting a merchant's bank notes was a display of faith that they would prove to be worth more than mere paper. The most common form of organization was a partnership, and family partnerships were the rule—brothers and brothers-in-law or father and son, father and son-in-law, or cousins.[4] These were men one knew and could trust. In the absence of forms of corporation, at a time when one was liable for a partner's debts, ties of kinship through birth or marriage were considered the most reliable.

Like the patriarch of a lineage whose corporate nature was based on land or cattle, Samuel Watkinson faithfully husbanded the family's capital by guiding his sons' entry into the commercial world and, with the help of his wife, by training both sons and daughters to expand and strengthen the family's connections.[5] John, the oldest son, twenty-four years of age, began several commercial enterprises immediately upon his arrival in Middletown. Within his first month there he, along with three fellow emigrants, purchased a mill seat and began to erect a flour mill. Shortly afterwards he also began building a brewery with his brother-in-law and several Middletown entrepreneurs. By spring he had been offered partnerships by two of the most important merchants in town. He retained an interest in both the mill and brewery and became a partner of Elijah Hubbard's, devoting most of his time to this enterprise. Under the name of John R. Watkinson & Co. the partnership engaged in trade with the West Indies and, to a lesser extent, in the coastal trade to New York and Virginia. Ten years later his marriage to Hubbard's daughter would further connect him with one of the wealthiest and most respected families in the city.

John had the experience and capital, assisted by a generous loan from his father, to start as a full-fledged merchant. His younger brothers, however, were not yet prepared to set up on their own. With Hubbard's recommendations to several of his contacts, Samuel Sr. traveled to New York City and Philadelphia, accompanied by his two eldest sons and his son-in-law Jacob Pledger, to find positions for four of his sons as merchants' clerks. He was able to place Samuel Jr., 23, Richard, 20, and David, 18, with merchants in New York City and William, 17, in Philadelphia, where several of their former Suffolk neighbors had established themselves. Samuel Sr. continued to advise his sons and provided each of them with a generous stipend of $100 a year, which allowed them to accept positions in which they received only room and board or a small wage which included an allowance for room and board. "I have been spreading my sons about," wrote Samuel Sr. to Meeking. "William is in Philadelphia and Samel and Richard in New York whither David is going in a few days all in the mercantile way."[6]

Connecticut merchants frequently sent their sons to work in merchant establishments in the larger cities. It served the dual purpose of occupational training and of expediting the families' commercial interests. New York, Philadelphia, and Boston were the major seaports on the Eastern coast. Their merchants carried out long-distance trade with Europe, China, and the West Indies as well as domestic trade with Virginia and Delaware. Connecticut merchants were dependent on New York and Boston to market rums and sugars from the West Indies to Europe and England. The credits they received were used to purchase the imported goods that Connecticut's farmers sought in return for their produce, which, to complete this triangle, was the necessary and desired commodity for the West Indian sugar plantations. Having good connections to one of these cities was extremely important for a Connecticut merchant.[7] If the young Watkinsons succeeded in establishing themselves, it would extend the family network in a valuable way.

Even as beginning clerks they were in a position to contribute to the family capital by providing information and services to their Middletown relatives. There was no bank in Middletown at the time, so Samuel Jr. carried out all of his father's and John's banking transactions at the Bank of the United States in New York. He provided his father with firsthand information on the prospects of companies in which he was considering investment or in which he already held shares. He held a power of attorney for his brother-in-law, Jacob Pledger, which enabled him to collect and bank the interest on his shares, and he kept the family informed of current prices, sales, and discounts on goods they wished to sell. He marketed Pledger's barley to New York brewers, took orders for the Middletown brewery, and purchased hoop iron for its barrels, receiving a small commission on goods that he purchased or sold for John and Pledger.

Richard carried out a much smaller amount of business for John, also providing information on goods and prices, acting as a middleman between his employer, a Mr. Kershaw, who was interested in purchasing flaxseed for export, and John, who could buy directly from local farmers. Richard obtained small amounts of cloth for John to sell in Middletown and settled his accounts with New York merchants.[8] John paid him a commission and assured him that having "an eye and brain in New York" was valuable for his trade.[9] While there are no records of William's participation in the family network during this period, there is a mention of David as well as Richard and Samuel Jr. helping to market beer from the Middletown brewery, though, at least once, David drank up his portion instead of distributing it.[10]

Samuel Jr.'s and Richard's years in New York are richly documented in their letters and in Samuel's journals, providing a glimpse into the life of the city in the years 1795–1798 from their points of view as they each in somewhat different ways and with very different temperaments strove for success as merchants and as men. Their family in Middletown remained a meaningful presence kept close by correspondence and by occasional visits. Though their sisters' letters have not been preserved in any archive, a faint image of who they were and who, as women, they were supposed to be can be discerned through the letters that Samuel Jr. and Richard wrote to them.

Samuel Jr. was the first to leave Middletown, moving to New York in December of 1795. His father traveled with him and remained a few days as he settled temporarily in a boardinghouse. Samuel Jr. moved two weeks later, when he took up his position with Galbraith & Sing, wholesalers of "ironmonger cutlery" (cutlery made of iron), "japan ware" (dishes decorated with painted or raised figures), and hardware. It was agreed that Samuel Jr. would clerk for Mr. Sing through the winter months, which promised to be busy, and decide in the spring if he wanted to remain. Mr. Sing offered Samuel room and board but no wages. Working without wages was a way of starting, a form of job training in the merchant trade, but only young men, such as the Watkinsons, with money of their own and/or an allowance could accept a position on these terms.

Samuel Jr. described this arrangement with Mr. Sing to his father. "With respect to wages, he [Sing] did not wish to make any bargain at present any otherwise than that, I should live with him as his other Servants did."[11] The ambivalent term "servant," which had a wide range of meanings, covered here a sense of informal apprenticeship and of being a part of the household.[12] Samuel described his new place favorably in a letter dated two weeks later. "Mr and Mrs are about 28 years of age and live very happily with their two children which they are very fond of. The Nurse who takes care of the children, the young man who waits in the store and myself always set down at meals with family. Mr. S is a very agreeable man and very much respected by his family; the servants are very much attached to them both."[13]

In the spring, however, he left Galbraith & Sing's, having found a more promising position, again through a recommendation of Hubbard, at Rogers & Woolsey, which he described as "one of the first houses in this city in the hardware business; importing, very largely from England, Holland and Germany."[14] Samuel Jr. agreed to work for a year's time or to give "timely notice of quitting them," in exchange for a small wage of £150. Although he was no longer part of his employer's household, his board and lodging were seen as the firm's responsibility; he had been promised that if

Supposed Annual Expences in the City of N York.

Boarding & Lodging 5 doll^{rs} P^r week	260.—
Porter & Brandy. 6/. P^r week	39.—
Hats	8.—
1 Broadcloth coat	16.—
2 Gingham Coatees	8.—
½ a Surtout $12/	6.—
1 Kerseimer or Swansdown waistcoat	5.—
2 Summer vests	6.—
1 Flannel vest	1.—
2 Pr Kerseimer breeches with drawers	13.—
2 Pr Nankin — do — without do	6.—
5 Pr Shoes	12.—
1½ P^r bootees $6.— (or 1 P^r whole Boots)	9.—
mending shoes & boots	6.—
Buckles & ribband	5.—
1 P^r supporters	1.—
2 P^r silk stockings	7.—
2 P^r cotton do	3.—
2 P^r patent worsted do	4.—
Hair cutting & dressing Powder & Pomatum	20.—
½ doz shirts	18.—
4 cravats	3.—
2 Pocket hdkfs	1.—
4 Pr Gloves	2.—
Postage	5.—
Pens Ink & paper	1.—
Cloaths mending	5.—
Linen washing & mending	20.—
Church subscriptions & Charity, watch mend^g knives scissars razors Brushes sleeve buttons &c }	5.—
Sundries	45.—
	$540 —

he should have to pay more in board for a place he liked than the firm's usual rate, his wage would be adjusted accordingly. He went to board at William McEwen's at Sixth and Pine Street.[15]

Boarding & Lodging 5 dollars pr week	260.—
Porter & Brandy 6/ pr week	39.—
Hats	8.—
1 Broadcloth vest	16.—
2 Gingham bootees	8.—
½ a Surtout $12/	6.—
1 Kersimer or Swansdown waistcoat	5.—
2 Summer vests	6.—
1 Flannel vest	1.—
2 pr Kersimer breeches with drawers	13.—
2 pr Nankin do without do	6.—
5 pr Shoes	12.—
1 ½ pr bootees $6.— (or 1 pr of whole Boots)	9.—
mending shoes & boots	6.—
Buckles & ribband	5.—
1 pr supporters	1.—
2 pr silk stockings	7.—
2 pr cotton do	3.—
2 pr patent worsted do	4.—
Hair cutting & dressing Powder & Pomatum	20.—
½ doz shirts	18.—
4 cravats	3.—
2 Pocket hdkfs	1.—
4 pr Gloves	1.—
Postage	5.—
Pens Ink & paper	1.—
Cloths mending	5.—
Linen washing & mending	20.—
Church subscriptions & Charity, watch mending	5.—
knives scissors razors Brushes sleeve buttons &c	
Sundries	45.—

$540.—

It was a traditional practice for merchants to place their sons as clerks with a relative or business associate to learn the trade and eventually to become a partner. Frequently such partnerships were further cemented, as John's would be, by marrying the merchant's daughter.[16] Although Samuel entered this position with the expectation at least of a future partnership, his hopes were not met, and eight months later he wrote to tell his father that Mr. Woolsey had turned him down and that he was, therefore, making a new plan, He would go into "the business of importing hardware," with his promising younger brother David in a year, when David's obligations to his employer were completed.[17] Samuel Jr. added that he would not tell his brothers Richard or William about his plans as they might become jealous. His choice of David as a potential partner was based on more than kinship. Richard was closer in age to Samuel Jr. and two years older than David, but David at eighteen had already revealed the promise that would eventually lead him to great wealth. In contrast, Richard showed signs of a frivolous and mercurial nature.

Richard had followed Samuel Jr. to New York in March of 1796, taking a position where he clerked for and lived with Mr. Kershaw, a dry-goods merchant. Richard was soon dissatisfied with both his work and his lodgings, however. Business was slow, and in the fall he began to think of leaving: "the Business which have been done in this House these 12 months I alone could do in 6 weeks, next spring I intend altering my situation But do not expect as much wages in any other Place."[18] In December he moved to Samuel's boardinghouse, which at first seemed pleasant,[19] but within two months he was again looking for a new place to board. He continued to write about his hopes of changing jobs, but there were few to be found, as merchant houses were being affected by a sudden shift in the international climate.

Until this point the ongoing war between England and France had benefitted American merchants in the West Indian trade as both antagonists had opened their Caribbean ports to neutral American shipping. But in a sudden reversal of policy the French had ceased treating American ships as neutrals and were firing on trading vessels bringing supplies to the British West Indies. Many businesses had failed, "among them the house of Galbraith & Sing," Samuel Jr.'s former employer.[20] With the closing of numerous merchant firms, many other young men were competing for positions.

Richard described the scene to his father in a letter in which he tried to get paternal approval for a change in employment. He first justified his desire to leave the old and then supported his choice of a new position by suggesting that he was following his friends' advice.

Dear Father Being now upon the lookout for a situation for the ensuing Spring, I have taken the liberty to address a few lines to you concerning the same. It's unnecessary to mention the few advantageous to be derived from being in such a store as Mr Kershaw's having the last fall had little or no business as you may judge by our not having sold more than 700 Dolls value in goods these six months past. — I have advised with several of my friends what situation would be most proper for me to engage in and they seem to be of opinion that an office in some shipping house would be far more advantageous than one in a dry good store.

He pointed out that the difficult times and the number of young men looking for fewer situations were leading merchants to offer no wages, only board and lodgings. Then in a tricky sentence he slipped in the fact that the position he would like to take was not even offering that. He clearly anticipated his father's disapproval and tried in vain to circumvent it. "Therefore have made application at several houses but have met with little success owing to the many failures that have taken place which have caused many young men to be out of employ: therefore the most I can expect for my time in the best situations is board & Lodging Your advice I now solicit respecting a situation I have now in view where neither can be procured that of Edw Good & Sons a Shipping House largely in the East India European & West India trade also the Commission Business."

The firm, he suggested, was one of the best and, furthermore, his brothers believed he should take it. "It's as respectable (if not more so) than any other in this City in point of credit connexions & the regularity with which they manage their business. My brothers & myself thinking this situation too advantageous to be slighted have thought proper to communicate it to you your sentiments upon what this subject by return of post will much oblige your Dutiful Son R Watkinson."[21]

A note at the bottom of this page in Richard's letterbook indicates that, indeed, his father was quick to respond: "Received an answer to the above by Return of Post." Samuel Sr. made short work of the notion of entering a shipping firm and strongly disapproved of Richard's taking a position without wages, board, or lodging. "I do not see what particular use it can be of to you to be in a house which is in the Shipping business only—I have always been of the opinion and am yet that a large retail or wholesale and retail store and not a wholesale store only was the best situation for you, having no idea that the shipping business was that you was likely to engage in to advantage—But moreover if I read your letter right in the house you mention you was not only to have no wages but neither board nor lodging nor allowance for them, you know you are not able to engage with anyone on such terms."

He went on to criticize Richard for the sloppiness of his letter, implying that it was because of his shortcomings that he had received such a poor offer.[22] "If they had read your letter, I would not have been so much surprised at them, there being sundry words omitted and other spelt Wrong. It surely shows great carelessness or something worse to let a letter pass out of your hands so exceptionable—You can live without wages but board washing and lodging you cannot and they that expect you should work for them without those and after having been near a year in [New] York pay a very poor compliment to your abilities."[23]

The previous year Samuel Jr. had made a similar criticism when Richard was first setting out, exhorting him to: "increase your knowledge of accounts or improve your handwriting," adding that "if David can do the same he will reap the benefit of it himself and indeed without these provisions I cannot venture to recommend either of You."[24] David had surely listened, but Richard apparently had not taken this good advice. More was at stake than simple neatness and clarity; sloppy handwriting was an indication of moral weakness. It suggested debility of character in an untrustworthy person. Correspondence was not a casual undertaking; the presentation of self in this form was carefully constructed.[25] Letters were first drafted into a letterbook and then corrected and copied with the best possible handwriting.[26] Even or especially in these letters within the family the aim was to communicate a picture of a proper self, one who could be respected and trusted. Both Samuel Sr. and Jr. were addressing serious matters.

Other worrisome signs indicated that Richard was not demonstrating the proper attributes of a successful merchant. His next employment lasted only a few days before he was asked to leave. "I had engaged to serve as Book Keeper after the rate of 450 dollars per annum after being with Mr Cruger but three days he informed me that I did not suit him he having met with a more able accomplant." He could not return to his old place and was using up his savings, $300 from his previous employment and the $100, which he received as an annual allowance from his father, so he asked William to help him find a job in Philadelphia.[27]

By May, however, he had found a position in New York, but, despite his father's advice, it was in a shipping house. Richard thought it a good place where he would earn "400 Doll per year and [have the] liberty of putting an adventure in each of his vessels—which probably would be advantageous at any other than the present critical times."[28] He and Samuel Jr. took advantage of this opportunity, investing in butter and smoked herrings to be shipped to ports such as Tenerife (in the Canary Islands) or Surinam. Richard wrote to his father requesting $100 toward one of his adventures, but his father's response, though unknown, was undoubtedly negative. Richard's records show a loss on one adventure of $25.90 and a gain on another of $39.60.[29]

Trade continued to falter during the rest of the year and into early 1798, but Richard nonetheless wanted to invest in a more ambitious adventure. He wrote to his father in February that he was planning to ask for a raise and requested that Samuel Sr. send him a sum of £500 which, he believed, had been promised, arguing that despite the gloomy times for business there were opportunities for those with money to invest. "The prospect for doing business in this city is at present very gloomy especially for young beginners, tho many opportunities offer when a person in my situation with some property at his command do business often to great advantage." He gilded his words with filial gratitude. "The pleasing recollection of your generous promise last fall to advance me the ensuing Spring 500 £ Sterling to do the best for my own accounts which with the many favors you have and are continually confering upon me ever commands the gratefulness and affection of Your dutiful son."[30]

His father responded sternly on both the raise and the adventure, questioning Richard's appraisal of his own worth, denying that any such sum had been promised, and rebuking his recklessness and arrogance. "I observe what you say about wages and I expect you will overate your services, and think you ought to be content...I was much surprised at your Idea you have formed of my promising you 500 £ this Spring as I do not remember any thing of it—but only of the interest of it—You have been but about two years in the Mercantile World and but just turned of twenty one—in england young men of your standing very seldom think of going into business for some years—And to be so very desirous of it in such unsettled times as these do not appear very prudential."[31] In his father's view Richard was clearly reckless and lacking in judgment, serious faults in a man seeking to find his way as a merchant.

Practical skills of keeping accounts and copying letters and orders were necessary to the aspiring merchant, and a grasp of the fluctuations and dangers of the market was essential; most important, however, was to gain a reputation as a serious and dependable person. A man had to learn to act in such as way as to present himself to other merchants as a person worthy of their trust. In what has been likened to the theater—the merchant world—Richard was having difficulty in learning his part, while his brother, Samuel Jr., had both the skills and the inclination to play the role.[32]

Both brothers had brought to New York a number of books and objects, props that helped to define them socially as educated young men. Richard's library consisted of "Brooks Gazetteer Carreys Guthries in two Quarto Volumes with a large Folio Atlas of every Country and each of the United States, as well as Shakespears works compleat in Octavo Vol," and he had added to these some smaller books purchased with his first year's salary.[33] Samuel's library was composed of a French dictionary, grammar, Bible, Roman history, *Recueil Dialogues des Morts,* psalms, Dilworth, English history, and geography—all of which he had requested Richard to forward to him from Middletown when he first came to New York, along with his shaving box, brushes, pumps, spurs, whip, writing box, papers, knives, and scissors.[34] Samuel's list of books reflects his serious self-image. He had probably purchased the French dictionary and grammar when he began studying at Lacotte's French Academy shortly after he started his first job, believing that it would prove useful. His mention of "Dilworth" may have referred to Thomas Dilworth's *The Young Book-keeper's Assistant: Shewing Him the Italian Way of Stating Debtor and Creditor.* It was published in London in the 1760s and went into at least twenty-one editions. It might, however, have been W. H. Dilworth's *The Complete Letter-Writer,* a volume originally published in 1786 in Edinburgh which then went into several editions in New York in the 1790s. He left his drawings, music, skates and, presumably, any other remnants of his childhood behind in Middletown.

Appearance was important. Samuel kept a careful record of his weight, and he advised his younger brother William "to be careful how you spend your money; to dress yourself genteely with neatness and plainess and without foppery so will you command respect from all. I think you might spare the expence of hair dressing by doing the job yourself."[35] His views on proper hairdressing changed over the next two years, and he made note in his journal on September 19, 1797 that he had begun to have his hair dressed three times a week. In January of 1798 he began to be dressed and shaved four times per week. He also noted that during that same month he began to be taught dancing.[36]

Samuel criticized merchants who lacked stability. "The people in the Country as well as the City are continually changing their connections in business, trying new places, there are but few merchants whose firm continues the same more than two years and very often not so long as that." From the vast authority of his twenty-four years he blamed "their unstable and speculative turn of mind" on their immaturity, which, he suggested, was due to the climate. "The greater part of the merchants begin to trade before they are arrived at years of discretion. The young men are ready to undertake business at 18 or 19 years of age and the young ladies are marriageable at 16 or 17. It is a warm climate and they as well as the fruits of the earth ripen quick."[37]

He, however, was concerned to present himself as a serious and mature person. Even when he felt dissatisfied with the wages he received at Rogers & Woolsey he was loath to leave for fear that "if I changed it some perhaps would say that I was an unsettled being."[38] Careful of his reputation, Samuel appears to have been shaped and to have shaped himself into a dependable, serious, and promising young man with his feet set in an approved direction. His most frivolous statement in all of his correspondence or journal entries was a request to Meeking to send some songs from England, but he specified that these should be suitable for young ladies. "If you have an opportunity of selecting about 1/2 dozen good songs such as are not unsuitable to the ladies and such likewise as are new and charge them to my fathers accot I shall esteem it as a favor conferred on me."[39] Letters certainly do not reveal the whole story about anyone, but the willingness to say what may be expected and not to say anything else even in the privacy of a journal was part of being the trustworthy and respected merchant that Samuel showed promise of becoming, while Richard was volatile and imaginative. In the social world beyond the merchants' counting houses Samuel Jr. followed a straight path, while Richard wandered, dreaming of pleasant byways.

Richard's letters to his father were respectful and serious; he shared some personal news with his brother, John, but these letters are careful and somewhat reserved when compared to those he wrote to his younger brothers and sisters. With them he displayed a rambling, newsy, and charming style. Unlike Samuel Jr. he never employed an authoritarian elder brother's tone. He shared a thought with William that revealed a less than businesslike frame of mind: "having just awaked from an agreeable reverie that was most pleasing from which I am now plunged by the call of the world to business but oh, how painful to be awaked from our pleasing immaginations!"[40]

Another letter to William displays his sense of humor as he teased his younger brother about a playful interaction with a young woman whom William had described. "You were indeed unlucky when in swinging a young Lady to have a rope so weak as not to bear her weight [!] but your medical aid (which I presume was nothing more than a few kisses) made all right the next morning. I hope you will be as fortunate in applying the same to your foot."[41]

He complained of the hours shut up in the counting house. To Mary he wrote, "I am not situated as you are, my days are all alike. I am continually kept in the Counting Room. Whereas in Middletown your amusements are various and pleasing." To Eliza he sent a similar reproach, comparing her fortune to his: "The charming Spring now approaches and call forth those Ideas which have been laying dormant so long, to you, I look for new Ideas; as for us Cityzens winter and summer are all one, the *Desk* is Hard." Richard probably exaggerated the tedium of his days, since despite the long hours that clerks were expected to work, they were generally able to take several hours away from their offices for lunch or to go for a walk with friends.[42]

While Richard imagined his sisters' pleasant lives, envying them the country pleasures of Middletown, they undoubtedly were much occupied in household work, the care of the younger children or the sick, and the preparation of food as well as sewing for the entire family. Servants, as Samuel Jr. had noted, were far fewer than in England, and though he believed that the reason that men were less disturbed by this fact than women was because they did not require "so much to be waited upon,"[43] he ignored the extent to which his sisters were the ones who did the "waiting upon." Perhaps their hours of work were shorter than their brothers' and their days less tedious, but it appears that their daily tasks were not defined as work.

Richard had also expressed this gendered blindness to women's work within the household in an earlier letter to Eliza. Although he acknowledged that the absence of servants limited her time, when he complained about some shirts she had sewn for him he nonetheless implied that her social engagements kept her from more strenuous efforts, "...and of course [you] have but little time to devote to the needle after having returned the visits of your friends...hope you will wait your own pleasure in making me more."[44]

Unfortunately Eliza's reply is not preserved in the archives nor were any of her sisters' letters. Their brothers refer to these vanished letters, and it's clear that they wrote each other frequently. The interchange of letters and favors between brothers and sisters reflected their gendered roles, modeling a reciprocity that would eventually take place in the married relation.[45] Though letters were exchanged between several of the brothers and sisters, each brother seems to have been paired with a particular sister who sewed for him: Mary for Samuel Jr., Eliza for Richard. Thus Samuel wrote to his older sister Mary,[46] itemizing what he had and had not received from her in the way of shirts, requesting a new vest, and assuring her that he had sufficient cravats.

> Your favor by brother JRW I recd with 2 shirts and a silk handkerchief and return you my thanks for the trouble you have taken with them; but if I recollect aright I sent by brother 2 shirts in October and in Feb 1797 2 more by G Phillips and you do not accot for more than three—I have taken the liberty of sending you two more which I should be obliged to you to repair. I believe Brother JRW will be able to show you some handsome patterns for vests of which be so good as to make me up one and send by the first opportunity he will be able to give you particulars. As to the cravats you need not trouble yourself to provide them having already provided them.[47]

Samuel's tone has an authoritative edge, expressing his need for his sister's services as a request, but one with which she will surely comply. His letters tended to be formal, almost stiff, even when he responded to her invitation to attend one of the Middletown assemblies, referring to "the obligations I am under for your kind invitation to come and dance at your assemblies. At present my time is fully occupied." This letter, too, concluded with a request for a vest.[48]

Richard expected his older sister Eliza to meet his requests, and in his letter, complaining of the coarseness of the shirts she had sewn for him, he said, "I should be much obliged if you would procure the finest and best piece of Irish Linnen brothers store produced for the frills." However, in addition to thanking her for her work he reciprocated with gifts, on one occasion with a bonnet of "very newest fashion," and on another with a "special face wash" that he sent to Mary as well as Eliza.[49]

His letters to his youngest sister, eleven-year-old Jane, show him to be a fond older brother. He congratulated her on her successes in school, described fires in New York, and asked if she felt like making him some shirts, handkerchiefs, or cravats. He approved of her dancing lessons and wrote that, "I anticipate the time when I may have the pleasure of seeing you grace the floor of a New York Assembly Room."[50] In the tone of the suitor she would one day meet, he gently chided her for not writing. "I am writing tho I believe you owe me a letter, but my love for you keeps alive our correspondence, which I hope fails not in your quarter."[51] On another occasion when he was the delinquent writer, he assured her that he was indeed willing to correspond with her. "I am happy that your apprehensions respecting my negligence in not writing are vanished—for believe me it is and ever will be a great pleasure to me to continue upon the list of my correspondents my amiable sister Jane."[52]

Entering into a correspondence was an important part of building and maintaining relationships. Sentiment was involved, but survival, security, and success also resided in these ties. The simple fact of biological relationship was not sufficient; it had to be reinforced through continuing acts of communication and reciprocity.[53] Breaking off correspondence or tardiness in replying was taken seriously, as a threat to these important ties. A letter from Richard to his older sister Mary, although written with his customary lightness, expressed a serious concern at her failure to write.

> I would, it were in my power to engage my Sister to correspond with her Brother tho it were not often, a few times in the course of a year, but I fear Sister's too far gone! lost in melancholy thoughts! believe me, the last letter from you was dated the 11th Feb—just six months since I have had the pleasure of receiving a letter from my sister, who promised during the cold season of Winter that when the all enlivening Spring should appear and her spirits be renewed by the appearance of summer to be a generous correspondent and not require this harsh language which is most disagreeable to me. I yet flatter myself that you my dear sister will not be so dilatory in your writings as you have been.[54]

The archive does not contain Mary's response, but she undoubtedly answered him, since in a letter written to her in November he accepted her excuses: "You plead so well for an excuse for your long silence that all I have to say, my hope is that you'll not forget me so long again."[55]

Although occasionally laggard in his responses, Richard was for the most part careful in extending and maintaining his kin relationships. He initiated a correspondence with his married sister, Sarah Pledger, by sending a gift as well as a letter. "After my long absence from you dear Sister and my friends in Middletown I now solicit a correspondence which I have comenced by these few lines ... and accompanied with a ... (a small present) which I hope will be acceptable from a Brother, whose long absence has not in the least abated his affection."[56]

The term "friends" referred here to relatives and suggests the importance and the social as well as the given nature of these relationships. Kinship terms and the term "friend" were extended to relatives through marriage, and these "brothers" and "sisters" were vitally important to the continuance of the family. Connections established through marriage held the possibility of extending networks and capital, and finding a suitable partner, therefore, was not only a consuming personal concern; it was also a matter of material interest as well as personal interest to all of one's family.

Not long after he came to New York, Richard received a stern letter from his eldest brother, John, interrogating him about a rumor that he had formed an improper connection with a young woman. "Dear Brother, Report here says you correspond with Miss Fouchong and that you are coming to Middletown to see her this summer—I wish to know if I may contradict or confirm it from you. I should not have troubled you with a letter but from a wish of your being acquainted with what nearly concerned you—I hope you will not by any indirect answer to this letter forfeit the friendship of your affectionate brother."[57] These are strong words—this threat of alienation from kinship ties. The archives are silent on Miss Fouchong's identity, and no family by this name is listed in the census, so the reasons for John's disapproval remain unknown.[58] Richard must have answered immediately and convincingly, however, since a few weeks later John responded favorably, expressing his relief that the rumor was false and offering to engage with him in some commercial transactions. The connection between proper social connections and mercantile success could not have been made more strongly. "I received your letter dated 16 July in answer to my last it fully satisfied me this town has its lovers of scandal. . . . If you remain in your present situation and can find leisure—I should probably have some business which I should wish to pass thru your hands and on which I would allow you commission."[59] The incident was apparently closed, and over the next months they corresponded about the price of flaxseed and cloth.

Away from the surveillance of his father and oldest brother, Richard attended the fashionable balls known as "New York Assemblies" or "City Assemblies." Although one paid for a subscription to these dances, entry was only for those who were regarded as belonging to the upper reaches of society.[60] Richard's attendance marked him as an up-and-coming young man, who was welcomed to enjoy the music, the dancing, and, especially, the opportunity to become acquainted with young women. He wrote to William and Eliza about the Assemblies, cautioning each of them not to tell his parents.

His letter to William included a complaint about his limited resources, but he seemed to find the means to enjoy his life in New York. "I have not been to many places of amusement since my arrival in this city finding it too expensive for my salary—tho I have not debarred myself from company—brothers & myself often walk out a few miles for the fresh air on the Sabbath—some times ride a few miles tho very little of the latter—I have attended the theatre but thrice, the amphitheatre once & three public Balls this Winter — And the latter I should have appeared very awkward had I not attended a dancing school for three months preceding which I wish to keep from the knowledge of our friends in M—on [Middletown]."[61]

He described one of the Assemblies to his sister. There were "250 ladies and about 200 gent." One young woman impressed him, "surely the most handsome, eyes ever beheld!!! and a very amiable Lady of a respectable family in this city." He enjoyed the music, "had you but 1/5 the music in Middletown I should prefer being there but as it is, I think these assemblies far preferable." He ended the letter with a postscript, "Show this letter to no one as my parents would not be pleased to hear of my going to the assemblies."[62] The lure of New York and independence was clearly at odds with Richard's sense of familial bonds and expectations.

His parents would not have objected to the dancing or to the music but to the fact that they were unacquainted with most of the families of those who attended. A young man such as Richard might become entangled with a woman from the wrong sort of family. In contrast, invitations to the Middletown Assemblies were proffered by a group of known and respected men. Membership in this Assembly Committee was by election of the Committee and implied a recognition of high social rank and the ability to wisely choose only the proper young people to invite. When John Watkinson was elected to the Committee, Richard wrote to congratulate him and to recommend that he invite a young lady with whom Richard had become acquainted. Despite telling his younger sister that he preferred the New York assemblies since the music was better, Richard's letter to his older sister Mary expressed approval of the more restricted gatherings. "I understand you are going to dances at Middletown after the same plan as at Lanham, which I highly approve of I think far more agreeable than dancing in company of *we know not whom.*"[63] It is unlikely that Richard had changed his mind during the year's interval that separates these two letters; rather, he probably knew what his older sister would consider a proper response.

The Middletown assemblies provided entertainment, but their primary function was to introduce respectable young people of good society to one another to facilitate marriage connections between well established families. Although the assemblies may have been unfamiliar to the Watkinsons, the desirability or even necessity of seeing that one's children were suitably married was as much a part of their old culture as of their new.[64]

As commonplace as this may be, in societies where marriages are not overtly arranged by the families, the structuring of experience that is necessary to guide children to make the correct marital choice is a complex matter. The obvious and overt moves were in the assemblies, which were kept exclusive to families of the correct social standing. John's disapproval and open threat of breaking ties with Richard on the suspicion that he was associating with an unacceptable young woman was an indication of the overt policing of sentiment. However, more subtle and harder to trace are the ways in which young people succeeded in learning to be attracted to the right and not the wrong kind of person and to present themselves as desirable and appropriate marital partners.

The family's daughters as much as the sons had parts to learn and important roles to play. The marriages they would make were a crucial part of enhancing the family's associations and capital. Learning to become the expected and respected kind of person was coded into roles that were defined by gender and class in very specific terms in the elite mercantile culture of late eighteenth century New England. Such roles demanded a carefully cultivated appearance of openness and sincerity, which led to a fear that others might be only playing a part and presenting a false mask that concealed a potential betrayer—a business partner who would lead one into bankruptcy or a suitor of no enduring worth.[65] Knowledge of family background was a partial guarantee that someone was who he or she seemed to be.

Like a lineage or a clan, these networks of family connections were bulwarks of security in an extremely dangerous and unpredictable world in which seemingly healthy persons and secure businesses might be destroyed overnight. Death and bankruptcy were common and sudden; both struck without notice, attacking young and old alike. Merchants were at the mercy of political and economic forces. They controlled neither labor force nor polity. The safety of their capital and their selves depended on their abilities to strengthen ties within the family and to fashion connections with other well established families.

All but one of the Watkinson daughters married successful merchants, and Eliza, the exception, married a well-connected lawyer. All but one son became a prosperous merchant and married into wealthy, important families. William was, as his brother, David, noted, "unfortunate in business a few years since, as well as in his marriage connection."[66]

Late in the summer of 1798 yellow fever swept through New York City. All of those who could had already fled, aware of the frightful toll that had been exacted there and in Philadelphia in previous years. The illness was known to have come from the West Indies, but its mode of transmission was mysterious. Samuel Jr. and Richard had planned to leave for Middletown, but on the very day they were to go Samuel Jr. fell sick. He survived for nine days, nursed by Richard, who also caught the fever and died two days after his brother. William fell ill at the same time as Samuel Jr., and David, who was caring for him, was infected as well. Slowly, however, both David and William recovered. Samuel Sr. wrote back to his family and friends in Suffolk of this great loss. "Dear Cousin, I wrote you last August all in good health and spirits, but in less than a month what a sad reverse—The Plague or Yellow Fever as it is called broke in NYork and it has been the will of the Almighty to bereave us by that dreadful visitation of his Providence of our two Sons Samuel and Richard . . . Wm also was seized with y[ellow] fever about the same time as Samuel his case was thought dangerous for some time David attending him also caught the disorder but thro mercy they have both recovered. In the midst of Judgments God has remembered mercy."[67]

After his brothers' deaths, David left New York and spent a few months regaining his own health in Middletown, and then settled in Hartford, where he began to build an extremely successful mercantile career. Hartford was close to the family and showed signs of becoming a more dynamic and prosperous center of commerce than Middletown. William, who had come to New York a year before the epidemic, continued to clerk there for several years, after which he joined David as a partner in the firm of D & W Watkinson. Like John, who was well established in Middletown, their main business was trade with the West Indies. New York held sad memories and it was also, as Samuel Jr. had noted, a place where it was difficult for strangers to be introduced to respectable people, a serious limitation to prospects of success.[68] In contrast, the Watkinsons fit easily into the prosperous Connecticut River Valley network of commerce. Recovering from the recent tragic loss of their brothers, they continued to expand their connections, add grandchildren to the family, and increase their capital.

CHAPTER 3

Balancing the Books

John Watkinson entered the West Indian trade at a high point in New England's long history of commerce with the islands. It had begun with the infamous triangular trade in 1644, when a New England ship sold Africans carried away from Cape Verde to Barbados in the West Indies for a cargo of tobacco (Bailyn 1984, 84). Within a few years Boston and Rhode Island were preeminent in this slave trade, which provided first Barbados and then other Caribbean islands with African slaves in exchange for sugar, tobacco, and cotton. Inland, from Vermont to Connecticut along the Connecticut River, the West Indian trade developed on different though related foundations. Although the region had a few slave traders, most of its merchants shipped produce, livestock, and wooden barrels—rather than slaves—to the plantations. As the Calvinist governor of the Massachusetts Bay Colony, John Winthrop, had noted as early as 1647, the planters of Barbados were "so intent upon planting sugar that they had rather buy foode at very deare rates than produce it by labour, soe infinite is the profitt of sugar workes after once accomplished" (quoted in Bailyn, 85).

Winthrop's observation has been echoed by historians ever since as they have traced the growing symbiosis between New England and the West Indies in which New England supplied the provisions essential for the survival and spread of the Caribbean sugar plantations.[1] Other forms of trade were added, but all depended on the ability of New England to produce food, livestock, and lumber in exchange for high-profit goods, such as sugars and rums, tobaccos, salt, and, later, coffee, which could be sold to earn credits for English manufactured goods.

The development of New England was closely linked to the expansion of the West Indian trade.[2] It was the impetus that roused the small farms of New England into surplus production, a surplus frequently minimal in quantity, two or three hogs or a few bushels of grain (Martin, 6). Gathered up with the assorted gleanings of a hundred or a thousand farms, however, they were worth a wealth of credits in the merchants' pockets.[3] Some subsistence farmers turned to raising cattle and horses; others produced handicrafts for export. Trade also provided incentives for shipbuilding and allied crafts such as sail making, coopering, pickling, and carpentry.

The merchants of the Connecticut Valley were neither as rich nor as powerful as the most successful merchants of New York, Boston, or Philadelphia, yet they were the dynamic force that transformed sleepy hamlets on the Connecticut River into small urban centers. Merchants had shaped the countryside to their needs, deepening the channel between Middletown and Hartford and building canals to circumvent waterfalls at Enfield, Connecticut, at South Hadley, Massachusetts, and at Turners Falls above Greenfield, Massachusetts. The merchants had arranged public lotteries to collect funds to build wharves and bridges and supports for the riverbanks (Martin 1939, 9–10; Saladino 1964).

The Revolutionary War interrupted trade and bankrupted many New England merchants, who saw their ships lying useless in the harbor, while providing opportunities to others who turned to privateering—legalized piracy, which involved boarding and looting British ships. The war was also a source of wealth for some of the merchants who helped provision the Continental army. Safely inland, away from shore and the marauding British Navy, which had burned down their sister cities of New London and New Haven, Middletown and Hartford became centers for storing the Connecticut Valley's agricultural produce. Two of Connecticut's leading merchants, Jeremiah Wadsworth and Elijah Hubbard, advanced their careers and expanded their fortunes through their official duties of supplying the army.[4]

After the war Britain closed off its West Indian islands to American ships, and though a few merchants prospered by sailing legally to the French, Dutch, and Danish islands, and illegally to the British (Lee and Passell 1979), for most the times were hard and unrewarding. But with the beginning of the war between France and England in 1793, trade boomed. This war, which had led indirectly to the Watkinsons' leaving one side of the Atlantic, was to assist their fortunes on the other over the next fifteen years, during the most lucrative period in history for the West Indian trade.

Middletown and Hartford had become the most important of the Connecticut River towns, with harbors sufficiently deep to provide safe anchorage for the small sloops, schooners, and brigs that plied the coastal and Caribbean trade, carrying crews of only seven, eight, or nine men. Both towns were within easy reach by river or, more expensively, by wagon to receive goods, which were processed and assembled as outward-bound cargoes. The merchants' warehouses provided storage for these goods, for the rum, molasses, coffee, and salt arriving from the West Indies, and for manufactured goods imported from England and shipped from New York.

The West Indies were also part of the social geography of Middletown's merchants. News of the West Indies was carried by the *Middlesex Gazette*, under the heading of "Domestic Politics," while news of Europe ran under the heading "Foreign Politics." The *Gazette* also featured "Maritime News," reporting on ships sailing to and from Middletown. Its advertisements listed the goods to be bought at a merchant's store or directly from a docked ship recently returned from the West Indies.

The Connecticut River was the source of Middletown's wealth, and Samuel Sr. likened it to the "Nile...carrying fertility wherever its waters expand."[5] Its fertility was not only in the soil deposited along the narrow strip of rich farmland lining its banks, but also in the trade flowing from Vermont through Springfield, Massachusetts, to Hartford and Middletown, carrying the promise of a rich return on capital invested in the products shipped to the West Indies.

That promise was usually, though not always, fulfilled, despite the dangers to captains, crews, and cargos from weather, disease, and attacks by foreign ships. The *Middlesex Gazette* reported many disasters—captains captured and jailed by the French, ships sunk in storms, or crews devastated by sickness—but when merchants spoke of "risks" and "adventures," they were referring to the capital they had invested and the possible increase that a shrewd and lucky trader might garner.

John Watkinson was not only shrewd and lucky; he was hardworking as well. His partnership provided him with the substantial backing of father-in-law Hubbard's capital and access to Hubbard's extensive network of connections in the Connecticut Valley, New York, and the West Indies (Young 1979, 11).[6] The partners owned several ships and a general store in Middletown.[7] Watkinson ran the store, selling groceries and dry goods: butter, eggs, and chickens from local farmers, imported cloth, laces, cutlery, shawls, and stockings from New York, tobacco and flour from Virginia, and, most important, rum, sugar, salt, molasses, coffee, and teas from the West Indies.

He sold for cash and credit, retail and wholesale, and his store accounts are filled with the names of family members and neighbors who bought small amounts of goods—a quart of rum or a pound of sugar each week. His main concern, however, was with the large-scale export-import commerce, which he and other merchants called "navigation"—the West Indies trade. He bought produce and goods from upriver merchants to assemble the outbound cargoes: thousands of wooden staves or thirty horses, barrels of preserved beef, and bushels of oats. He sold hogsheads of sugars, molasses, rums, and coffee to merchants or purchasing agents in Connecticut, Massachusetts, and New York.[8]

Like other merchants John Watkinson kept careful books, which might at all times be opened to the inspection of his partner, or, in cases of financial difficulty, be perused by a creditor to ascertain that payment might be forthcoming and that no assets were being concealed.[9] The entities in these account books were individuals, merchant partnerships, the ships, and even the Town of Middletown. There are entries for his father and mother, sisters, brothers, and neighbors; entries too for merchants such as Watkinsons & Co. (the Hartford firm of three of his brothers), Southmayd & Redfield, S. Pulcifer & Co., and *Schooner Sally, Schooner Hannah, Brig Two Brothers,* and *Sloop Industry.* In Watkinson's account books the large and small customers appear in the same manner, so that an entry debiting a neighbor for one quart of rum and another entry for one of his sisters for two pairs of stockings might share a page with a debit for three hogsheads of rum or molasses.

Watkinson's accounts followed precisely the form described by the earliest known treatise on double-entry bookkeeping, written by Luca Pacioli in 1494. Pacioli's textbook formulated the practices already common in several northern Italian cities, among merchant partnerships engaged in overseas trading (Chatfield 1977, 19). Pacioli's text described keeping a shop outside the home. "For all the goods which you supply it day by day, you shall debit the shop in your books, and credit the particular goods which you put in it one by one, and imagine that the shop is a person, your debtor for the amount which you give and spend for it in every manner. And per contra you shall credit it with everything you make and receive for it as if it were a debtor who would pay little by little" (trans. 1924, 68).

Historians of accountancy trace the diffusion of the double-entry system of bookkeeping from Italy to the Netherlands and to England and America. It was a system of codifying transactions by separating the elements relevant to the merchants' concerns from the myriad interactions, perceptions, and

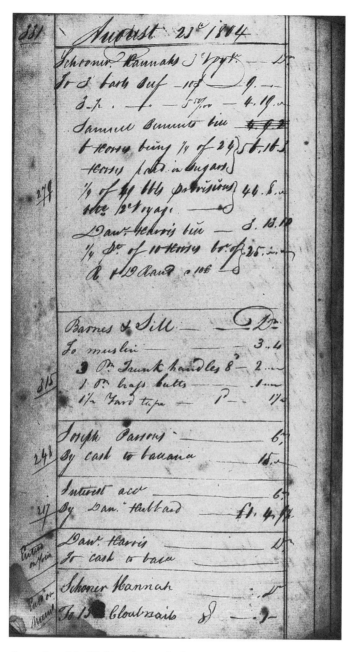

A page from John Watkinson's waste book, August 23, 1804. Watkinson, John R. & Co. Records 1796–1819, Olin Library, Special Collections & Archives, Wesleyan University, Middletown, Connecticut.

experiences involved in their commerce, carefully describing quantities and prices but neither production nor use.[10] This form of accounting is still in use, although it has become more complex than it was in Watkinson's time.

Block likens accounting to kinship: "The dualism of double-entry book-keeping bears a similarity to the complex kinship systems analyzed by structural anthropologists. In both cases a typological system operates to defend against uncertainty and ambiguity" (1990, 31). Like other folk models, double-entry bookkeeping is not a representation of reality but a language and practice that order an uncertain and dangerous world. For John Watkinson, whose livelihood and security depended on his ability to plot a prosperous course through unpredictable and changeable currents of supply and demand, carefully kept accounts provided the charts, the means by which he understood and negotiated a far-flung market, which he could not control.

Following this form of bookkeeping, Watkinson listed debits as "D to" while credits were entered as "C by." For example, there are many entries for Elijah Treadway, written as "D .27 to 1 quart rum" and several credits written as "C by bill for coopering [making a barrel]." On a larger scale there are items such as those entered on November 10, 1809, for his brothers' firm, Watkinsons & Co.: "D to sales of rum $1557.82" and "sales of salt $783.44." This entry was coupled with credits: "C by charges [customs duty] on rum & salt 45.99" and "C by cash pr JRW 10/4 $540.00," plus "cash pr JRW $380."[11] Some credits, such as these, were in cash or in notes on another merchant or bank; some were credits for goods that Watkinson had purchased, such as the entry for May 14, 1810: "Samuel Allison, C by his bill of candles, 120 boxes—$783.41; 10 boxes soap —$41.80."[12]

These were ongoing accounts; additional debits and credits would be entered throughout the year and finally totaled and balanced in a separate ledger. Merchants kept three kinds of books: waste books (also called day books), account books, and ledgers. Every day as a purchase or sale took place the merchant or his clerk made an entry in the waste book which noted the date, the name of the person buying or selling, and a debit or credit. Every day or several times a week the merchant would transfer these entries to his account book, in which the credits and debits of an individual or partnership were matched up and marked "settled" when they balanced. An account book would contain several entries for each account as new credits and debits occurred throughout the year. At the end of the year all of the entries for each account were entered into a ledger with its debits on one page, its credits on the facing page, and its totals balanced.

Although cash was rarely exchanged, all transactions were given a cash value, which made it possible to equate objects, work, animals, and other goods or services. The account books were based on a familiar yet extraordinary shared belief that everything could be translated by money. Rum could be transmuted into eggs or a day's roofing or a piece of fine lace. Barrels of beef could be added to horses or divided. The debits listed to *Schooner Hannah* on August 23, 1804, read: "S Hannah, Ds to 3 barrels beef, Samuel Bennet's bill, 6 horses being 1/4 of 24 horses paid in sugar, 1/4 of 49 Hhds provisions...2nd voyage, Danl Harris hire, 1/4 pt of 10 horses bot of R & D Rand @ 10 £."[13]

Through Watkinson's account books and other archival sources—his correspondence, bills and promissory notes, customs declarations, ships manifests, and newspapers—it is possible to reconstruct a few of his ships' voyages and thus to gain a view of his daily concerns and the cultural screen through which he viewed them. The goods, ships, and sailors have long been gone, but the paper trail still exists, showing not the wake of a small schooner plying the trade winds south, but the trails of relationships, networks along which money and goods moved. The goods were no longer earthbound by the hands of their producers—the farmers who raised the pork and beef, corn and oats; the lumbermen who cut the trees and shaped staves; the slaves who cut and processed the cane—but were free to move and to circulate for the purposes of the merchants. The uses that these objects fulfilled—sweetening food, easing spirits and souls, provisioning the sugar plantations—have left no marks on time, but the profits and losses, the credits and debits of these voyages survive in the careful entries of the merchants and their clerks, creating a reality of their own.

In the spring of 1804 Watkinson organized several voyages of *Schooner Sally* and *Schooner Hannah*. Each voyage began and continued a set of relationships, documented in the account books, between the ships, their owners, the captains, and an array of other individuals and firms. These included those who brought goods to be carried to the West Indies, those who would purchase parts of the returning cargo, those who worked in some way on the ship, and those officials who inspected, certified, measured, and collected duty for the imports.

The representations of the ships in the account books bore little resemblance to the ships anchored in Middletown's harbor—objects of wood and nails, sails and ropes—or to their voyages. *Schooner Sally* appears in the two separate account books of her joint owners, John Watkinson and Elijah

Hubbard, enmeshed in debits and credits for past, present, and future cargoes; while long lists of debits clustering around the date of her departure signify some of the cargo she actually carried, many of these debits are for items that were carried on an earlier voyage or were secured in the warehouse for her next. The cargo she returned with might not be credited to her account for months, until a buyer was found. Only the manifests and the inspection forms, which were prepared for customs and other port officials, listed or were alleged to list the actual cargo.[14] These documents, of little relevance to the merchants, have come to rest in general collections of shipping records or in the national customhouse records, whereas account books formed part of a merchant's personal papers.

The *Schooner Sally* sailed for the West Indies, with Joseph Hubbard as master, on Saturday, March 23, 1804, according to the "New London Marine List" printed in the column "Marine Intelligence," of the April 6, 1804, *Middlesex Gazette*. She had been in port a little over a month. In John Watkinson's account book for 1804 the *Schooner Sally* showed debits for a wide variety of objects and services, some of which were clearly cargo while others were charged to the schooner's account to balance a credit earned by a worker for repairs on the ship, or for 1 quart of rum, or to repay her captain for mailing a letter.

The debits that made up a portion of her cargo included: 25 bushels of corn, 21 ½ bushels of oats, some 20 pounds of nails, 35 1/2 yards Tuklinburys [a coarse cloth], and 1,800 staves taken from a store of 7,000 staves, which had been purchased from four persons. Those staves that were not put on board might become part of the cargo on the ship's next voyage or would be credited to her if shipped on another vessel or sold to another merchant. An entry for Captain Joseph Hubbard on March 18, debiting him nine barrels of prime beef No. 1, was probably shipped on the *Sally* and would have been his own adventure.[15] Like other captains, he had the right to invest in an adventure on the ship he commanded. In this way many captains built up the capital to become merchants on their own.

Elijah Hubbard owned part of the *Sally*, and his account book includes an entry on March 19, debiting the *Sally* to 10 horses and on March 20 crediting Robert and Dan Rand by 10 "shipping horses." Hubbard's entry for *Schooner Sally* included many other items, all unfortunately illegible.[16] The *Sally* returned on May 31, two months later, from Guadeloupe and Montserrat.[17] Her arrival generated numerous forms to be filled out, and the two that still exist were signed by John R. Watkinson. On June 9, he "solemnly, sincerely, and truly" swore on the collector's form of the Port of Middletown that he was giving a "true and full account of the Goods, Wares and Merchandize" contained in the entry, i.e., the ship. The second form, dated June 11, 1804, certified that he had paid the duties on the merchandise. This form was addressed "To the inspectors of the port" and signed by "Customs." The cargo was itemized under the heading "Marks," which identified the barrels and sacks of four owners: SS, standing for *Schooner Sally*, received 66 hogsheads of sugar, 32 of molasses, 18 bags of coffee, and 4 hogsheads of rum; JH, Joseph Hubbard, the ship's master, had 4 hogsheads of sugar, 4 of molasses, and 21 bags of coffee; EH, Elijah Hubbard, received 2 hogsheads of molasses, 2 bags of coffee, and a "quantity" of oranges, limes, and tamarinds. SR stood for Southmayd & Redfield, a closely connected Middletown merchant partnership, which received 1 hogshead of rum.[18]

The certificates of duty paid were required by any merchants who purchased the molasses, sugars, and rum, and additional payments and certificates followed each shipment and wholesale transaction. These show that the *Sally*'s 41 bags of coffee and 43 of the hogsheads of sugar were shipped to New York and then on to Amsterdam, Holland.[19] Part of the remaining cargo was sold by the hogshead to other merchants, many of whom had helped to stock the ship's cargo for its West Indies adventure, and some was sold in small quantities in Watkinson's store.

In some years or seasons the market was difficult, and hogsheads of sugar and molasses remained in Watkinson's warehouse or were shipped to an agent in New York or Boston to await a good market, a process that might take a long time. In the warehouse, the goods lay mute, devoid of meaning. Only the act of exchange brought them to life and substance as they entered the account book, credits to balance the debits.

A series of letters from an associate, Noah Talcott in New York, indicate a poor market in 1806. "After the strictest attention to your 40 Hhds molasses since the leaving of your Mr. W. the sale was this day effected at the miserable price of 33 cts @90 days for paper which I think indubitable ... it is the most that it was possible to make of it this place is completely overstocked with the article."[20]

A few months later, in July, Talcott wrote to Watkinson that the price of even the best sugars was very low, and in a letter dated August 18 he reiterated that only a very decent lot would readily bring $9.[21] A letter in the fall of the same year was still discouraging: "D Sirs your favor of the 16th I recd this day but cannot say much in favor of this place, for sugar shippers are idle waiting to know the effects of the negotiations. The prices nominally are about the same as when you was here, the first qualities of Muscovadoes are wanted by the grocers—but 8 1/2 to 9 is as much as there would be any possibility of obtaining at this moment from a common lot of Gaudaloupe your respectfully."[22]

Merchants were forced to pay close attention to European politics, which opened and shut markets for their wares and created fluctuations in the market price. At this time New York exporters were hesitant to make any purchases. After his victories in Europe, Napoleon had forbidden trade with Great Britain, which, in turn, was threatening a blockade of the continent. Watkinson's New York connection held his barrels of sugar for several months before finding a buyer. "We have this day sold your sugars to J W & P Kearney @ 9$ ninety days, which is the best offer we have had since your JRW left us, Since ours of the 14th inst there has been little or no sale of — Produce owing to the French Emperor's Decree. It is expected by our merchants that Great Britain will follow the example and declare France & Holland in a State of Blockade which (if it should) be the case would put our merchants in a very unpleasant situation."[23] Watkinson had placed some of his sugars with a Boston firm as well, but that firm faced the same problems.

In 1809 Watkinson and Hubbard turned to the "coastal trade" with New York and Virginia as an alternative to the West Indian trade, which had gone from bad to worse, after Congress in December of 1807 placed an embargo on exports in an effort to force England and France to respect the neutrality of American ships (Martin 1939, 65).[24] The embargo was revoked in 1809 but immediately was replaced with a Nonintercourse Act, which seriously disrupted mercantile trade. In preparation for the coastal trade Watkinson & Hubbard purchased one and a half small coasting sloops, half of the *Sloop Industry* and all of the *Sloop Leopard,* and tried to sell their two larger ships, *Brig Samuel* and *Brig Two Brothers.*

In January of 1810 a letter arrived from New York with an indication that the Congressional wind was shifting, restrictions might be removed, and a strong demand was being felt. "Business is still very dull here owing to the season and the uncertainty of what may be done by Congress. War seems to be the rumour of the day and many articles of produce are affected by it. Still we are strong in the belief that commercial restrictions will be in some degree removed—West India Goods must advance in the Spring as the quantity in market will not answer the demand—nor can sufficient quantities be imported in season unless the restrictions are shortly taken off."[25] The letter concluded with a list of current retail prices for molasses, refined and unrefined sugars, coffee, West Indian rum, pimento, brandy, cognac, and flaxseed.

The *Brig Samuel* had already been sold and *Sloop Industry* was on her way to New York and Petersburg, Virginia, but in response to the lure of an unmet demand and the faint stirring of movement in Congress that suggested that the Nonintercourse Act would be lifted, Watkinson & Hubbard made a quick turnabout; by early March the partnership was readying to venture once again into Caribbean waters.[26] *Brig Two Brothers*, which had not been sold, and *Schooner Hannah* were rapidly being outfitted and cargoes collected for the West Indies. By early May the partners had called back the *Sloop Industry* to join them. The eagerness and alacrity with which they shifted their heading make it clear that there was a sizeable difference in the returns on capital between the coastal trade and the West Indian trade.

A fairly extensive collection of letters still remains of the correspondence involving John Watkinson, his suppliers, and one of the captains of these three ships, which cleared Middletown's port in the spring of 1810. These letters provide a fuller picture of the process involved in assembling a cargo and setting sail than the limited discourse of account books.

Early in March Watkinson had written to Messrs. Sylvester Pulcifer & Co., Plainfield, Massachusetts, who were part owners of the *Brig Two Brothers* and who were located in the Berkshires of western Massachusetts, suggesting they send horses and asking what other cargo they would like to send. "Gentlemen: It is probable our commerce will be free in a few days and the prospect is very good for a cargo of horses sent out early in the Spring as Stock vessels are very scarce—we wish to know immediately your intention as to the Two Brothers and what you have on hand and will procure to put in her—for our government as we shall get her ready to take on board as soon as she is graved [out of dry dock] Yrs etc W & H."[27]

A letter of Pulcifer's dated March 10, which seems to have crossed Watkinson's, shows that he, too, was responding to the reawakening of the trade winds. He wrote: "We also wish you to write us the prospect of sending out the Brig and your opinion respecting Commerce should it be warm weather our beef may take damage unless overhauled which we wish you to attend to."[28] "Overhauling" beef meant salting it, and a certificate guaranteeing that it would remain edible was supplied by the overhauler. Pulcifer wrote again on March 19 asking to be informed about prospects for sending the brig. Watkinson, having put up their bond for duties at the Middletown bank, made an entry in his account book dated March 21, debiting Sylvester Pulcifer & Co. for the amount of $71.94.[29] He replied to Pulcifer, suggesting again that Pulcifer's company supply horses for the cargo and asking for information as to what other produce they might supply. "Your letter ... is just received—we have not much to day ... the Brig Two Brothers is preparing to take a cargo—and the general opinion is that when Congress rises vessels will be at liberty to go where they please ... with respect to cargo perhaps horses will do as well as anything and wish you to inform us what else you have to put on board and if we are to buy the water Hhds and oats etc. we shall overhaul the beef and put it on board as soon as she is graved, which will be in three or four days."[30]

An entry was made in the account book dated March 31, "*Brig Two Brothers,* D to 10 Barrils beef @ $9–$90.00; to 2 half barrels beef @ $6—$12.00." Another entry, dated April 2, debited the ship and credited Barzilla Cone for coopering beef; that is, building the barrels for it.[31]

The horses had still not arrived from Plainfield by the end of April, and Watkinson was urging Pulcifer to make a move.

Although nothing new has occurred since your S Pulcifer was here yet on reflection as the nonintervention will probably expire in a few days we are of opinion no time ought to be lost in sending the B[rig Two] Brothers to sea, and as you are so far distant it is necessary for you immediately to be collecting your horses for notwithstanding all the dispatch you can make she may be the last to sea. If you conclude to send her to Guadaloupe it may be well to ship 100 barrels beans or more—we have bot [bought] some staves and are engaging oats and wish you to answer us pr mail what you shall send and when you will be here.[32]

Another letter from Pulcifer, dated May 2, crossed Watkinson's, informing him that he had sent a load of shingles and that he wanted a hogshead of rum to be sent to him.[33] His response to Watkinson's letter of April 30 followed eleven days later, discussing the cargo of horses for *Brig Two Brothers.* He wrote that the rafts which were needed to transport the horses down the Connecticut River to Middletown were not available and further, that "the horses in this part of the country is poor on account of Hay being so bad." However, he assured Watkinson, "We shall calculate to get them as soon as we can."[34]

Watkinson replied with annoyance that the delay in shipping the horses was holding the brig in port, that the trip underwriters were already paying the crew, and, further, that a late departure would bring them to an already glutted market and would limit the number of trips the brig could make as the lateness of the season brought them into bad weather. "We see your letter dated 13th Inst [of this month] wherein you remark that business with your rafts etc would prevent your purchasing horses at present. The *Brig Two Brothers* is only waiting for cargo to go to sea the water Hhds are filled the oats bot and part of the Crew shipd and on expense—this delay may be the means of her going to a glutted market and ruin the voyage and bring the time into the hurricane months and will also prevent her making so many voyages as other vessels it is impossible to make anything by navigation without dispatch. Your humble servants W & H."[35]

The ships had been made ready for the voyage. Entries were made in the account book for seven days' work in March and three in April on *Brig Two Brothers*. *Schooner Hannah* was debited for one day's work and caulking, and the sails of both ships had been replaced or mended.[36] Their cargoes, however, were still not on hand. Watkinson wrote another urgent letter to another merchant house, D H and J B Sumner in Hartland, Vermont. Sumner's was stocking the *Schooner Hannah* which was anchored, eating up money, and also waiting for horses to arrive. "We remark what you say with regard to horses in your letter dated May 20th the Hannah has been ready for sea a week we had already proceeded with your provision…as you directed in your letter the Hannah has all her hands shipd and is under considerable expense it is therefore necessary for you to make all possible dispatch."[37] The *Hannah's* crew had to be fed, and the *Hannah* had been charged $23.62 1/2 for their board and for three barrels of flour for their bread.[38]

Sumner's responded a good deal faster than Pulcifer, and a bill they submitted to Watkinson & Hubbard on June 6, 1810, included 35 horses, 29 barrels of beans, 15 barrels of yellow peas, 7 barrels of green peas, 26 1/2 barrels of beef, 14 barrels of pork, and 4 illegible items, for a total of $1,828.97 1/2.[39] This company was charged for inspection of their beef and pork and for the guarantee that it was edible. Almost all of Sumner's stock was debited to the *Hannah* on June 4, even before the bill was submitted. The entries balancing out D H & J B Sumner's account were complicated, since they were regular buyers as well as suppliers, purchasing large amounts of rum, tobacco, tea, sugar, raisins, and other goods from Watkinson's. The entries debiting their account in May and June totalled $1,218.95, and their account was balanced on June 4, with a credit to Sumner's "by amt of his acct in the amount of $1911.90."[40]

The *Hannah* was loaded, the barrels of meat and legumes from Sumner's stowed in the hold along with bushels of corn and oats, boxes of soap and candles, tobacco, staves and cloth, and some six tons of hay for thirty-three horses and eight head of cattle secured on the deck.[41] The mate and a five-man crew boarded, and on June 6 Captain Daniel Hubbard was given his sailing orders. The schooner was under way on June 14, clearing Middletown for Barbados.

Sir, You being Master of the Schooner Hannah will proceed to sea with the first fair wind and make the best of your course to the Island of Barbadoes if you can sell for cash you may bring a load of salt, but as your dependence is entirely on your Stock you must make yourself acquainted where the best mark is for such lively moving horses as you have on board in fine act your own judgment and make all possible dispatch and write us every opportunity wishing you a prosperous voyage we remain Your obliged friends, Watkinson & Hubbard. NB: we believe quick dispatch is of the first importance to the owners and we recommend it particularly to your notice.[42]

At the end of May, Watkinson had written to Captain John Loveland to bring *Sloop Industry* back to Middletown. "Sir, We recd your letters from Norfolk & Richmond and in expectation that this will meet you in N York we wish you to return with the Industry to Middletown, as soon as possible if no freights should offer as we have some thoughts of fitting her out for the West Indies; you may buy 10 or 15 barrels good flour for us."[43]

The entries debiting the *Industry* indicate that her cargo was being stowed during the last weeks of June and first few days of July. This cargo was similar but not identical to that of the *Hannah:* oats but no corn, codfish, soap, candles, beef, empty hogsheads and hoops for making barrels, some six tons of hay, and horses but no cattle. The captain, first mate, and three members of the crew were paid one month's wages.[44] One of the *Sloop Industry's* debits was to Mr. Goodrich, the first mate. "The mate agreed to receive instead of half a horse, the freight of half a horse—but we afterwards agreed to consider him on acct of his going in the Sloop as he was offered elsewhere a whole horse priviledge." Insurance was purchased, the fees at the customhouse were paid, wharfage was debited,[45] and Captain Loveland was given his sailing orders. "Sir, You being master of the Sloop Industry will proceed with the first fair wind for Barbadoes where if you can sell your horses and fish for cash, paying a freight we should advise you to do so in which case you will take a load of salt but if you can't sell in Barbadoes after having informed yourself where you can do better, you may proceed where you judge best for the concern—we would recommend your taking molasses in preference to Rum—but you will proceed in the voyage as you judge most for our interest wishing you a safe voyage and quick return."[46] The *Sloop Industry* sailed from Saybrook on July 5th, a week before *Brig Two Brothers*.[47]

Watkinson had written again to Pulcifer & Co. on June 5, 1810, reviewing their correspondence of the last months and reproaching them for the loss of time and, therefore, profits. "Several cargoes of horses and cattle have been bot in this neighbourhood since April 30th and we could have sent her to sea before this time if we had depended on purchasing here, we would recommend it to you to buy or sell, we are willing to do either; or in any other way agreeable to yourselves will settle this concern—W & H."[48]

Pulcifer's responded. They bought Captain Enoch Hubbard's 1/8 share in the ship and cargo and sold their half interest in the *Brig Two Brothers* to Thomas Mather, who transferred it to Watkinson & Hubbard for $2,500. They paid the crew's bill for board and in early July they finally came through with eight horses. *Brig Two Brothers* took on the rest of her cargo of beef, staves, oats, corn, hoops, cloth, candles, soap, empty hogsheads, and some five tons of hay. Her crew of nine, including Captain Enoch Hubbard and the mate, Joshua Miller, had received a month's wages in advance. *Brig Two Brothers* at last got under way, clearing Middletown and sailing out of Saybrook into the Sound on July 12, 1810, heading for Antigua.[49]

Letters were the only source of information on a merchant's investment of time and capital, and Watkinson added a postscript to Loveland's shipping orders: "write every opportunity." Captains from the same home port regularly carried mail back and forth for each other when they met in port at one of the islands.[50] The three ships vanished briefly from the account book. The first news about them was in a letter from St. John's, Antigua, addressed to Thomas Mather and Watkinson & Hubbard, announcing the arrival there of *Brig Two Brothers*. The letter was from a commission agent, apparently a relative of Mather's in St. John's, describing a poor market.

I have the pleasure of informing you of the safe arrival of your *Brig Two Brothers* last evening all well the stock in tolerable order, but am afraid to a bad market, the crop is now entirely off and very little use for horses on the estates, the island is fully supplied with every kind of american produce it seems as if the united states had let loose the whole of her produce and sent it to the west Indies, but we must make the best of it, I have not yet had time to make sale of her Cargo you may probably calculate on the following flour 12, corn meal 32, corn [illegible], staves 30, beef 12., port

20 etc The horses will be the worst article but you may be assured I shall do every thing in my power for the good of your interests. I had no information of her coming until she came in. it was very unexpected.[51]

Both *Brig Two Brothers* and *Sloop Industry* had first made for Barbados, but a letter written only a few days later from Captain John Loveland makes clear why both ships then sought more favorable harbors. Captain Loveland wrote from St. Kitts in the Leeward Islands, informing Watkinson of the difficulties of the voyage.

I arrived at Barbadoes in a passage of 27 days, very rough weather in which we sprung a leak the 5th day and which obliged us to keep a pump agoing constantly till a day before we arrived when we found the leak. I could not sell the horses at Barbadoes and from that went to St Lucas where I sold them at 75$ a head payable in a bill drawn by Peter Muter & Co the first merchant in St Lucas one of which I have send enclosed in a letter from St Lucia another Capt Alsop will deliver you from that I anchored at Montserrat where I sold the onboard cargo at the following prices...: corn 3.00, staves 30.00, Hhds 3.00, soap .15, candles .25, oats .55.

The terms of payment were written illegibly, but it is clear that payment was not in cash; he added that he was going to Turks Island but would not be able to pay cash for salt. "I am going to Turks Island for Salt with no money but have got a recommend from Capt Alsop to draw on you as you wrote nothing in your letter to that purpose. NB I lost a horse on the 2nd night out."[52]

Turks Island, the main source of salt in the Caribbean, lay north of the island of Hispaniola. It was a final stop in the West Indies for many ships on the homeward passage with room in their holds for a profitable addition to their cargo. Loveland followed the advice of Captain Alsop, whose home port was also Middletown, and was able to purchase the salt on Watkinson's account. The merchant from whom he purchased it wrote to Watkinson & Hubbard of his willingness to engage in business with them. "Your estemd favor was duly handed me by Capt John Loveland and the contence noted and agreable to your request I have put as much salt as the Capt could take, Gentleman you wil be pleased to lay your commands on me at all times."[53]

An item in the October 11 issue of the *Middlesex Gazette* under its "New London Marine List" reported that a ship returning thirty days from Turks Island left five ships there, one of which was the *Sloop Industry;* all were to sail within two days. Two weeks later the "Ship News" listed the *Sloop Industry* as having entered the Port of Middletown from Montserrat, the *Schooner Hannah* from St. Vincent and the *Brig Two Brothers* from Antigua.

The revenue inspector surveyed and issued a certificate of the proof of the rums; a customs official collected the duties, certified that payment had been made, and gave permission to land the cargoes. *Schooner Hannah's* cargo consisted of 51 hogsheads of rum and 26 hogsheads of molasses. *Sloop Industry* carried 25 hogsheads of rum, 6 kegs of tamarinds, 600 oranges, and 2,000 bushels of salt, while 1 cask of rum and 1 bushel of sugar were listed as "stores," presumably having been consumed during the voyage. *Brig Two Brothers'* cargo was composed of 116 hogsheads of rum and 2 of molasses, while stores consisted of a barrel of sugar, 5 kegs of tamarinds, and 400 oranges.[54]

After three months of calm in Watkinson's account book, broken only by a few entries for postage to and from the West Indies, the arrivals brought a flurry of activity around the docking and unloading of the three ships' cargoes. Two entries dated October 8 and 10 debited the *Schooner Hannah* to cash paid for her captain and crew. An entry October 18 balanced John Loveland's account in cash and credited him by nine bushels of salt.[55] On October 20 the *Brig Two Brothers* was debited $21.59 to fees at the customhouse for tea and sugar and $1,759.40 for rum.[56] A few days later her crew and captain received their wages.[57]

Some or all of the cargoes had already been assigned when the ships docked. Two of John Watkinson's brothers purchased significant amounts for their own trade. Edward Watkinson bought 26 hogsheads of rum and 24 of molasses valued at $2085.33 for which he gave two notes on Oct. 4, 1810: one to be paid in three months in the amount of $1042.67, the other in six months in the amount of $947.83. He was credited by an unspecified amount of cash mailed to Watkinson & Hubbard on Jan. 2, 1811, (of which Captain Hubbard received one quarter and John Watkinson the rest) and by his $244.83 bill for tallow, pork, butter, and cheese.[58] David Watkinson received 20 hogsheads of rum valued at $2,292.95. He paid for it with two notes and his bill of payment for pork, which had been part of the *Hannah's* outgoing cargo.[59] Some nine hundred gallons of rum were debited to D H & J B Sumner in the amount of $1,090.80, which included two months' interest.[60] Four hundred pounds of the sugars were sold, probably in New York, by Benjamin Strong, a commission agent.[61]

Although these three voyages had been somewhat disappointing in terms of the prices Watkinson received for his horses, the trade still looked promising, and he lost no time in assembling a new cargo for the *Brig Two Brothers*. Four closely written pages list entries for this cargo, which included forty-four horses, their qualities and worth individually noted.[62] The ship sailed from Middletown the first week in December, waiting at New London for a fair wind; however, political storms threatened, and Watkinson was worried. He drafted a letter to his brother William at his new firm in New York, asking what the merchants there thought about the effects of the new Nonintercourse Act enacted by Congress.

> Our Captn Hubbard was in the *Brig Two Brother* with horses...on board for Antigua...waiting a wind to go to Sea—this new Non Intercourse which takes place 2nd Feby making British productions seizable quite deranges us we shall expect the Two Brothers to return in March with Rum—we should be obliged by any information by which to guide ourselves in this affair pray what is the calculation of your merchants; as a great number are in a similar situation, is it probable the British order in Council etc will be so modified as to prevent the non intercourse law going into effect.[63]

This portion of his letter, which clearly communicates the difficulties of trading in these troubled times, had been crossed out in his letterbook and may never have been sent. But despite his worries, the *Brig Two Brothers* headed out from New London in mid-December.

Nature echoed the political climate, and Captain Hubbard wrote from St. Croix, describing a troubled passage. "We arrived here after a passage of 19 days very rough weather we had a violent gale the 2d day out which passed 2 days we lost 1 horse 4 bundles hay and 2 Hhds water. We had the wind to the eastward most of the passage and in consequence fell to leeward we made the Island of Saba the 17th day out, we tried one day to beat to windward but the weather being so rough we found it impossible and was, therefore, obliged to put in to some of the Leeward Islands."[64]

Although he had lost one horse in the gale, another in getting ashore, and four were sick, he was expecting to get a fair price on his cargo. Hubbard returned to Middletown in late March, sailing from St. Croix with a cargo of 130 hogsheads of rum, 1 barrel of sugar, 7 kegs of tamarinds, and 1 bushel of limes.[65] He returned again to St. Croix, arriving there in July. He sold his outgoing cargo, returned with his ship in ballast and carrying, in lieu of a return cargo, two promissory notes from West Indian merchants or purchasing agents. Both notes stipulated that payment would be made in dollars or doubloons if the Nonintercourse Act proscribed British rum. One such note was from a merchant named Rob Montgomery in the amount of $3,503.28, the other from James S. Bedlow for $995.80. The one from Bedlow reads: "St Croix 6th July 1811, For value received, I promise to pay Capt Joseph Hubbard...on order for account of Mr. John R. Watkinson of Middletown in Connecticut, the sum of nine hundred and ninety five dollars and eighty cents, on the fifteenth of February 1812, in rum at the current cash price then existing, or cash say Doubloons or Dollars; having signed this in duplicate one of which to be coply'd with, the other to be null and of no effect."[66]

The note was signed by Bedlow and witnessed by George Curtis. A letter from Captain Hubbard to Curtis stated that one copy of Bedlow's notes was entrusted to him, and that should Hubbard not return by the time the note was due, Curtis was to follow the directions of John Watkinson. A brief letter from Curtis acknowledged receipt of this note and instruction. These notes were marked "paid" and filed.

Watkinson's letterbook includes a copy of his letter, written six months later, to the other merchant, Montgomery. Watkinson addressed him as "Esquire," indicating that this was a person of some stature in St. Croix. "I wrote you by Capt Joseph Hubbard...of the Brig Lambert saying that his receipt shold be in full of all my demands on you from me which as Capt Hubbard had transacted the business and your note was made payable to him on order I supposed would be satisfactory as it is very probable Capt Hubbard will return from the West Indies before your note becomes due. I have formally given Capt Joseph also full power to settle the same."[67]

Hubbard's letters, like those of the other captains, provide a glimpse of the sea, the weather, the concern about securing the cargo, the islands they tried, and their struggle to find a good market. In the archives the captains' letters and a handful of letters and promissory notes from West Indian merchants or agents give the prices at which the outgoing cargo was sold and the incoming rum, molasses, or sugar was bought.[68] But neither these merchants' names nor these transactions ever appeared in the account books.

Consistent with the formal traditions of double-entry bookkeeping, no entries show a credit by horses sold, no debit to rum purchased. These may have been entered in the books of West Indian merchants, but in the Connecticut merchants' books there are only debits to horses (or beef, for example) when they were purchased, coupled with a credit by horses for the merchants who supplied them and a credit by rum (or sugar, or another product) when it was sold, coupled with debits to the rum for the purchaser. Thus the

Schooner Sally (or the other ships) was never credited with the sale of the horses she unloaded in the West Indies or debited for the purchase of rum that she took aboard. To put it another way: according to the bookkeeping system, in New England merchants sold horses that were bought by the ships or the merchant who was investing in the cargo. Neither ship nor merchant appeared to receive payment for the horses when they were sold in the West Indies. The rums, sugars, and other products that filled the hold on the return voyage were not charged against the accounts of ship or merchant, but a credit was entered when these products were sold, and the credit balanced the debits to horses. A typical entry was that for D H & J B Sumner, one of Watkinson's many accounts, which credited them by horses, beef, pork, peas, and beans, which were debits for *Schooner Hannah*. There were no entries under the *Hannah's* account, crediting her by the sale of these items. Sumner was debited to nine hundred gallons of rum, while the *Hannah* received the credits, but the *Hannah* had never been debited by this rum when it was purchased in the West Indies. In the ships' accounts Connecticut's produce quietly turned into rum.

In these accounts Watkinson's ship became an imaginary site located within the powerful discourse of bookkeeping. The balanced accounts fashioned an illusory though familiar world in which exchange was real, production did not exist, and use was meaningless. Certainly Watkinson and other merchants knew that the corn they shipped went to feed the West Indian slaves; that the oats fed the horses and cattle that powered the sugar mills; that horses were ridden by the planters or their overseers; that the beef and pork went to the planters' tables, while a bit of salt cod might occasionally be provided to the slaves; and that the staves and hoops formed the hogsheads in which slave-produced rum, molasses, or sugar was shipped. Assembling each of these elements of the cargo was part of the merchants' daily endeavors, but the ledgers helped to deflect their thoughts from the scenes of brutal exploitation which these objects so vividly embodied. The obfuscation was neither deliberate nor conspiratorial. It was a welcome artifact of the purposes and language of mercantile bookkeeping.

These purposes did not include estimating or keeping a record of the growth of the merchants' capital. Although accounts were entered into ledgers each year and neatly balanced, they showed neither interest gained on capital (Chatfield 1977, 106–07) nor the source of profits.[69] An inventory of a merchant's assets was compiled only when there was a particular reason to do so, such as bankruptcy, the dissolution of a partnership, or, as in Watkinson's case, when he was planning to invest in a new enterprise. If such inventories could have been compared over a period of years, estimating a merchant's overall gains or losses would have been possible. Unfortunately, only one such inventory exists in John Watkinson's accounts.

In 1811 John Watkinson began to turn away from navigation and two years later invested his capital in a textile mill. At this time he entered an inventory of his assets into one of his account books. It included his holdings in real estate, shares in stocks, property in two stores, livestock, half interest in *Sloop Industry,* and a number of outstanding notes and debts owed to him; the total, approximately $44,000, was a modest fortune for this period.[70] His fine brick house still stands on Main Street and, according to archaeological finds, "the quality of the artifacts shows a high standard of living." It had been well stocked with costly china, large serving dishes, and the remains included a "quantity of wine bottle glass" (Gray 1978, 84).[71]

Since there is no way of knowing how much capital John Watkinson brought with him to Middletown and invested in this partnership, determining exactly how much his capital earned in the West Indian trade is impossible. Some of his investments, especially those in real estate, must have earned well. Still, it seems reasonable to assume that as a young man of twenty-three in 1796, when he began his partnership with Hubbard, he would have been worth only a fraction of this amount and that he might have multiplied his capital five times over in the sixteen years in which he actively pursued "navigation." An authoritative work on the mercantile trade noted that at a time when 6 percent was the standard interest within America, the data, though fragmentary, suggest that merchants could expect a 12 percent profit on their investment (Doerflinger 1986, 127).

If asked where and how his capital had grown, Watkinson would have modestly credited it to family and business associates, his hard work, character, and Providence, as he would have blamed other merchants' failures on both their lack of social ties and their individual shortcomings (Ditz 1994).[72] He did work hard; he took risks with his money and to the best of his abilities he followed where the market led. And, it had led him to the West Indies.

Along with many other Connecticut merchants, Watkinson had found a place in the network linking the sugar plantations of the West Indies to Connecticut's rural produce and to the industrial manufactures of England. The network had allowed him to profit through tapping into the enormous surplus value that planters appropriated from a slave work force. The market for Connecticut's produce had been created by the planters, who preferred to pay the costs of importing food and every necessity to giving up even a small portion of fertile land to subsistence; sugar was simply too profitable. New England's farmers were beneficiaries of this market network, which buoyed the prices of their produce and allowed them to purchase both necessary and luxury items manufactured abroad.[73] The New York merchants to whom Watkinson sold most of his sugars and rums and from whom he purchased manufactured goods shared part of this booty and took a good-sized share from the profits created by workers in English factories.

In the mass of Watkinson's papers only one sentence in a letter from a West Indian merchant offers a glimpse at the cane fields that supported all of this—it was a bad year for the sugar crop, and no horses were needed on the estates. The places, the processes, and the people that generated profits went unnoted. The West Indian slaves, like the English factory workers, were nowhere to be found, while the merchants' ships, symbolically empowered in their account books, became magical sites where horses were transformed into rum.

CHAPTER 4

Continuity and
Change

Within the first decade of the nineteenth century all of Samuel Watkinson's sons had entered navigation, and all but one of his daughters had married into families with long histories of trade. By the second decade their enterprises had changed in ways that neither they nor other merchant families would have predicted. During the years leading up to the War of 1812, while John had settled and prospered in Middletown, his younger brothers had followed similar but separate routes. David had returned to Middletown after Samuel Jr. and Richard's deaths to recover from his own illness. The following year, 1799, having regained his health, he undertook a long trip to the South to purchase cotton for a New York firm, traveling by sea to Charleston and Savannah and returning by horseback along inland roads, a trip of some 1,100 miles. According to his father, he found business conditions poor in the South, but he established several useful connections.[1] In 1800 he moved to Hartford, where he opened a general wholesale and retail establishment with his younger brother Edward as clerk.[2]

William remained in New York in the position of first clerk in the house of Dunlap & Gennert, but he found living on his meager salary to be difficult, even though he also received an allowance from his father. His complaints earned him a stern rebuke from his father. "As to your absolute occasions for money beside the income of your clerkship appears to me a matter of blame—and this also is certain had I been no better Oeconomist in my young time it would not now have been in my power to answer your request. It is the business of Summer of youth to prepare for Winter of age."[3]

Nonetheless, the following year Samuel Sr. entrusted William with the responsibility of traveling back to Lavenham to check on his various properties and business affairs. Upon his return William joined David in Hartford "under the Firm of D & W Watkinson." He described himself "well pleased with my situation, finding a much greater field for Commerce than I had any idea of." Hartford was also part of the prospering West Indian trade, and William described their enterprise. "Our principal business at present consists in trading to the West Indies, and in supplying the store keepers in different parts of this State and up the Connecticut River with West Indian Goods and groceries in general, and our run of business has been such as to call one or other of us continually to New York or Boston to purchase goods for the supply of the store here."[4]

Samuel Sr.'s letters to his friends and family in England were filled with references to the marital connections of his children, the businesses of his sons and sons-in-law, and the birth and health of his grandchildren. "Since my last letter to you two more marriages have taken place in my family viz Jane W on the 28th May 1804 to Mr Samel Gill merchant in this city and JRW [John] on the 26 Janry 1805 to Miss Hubbard the daughter of his partner Mr. Elijah Hubbard Esq of this city. My grandchildren have increased since my last Mrs Perkins a daughter Mrs Pledger a son Mrs Wells a son and Mrs Collins a son—Edw W is now in business with his brother and W.W. and RW is clerk to them."[5] With the addition of Edward as partner in 1805, the enterprise was renamed Watkinsons & Co.[6] Seemingly a solid and secure foundation was here laid for all their futures.

For David this was certainly the case, as in 1803 he married Olivia Hudson, daughter of Barzillai Hudson, the well-known and influential publisher of the *Connecticut Courant,* Hartford's main news weekly. William described her with admiration in a letter written a few weeks after the wedding. "The young Lady is daughter of a Mr Hudson of this City, with whom David is very happy, and indeed it would be his own fault if it were otherwise for she possesses every charm that could make matrimony a state of felicity."[7]

Several years later, in 1810, Edward married Olivia's sister, Lavinia. The two families lived next door to each other in Hartford until Edward's death in 1841. David and Edward's sister Ann, who had been married the same year as David to James Hancock Wells, an established merchant, also lived nearby in Hartford.

Over the years Samuel Sr.'s letters to England continued to enumerate each additional grandchild and the sorrows as well as the joys of the family.

Sickness and death took their toll in the first decade of the nineteenth century. David had been afflicted with an asthmatic condition for several years and in 1806 went to Barbados to recover. Elizabeth Watkinson Collins lost her two-year-old son in a tragic accident. He fell into a kettle of boiling water.[8] John also suffered a serious loss. His first and, at the time, only child, a son eighteen months old, became ill and died in the summer of 1808. Overcome with grief, John "was attacked by a nervous disorder and a slow fever which brought him very low." He recovered slowly and was still in poor health a year and a half later.[9] William had caught a fever in the summer of 1809 after a trip to Carolina. He escaped with his life but required a long time to recover his strength.[10]

The family was afflicted by a commercial disaster when the brewery burned down. John lost only the small amount he had invested, but Jacob Pledger, his brother-in-law, had owned half of it and his loss was great.[11] On balance, however, considering the ever-present threat of fatal illness at this time and the frequency of failure among those who followed the mercantile trade, the Watkinsons had done well.

The year 1809 marked a time of change for the five brothers. In Hartford, after five years of partnership, Watkinsons & Co. was dissolved, and each of the brothers went into business on his own. Customers and suppliers were notified of their intentions by a series of advertisements in the *Connecticut Courant*. An advertisement for Watkinsons & Co. in the December 7, 1809, paper announced, "*West-India Goods at reduced prices.* The subscribers intending to close their business in January next, will dispose of their remaining stock of GOODS on such favorable terms as to be an object for Town as well as Country Merchants." A request followed that "all persons having claims against them" and "those indebted to them" settle their accounts, and a list of the "GOODS ON HAND" was included.[12]

On February 7, 1810, there was an announcement of the "*Dissolution of Partnership*" over the three names: David, William, and Edward Watkinson. On February 21, an advertisement appeared for "EDWARD WATKINSON at the store lately occupied by Watkinsons & Co.," on March 14 "DAVID WATKINSON...at his Store in State-Street, next south of the one lately occupied by Watkinsons & Co.," and on March 21, "For Norfolk, Petersburgh and Richmond. The Sloop Lucy, Lemuel S. Jenyns Master will take freight for either of the above places, if offered soon. Apply on board at Buck's wharf, or to WILLIAM WATKINSON, Hartford." Robert, who two years earlier had left his position as clerk to become a partner in his brother-in-law Samuel Gill's dry-goods store, now struck out on his own with plans to build a new brick store in

Middletown, specializing in the sale of dry goods.[13] All of them were leaving their partnerships with sufficient capital to begin their new, separate enterprises.

While dissolving Watkinsons & Co. was probably in part a business decision, for William at least it was also a personal one. "As I am sickened of *Partnerships,*" he wrote to John. "It is my intention to do business in my own name. Yours, in haste, Wm Watkinson. NB. Have you any freight for the Sloop.?"[14] William set out by himself to New York and for the next two years exchanged no letters at all with his former partners.[15] He wrote an occasional letter to his parents and kept up a steady correspondence with John which combined business and personal news. William was optimistic about his future. "Dear Brother I wrote you a few days since informing of my determination to establish myself in Business here. Since then, I have hired the 2nd floor of the Store No 87 South St. the corner of Burling Slip, being the same T & H Ely occupied, where I shall be happy to receive your commands and those of your friends, in the Commission line, whenever occasion offers. My Sloop Lucy arrived a few days since with a full freight from Petersburg, ship'd principally by D & H, but consigned to Ja Walsh; and she returns there immediately in Ballast. Goods are selling, in plenty, at V., where I have made some little purchases I think to advantage, and I feel quite encouraged that my Business here will be found to answer my expectations."[16]

Only two weeks later his tone was one of discouragement.

Dear Brother, Mr Bowers will hand you this, whom I am sorry to have seen so little of during his visit here, having been more occupied probably than if my Business had been of much greater magnitude; mine has truly been "much ado about nothing". For very good reasons, not necessary I trouble you with, I have given up the Counting room No 87 at the Corner of Burling Slip & South St. and taken one at No 68 South St (Corner of Pine & South) at a less price and vastly more convenient every way, much nearer the Coffe Ho. and on the lower floor, having the use of part of the lower floor for storage of my goods.[17]

Even though political tensions between England and America were growing, in the fall of 1810 both William and Robert were trying to maintain and expand trade connections with English merchants. William, who by then had entered a new partnership—despite his earlier strong words on the subject—was planning to ship wheat and flour to London. In a letter to

Meeking he stated that he and his partners hoped to engage in commission business from English merchants and asked for his help. "Our primary object is Commission Business which we should be glad to get some of from your side the water, but there is so little commercial intercourse with your part of the country that we cannot expect much from it, altho in your transactions with some of the distant counties you might sometimes have an opportunity to mention our names to merchants or manufacturers...which I would esteem a favour."[18]

He added in a postscript that Robert was traveling to England for the purpose of setting up connections for importing English goods and described him as the very model of a successful merchant. "I will just observe that his Capital is quite respectable, and his uniform correctness in mercantile transactions has secured him an extensive credit in this country. I understand it is his intention however to purchase for payment only, for which he goes provided, and letters also of the most useful kind to the principal manufacturing and commercial towns."[19] Robert was 24, William, 31, but Robert's degree of mercantile perfection would be forever beyond William's grasp.

Correct as he was, however, Robert made a serious misjudgment in the timing of this trip. Within three months of his departure President Madison had prohibited all trade with England and had decreed the confiscation of all English goods found on board Americans ships. Samuel Sr. wrote of the news, which would seriously affect all of the merchants in general and his son in particular. "The President's proclamation to stop all intercourse with the British and to seise all vessels after the 2 of Febry in which English goods shall be found although they may be the property of Americans and their being no reason to dout it."

He was especially worried about the possible consequences for Robert. "It has caused a general consternation amongst the merchants and failures to a very large amount have already taken place And if a war should follow I have very little hesitation in saying that I believe little respect will be paid to the property of Englishmen in any situation by the present ruling powers—My son Robert sailed for Liverpool the 3d of Nov. without knowing of the Presidents proclamation intending to purchase goods. It will be a most unfortunate affair for him if he proceeds in doing it under present circumstances."[20] Robert returned in May, but there is no mention of whether he bought goods or whether they were seized. Probably neither occurred, as Samuel would have mentioned it in the letter that told of Robert's return and subsequent marriage to the daughter of General Henry Champion.

The mercantile world that Robert left, seemingly secure and predictable despite the ups and downs of the past few years, was rapidly deteriorating by the time he returned. Mercantile connections that had been established for more than two centuries were breaking apart. The stormy relationship with Great Britain was one conflict, perhaps the most obvious one, among the numerous important struggles and changes that had been occurring within as well as outside the country over a matter of decades. Throughout the United States a tide of commerce, the "market revolution," was spreading into every rural nook and cranny, sweeping all before it into a flurry of selling, buying, and speculating.[21]

A vastly improved transportation system, which linked the inland regions to the coastal cities, had expanded the distribution of commodities to rural areas that had previously known only an occasional traveling peddler. A larger population, increased by an influx of immigrants, was becoming more dependent on purchased goods. More farmers found it profitable to ship produce to market with the new, lower costs of transportation, and more farmers, therefore, planted crops for sale. As men devoted their time to raising commercial crops, women spent more time in the home and barn, with greater responsibility for the dairy herd and for household manufactures. This rising tide of commodities and deepening dependence on the market had powerful effects on the lives of those in rural areas whose subsistence level had remained low but secure, whose communities had been small but closely knit, and whose culture had been parochial but predictable.

There was nothing new about raising crops and spinning and weaving for exchange, but in the frontier regions the exchange had occurred among neighbors. A small surplus of woven cloth, eggs, or corn from one household might be exchanged with a neighbor for help in haying or cheese or might be bartered with the local storekeeper for credit toward a purchase or for cash to pay a tax.[22] The increased dependence on selling the crop made some farmers rich, but it put others at risk. Borrowing to clear more land or to buy equipment for raising commercial crops might improve a family's standard of living, but poor weather, bad luck, and the ups and downs of the market could also lead to a bank foreclosure and the loss of the farm.

The resulting insecurities were expressed in a rise of religious fervor, spreading through the countryside, and the insecurities provided some of the fuel that politicians channeled into support of the Jeffersonian Republican platform. The Jeffersonians were challenging the Federalist elites' efforts to implement and control national economic development and primed their rhetoric with pictures of rich merchants and bankers, profiting from the destruction of simple farmers. The Bank of the United States became a convenient scapegoat for people's fears of change, and the Republican-dominated Congress's refusal to renew its charter was described as a victory for the farmers. Behind the scenes many enterprise-minded Republicans, and a few Federalists as well, promoted their personal interests in state banks, which stood to gain the national bank's federal deposits and the free-dom, without the bank's control, to lend far beyond their means.[23]

In a classic and familiar move politicians presented the Bank of the United States as a dangerous foreign institution, as many of its stockholders were English, though in reality most of the stockholders had no say in its management. Samuel Watkinson was one of those stockholders. Whereas in the past he had commented coolly on the party passions he encountered in Middletown, now he found himself threatened by them. "The Democratic Party [Jeffersonian] which is dominant increases and rages against any insti-tution where Federalists may be at the head and Englishmen have any in-fluence spurred on as it appears to me by a foreign agency. It is the apparent determination of the party to put it down that they may trample all under their feet that had any connection with it." The national bank had at-tempted to negotiate, he wrote to an old friend in England, but to no avail. "They offered a million and quarter of dollars for a renewal of their charter and that government might choose a portion of the directors and to allow 3 per cent for their money after a certain time and to allow them to subscribe into the bank, but they will not listen to anything."

As a stockholder Samuel believed himself to be in danger of being politi-cally attacked as well as being in danger of losing income as the bank cur-tailed its payments on dividends. "What think you of their insisting on the names and residence of the stockholders—As their charter has little more than a month to run they have been curtailing their disct for some time."[24] Samuel depended on bank dividends on his shares and feared he would be affected seriously by this loss of income.[25] At this unfortunate moment William, whose partnership was in serious financial difficulty, wrote, asking his father for help. John answered the letter, informing William that Samuel was in no position to advance him any funds. "There are none who were doing business at this time but meet with some trouble," he wrote. "Your Father is entirely destitute of money and is indeed somewhat alarmed for himself as his resources are considerably shortened by the United States & Jersey Banks not dividing any thing; and it may soon be the case with other monied Institutions."[26]

William's firm was forced out of business, but he and his partner were able to meet their financial obligations. John reassured William that this was only a temporary setback, while adding some heavy-handed advice laden with nautical imagery. "I was happy to find...that your house has been able to meet its payments & as your prospects are so favourable I have no doubt you will swing clear...when you have weathered this storm you will look out in future not to be caught with so much sail set. Long storms & heavy gales make the best sailors."[27]

John himself, like many other merchants, was planning to withdraw from the West Indian trade. "For my own part I am determined to keep my business within the limits of the United States & so much within bounds that Bank Charters shall not affect me in future. Enabled by Providence I will use the strictest economy & Industry in all my affairs; & though I may not be rich; I trust the good Providence which has hitherto protected me will enable me to spare something for the needy."[28]

Over the next months the increasing threat of war, coupled with the closing of the national bank, continued to wreak havoc on mercantile firms. In a letter to Meeking, William described the distress of New York's merchants and their belief, which he shared, that the Republican government had become an enemy. "The Commerce of this Country like that of England is very much deranged, as might be supposed when not only foreign nations but our own Government is at war with it and the non renewal of the Charter of the National Bank has had an effect in increasing the general embarrassment, which has been very general through our Commercial towns, but in none as much as New York, whose commerce being more extended has felt the pressure most, and the failures have consequently been very numerous."[29]

The president's proscription of all foreign trade in response to British harassment of American shipping was seen by much of the mercantile community as a deliberate attack on their interests. Although they deplored the English attacks on their ships, especially the seizure of American sailors to serve in the Royal Navy,[30] they were even more disturbed by the federal government's outlawing of trade, and they strongly opposed the declaration of war against England. Many of Connecticut's merchants, who were staunch Federalists, went so far as to discuss seceding from the Union.[31] The Watkinsons kept their distance from the political battles raging around them, which even in Middletown were intense.[32] Instead, they carefully followed the economic currents and changed course rather than engaging in the fight to keep the old ways of trade alive. While the Revolutionary War had broken many of the political ties to England, commercial ties had held firm and British manufactures had remained the key to successful trade.[33] But the War of 1812 severed most of those ties and reoriented trade to a domestic market. By 1814 the tonnage of American ships entering American ports had fallen to less than 10 percent of the 1811 level.[34] The Watkinsons were among the merchants who turned their skills and capital to new enterprises.

John had dissolved his partnership in navigation by March of 1811. An advertisement for S. Pulcifer & Co. in the *Middlesex Gazette* of March 16, 1811, offered goods for sale at the store "lately occupied by Messrs. Watkinson & Hubbard" (quoted by Young 1979, 25), and a letter to William the following year advised that he was now "clear from Navigation."[35] He still maintained a partnership in a grocery store with one of the sons of William Johnson, a fellow emigrant, longtime friend, and business associate.[36] He had chosen an opportune time to retire from the West Indian trade.

His brothers, as well, reoriented their commercial interests. They were able to import a small amount of steel and gunpowder from England but no manufactured goods, and they found new ways to remain successful in this period of flux. David's, Edward's, and, later, Robert's advertisements in the *Connecticut Courant* display the shifting patterns of mercantile enterprises in these tumultuous years. In February 1810, Edward was offering a mixed bag of wholesale goods, mainly foodstuffs, which included imported sugars, teas, brandy, wine, coffee, salt, and spices. He also sold New Orleans and Carolina indigo and Virginia tobacco, a variety of snuff, Nicaragua wood and camwood (a dye), and a large quantity of seasoned boards and shingles (Feb. 21, 1810). David's list of offerings was similar, but he also included Georgia cotton, shot, and whale and liver oil (March 14, 1810). In the fall of 1810 David also advertised for freight or passengers on his *Schooner Mars,* sailing the coastal route to Virginia's ports—Norfolk, Petersburg, and Richmond (September 19, 1810). At this time Edward offered rum and cotton in addition to his other merchandise. The following spring their lists were still similar, with Edward offering sperm oil and both selling lime, presumably to be used in iron manufacturing.

In the fall of 1811 David began to wholesale large quantities of iron from Sweden and Russia, steel from Philadelphia, and a small quantity of steel from England (September 25, 1811). The rest of his offerings were as varied as ever and now included American gunpowder, domestically produced nails, spikes, tar, pitch, and rosin. Edward advertised English gunpowder along with his general merchandise (October 16, 1811). In addition, both men were still importing rum, sugar, and molasses from the West Indies. Their spring advertisements were placed together, with David offering more iron, steel, and various products made of them, with a shorter list of other goods, of which only tobacco and snuff were not for use in manufacturing. Edward still maintained a large assortment of merchandise: sugar, cotton, shot, ginger, rice, tar, coffee, white lead, spices, duck cloth, and lime (April 15, 1812). By fall of 1812 the war had prevented any West Indian imports from entering Hartford. David's list consisted almost completely of hardware, except for salt, "a large assortment of Groceries and Dye Stuff," and "A second hand Copper Still with a new bottom" (October 20, 1812). He also advertised for freight for Boston on his *Schooner Two Sisters* (September 22, 1812). Edward continued to diversify, advertising a wide range of goods from many places, such as lime from Providence, cotton from New Orleans and Georgia, wines from Lisbon, and rum from New England. In May, a windfall of imported spirits appeared, and Edward topped his advertisement with capital letters reading 6 HHDS. GRENADA RUM while the rest of his advertisement remained the same (May 11, 1813). David was also selling "New Rum" but titled his advertisement "Indigo, Iron, Groceries, etc." (June 1, 1813).

The market for dyes that both men had been selling was in the domestic production of textiles by both households and factories, as imported British cloth was no longer available. In June of 1814, David began to sell the very fine merino wool (June 21, 1814), and in the fall he offered "a full blood Merino Buck 18 months old" and "1 first rate Cow 6 years" as well as 46 bales of upland cotton, cut nails, and shovels. A bit incongruously, the advertisement included for sale or rent "A front gallery Pew in the brick meetinghouse" (November 22, 1814). Edward's remained the same.

In fall of 1815 Edward's sales leader, "15 Hhds St. Croix Rum," reflected the reopening of West Indian trade, following the end of the war with England earlier in the year. The rest of his offerings included wines, oils, and foodstuffs. David's merchandise was composed solely of iron, steel, and wool (November 14, 1815). David leased out his flock of merinos in 1816 (June 11, 1816) and turned completely to hardware, with an occasional consignment of cotton. The brothers' distribution networks and markets were now almost completely distinct, and when Robert's first advertisement appeared in the spring of 1817, he was appealing to still another market. He offered a wide assortment of cloths, ribbons, buttons, laces, gloves, and handkerchiefs. His list was topped with a notice: "Will open this day a great variety of FANCY and STAPLE GOODS, which he has just purchased at the Auctions in New York for cash, and will sell at a reasonable advance for cash or approved credit to merchants only" (June 10, 1817).

Their shift from being generalized merchants combining exporting and importing, wholesale and retail, to becoming specialized wholesalers was part of the market revolution that became even more turbulent after the war ended. In urban centers where trade and the market had been a way of life for decades, merchants found it necessary to specialize: to be wholesalers *or* retailers but not both; to import *or* export, to learn a particular market and to sell fewer kinds of goods.[37] However, far more than a realignment of networks and increasing volume of trade was occurring. A significant number of merchants were deploying their capital into new methods and new organizations of manufacturing, development of which would result in even more far-reaching changes than the market revolution.[38] The Watkinsons continued to manage their wholesale stores, but they, too, began to invest their capital and become involved in the creation and management of textile factories.

Although manufacturing was already part of the American landscape in 1795, two major factors had inhibited the development of industry: the successful outcome of the Revolutionary War had opened up cheap lands in the West, thereby keeping the price of labor high and the attraction of working in a factory low; and the war between France and England had opened up the West Indies to American merchants, making trade a more attractive investment than manufacturing. In the second decade of the nineteenth century, however, the situation had changed. Land had grown scarce as population increased and speculators pushed up the price, and the War of 1812 had disrupted trade and cut off the importation of British manufactured goods. A potential supply of workers had been created from those with little or no land who sought a means of subsistence, and a potential pool of capital was available from a network of merchants who were turning to invest in manufacturing.

The market beckoned, and shopkeepers in Lynn put shoemakers to work (Dawley 1976, 25); mechanics in Rhode Island built the first cotton-spinning operation (Bluett 2000, 23), and in Boston, Francis Cabot Lowell, a merchant, and Paul Moody, a mechanic, constructed a power loom (Dublin 1979, 17). Throughout the country small industries of every sort were springing up as foreign imports ceased. Enterprises that could not have competed with the less expensive goods produced by more experienced British manufacturers became profitable, and the government itself, despite the Jeffersonian tradition of viewing industrial production as morally inferior to yeomen farming, lent support to these fledgling attempts.

John Watkinson was one of the merchants who turned to manufacturing. His interest in textiles dated back to 1809, when he had rented a mill in Middletown, but at that time navigation was still the major focus of his attention. He had gradually given up the West Indian trade over a two-year period, 1811–1813, retiring from active commerce for a year or so to regain his health. "I am so much out of health that I think it prudent to decline business if I can do so with enough to live on. I was ambitious to have been useful in business but my health obliges me to decline anything which affects my mind."[39]

In 1814 he returned to business and began to manufacture woolen cloths, at first in partnership with William Johnson. In his account books sugars, molasses, horses, and staves were replaced by wool, sheep, and cloths. His daily business correspondence contained receipts for fleeces and indigo, invoices and warranties for shearing and spinning machines, and bills from women who cleaned the wool.

The earliest attempts at woolen manufacture in the United States had failed at producing good-quality cloths, in part because of the difficulties in obtaining high-quality fleeces.[40] Efforts were made to improve the quality of American sheep by importing animals from Spain and by paying careful attention to breeding and nurture. The *Middletown Gazette* ran numerous articles on the care and feeding of herds of sheep and carried advertisements for Spanish merinos—both full-bloods and half-bloods. John, David, and many others at this time began to build up flocks. John and Pulcifer, formerly co-adventurers in shipping, became co-owners of a flock of fifty-eight sheep. Where earlier correspondence between John and David had concerned the sale of rums, it now dealt with David's charges for the services of his ram to John's twenty ewes—ten dollars, "whether they have lambs or not." He pointed out in his letter that this was a special price as he charged other people $1 per ewe.[41]

Along with his capital John brought to his new occupation many years of experience in trade, many useful family connections, longtime commercial relationships, and his early immersion in England in the wool trade. He was dealing with many new elements, such as maintaining flocks of sheep, constructing a factory, transforming flowing water into power, purchasing machinery, coping with the developing technology of textile manufacture, and learning the ins and outs of a far-flung and complex market.

In 1815, when he bought out his partner and became sole manager of the woolen factory, he wrote to one of their old customers, asking for advice on how to produce for the market. "Having taken to myself the woollen Factory which was carried on by Wm Johnson & Co. I shall pay all my attention to it and will expect from you every information on the subject of manufactoring cloth the colours qualities etc. and wish you to point our the deficiencies of mine, as the profits on a manufactory will arise from the goods suiting the market. I shall follow your recommendations with precision."[42]

At first he remained dependent on a network of family and old associates for buying raw materials and for selling his cloths.[43] From Edward he bought indigo and olive oil for cleaning the fleeces. Edward and Robert sold his cloths in Hartford; William became his agent in New York, purchasing fleeces and finding buyers; and his former partner, William Johnson, lent a hand with sales and credit. But the potential and pressures of industrial production for the market were more than the familiar mercantile networks could handle. Family and old friends could not provide adequate sources of supplies or distribution connections.

Perhaps these changes and the unpredictability of the future were on John Watkinson's mind on January 1, 1817, when he wrote a series of melancholy memorials on the front endpaper of his second factory account book:

> Tuesday August 28, 1798 my Brother Samuel Watkinson was seized with an Epidemic fever in the City of New York and died Thursday 6th Sepr at 2 o'clock in the morning in his 24th year and was buried between 5 & 6 o'clock the same morning in St Pauls Church yard——My brother Richard having performed the offices of a nurse to Samuel took the fever and died at 3 o'clock Saturday morning Sept 8th aged 21 years and was buried by his side
>
> Elijah Hubbard Esq my Father in Law died in Hartford on Monday evening May 29, 1808 at 10 o'clock and was buried in Middletown aged 63 years.
>
> Samuel Watkinson my son died August 10th 1808 aged eighteen months.
>
> Samuel Watkinson my Father died Oct 26 1816 aged 71 years.
>
> Sunday Nov 23, 1817 Resolved with the assistance of God to live in constant preparation for my own departure in joyful expectation of meeting my long lost friends.[44]

On the following page he again wrote that his father had died on Saturday, October 26, 1816. Although his wife, seven-year-old daughter, and two-year-old son were alive and well, on this first day of 1817 his thoughts turned to the past. Perhaps the first day of the new year had led him, like many other people, to ponder where he had been and where he was going; this list of patrilineal losses may have stood not only for the individuals he had loved, but also for a secure web of connections to the past and future. The times were changing. The kinds of relationships that had tied together businesses and families were taking on different dimensions.

The melancholy mood passed, however, and John became fully engaged in building different kinds of connections in addition to the strong links to the past. Establishing steady sources of the essential raw materials was difficult. John bought fleeces from local merchants and from New York. At times he was overstocked and was forced to turn away offers of wool; at other times he traveled to New York to help William find additional suppliers.

The cloths sold well locally, but as production increased finding more buyers became vital—and that was not a simple task. William had depended on friends and acquaintances, but with John's advice he tried new and unknown places to buy fleeces and indigo and to sell the cloths. He and John maintained a steady correspondence in which John informed him of what was needed and made suggestions, while William reported on his efforts and the state of the New York market. Their correspondence depicts an unorganized system of distribution. "You observe you have made no progress in the sale of cloth—would it not be well to try some one or more of the wholesale dry good merchants with one or two pieces and if they are successful to furnish them more or take them back. . . . I finished work in my Dye house 29th Nov which will be closed till March and have sufficiency of wool to work till 1st April before which time I will write you respecting dye stuffs etc."[45]

The manufacturer had little control over the price at which his cloth was sold. Merchants took the cloths on a commission basis, looking for a good price but taking what they could get. John wrote angrily to one such firm, Lobdell's, which had accepted a price of $1.75 per yard, an amount that he felt was far too low for his goods. "Your favour of the 27 Nov was recd informing the sale of my broad cloths with the acct and I should have been satisfied could I have known of the sale; that I might have been a purchaser." Some of the same cloth had been sold by a "merchant in your city at the same time at private sale at 3 Ds."[46]

John took advantage of any contact he could find and, for example, wrote that he had met the schoolteacher's brother, visiting in Middletown, who had a store in Charleston, South Carolina, and might be in a position to sell some cloth.[47] He urged William to search out new potential buyers.

"Mr Taylor's acct should be well looked after; and not offer him any more cloth——do not press Austin & Andrews any further but make new acquaintances; it is well to learn the different opinions merchants entertain respecting American cloths and if after all your exertions you should not immediately effect any thing; it is procuring for us the necessary information and acquaintance."[48]

He wrote a letter introducing a Mr. Fielding, recommending that William, if he saw fit, entrust some of the cloth to him. "Mr. Fielding is a poor scholar and bad penman; but has the character of being a very honest industrious faithful man and worthy of credit—but has no property—should you think proper to leave two or three pieces of cloth with him to sell on commission and to pay you as he sells it or any other way you judge best it will be agreeable to me."[49]

These problems of selling his cloths were made even more difficult by the onslaught of cheap European imports, which flooded the market after the peace with England. John's factory not only survived, however, but also grew and prospered. In 1819 John and William Johnson incorporated the woolen factory under the name of the Pameacha Manufacturing Company with a substantial capital of $200,000 (Martin 1939, 208; Young 1979, 69).

Watkinson had risked his capital on the market as he had once adventured in the West Indian trade and again he was successful. The most significant and, at first, the least apparent difference between his new endeavor and his old was the connection between himself as owner and his workers as a labor force. This time there was no slave production hidden behind the columns of his account book, but, instead, the beginnings of a new capitalist relationship.

Hiring men and women to work was by no means a new experience. His mercantile account books contain a range of forms of payment for services. These entries were listed along with the more numerous entries for objects, such as sugar and staves, as debits to himself or to one of the ship accounts either for money owed or as cash already paid for the work undertaken. One mode of entry was to list the specific tasks: coopering rum hogsheads, coopering beef, repairing and painting cart wheels, turning dung at the summer barn, hewing stone, carving beams for *Schooner Hannah,* or collecting of an overdue account by Alexander Collins, his lawyer brother-in-law.

Occasionally this type of entry included the number of days involved, such as 2 1/3 days carting ice or 4 days haying, but frequently the entries specified a number of days' work on one of the ships without mention of the task—for example, April 7, 1810, "Jeremiah Norton Credit by 3/4 days work .62; part day 1/3 21." A shortened version gave an amount based on the number of days but without specifying them, thus: April 6, 1810, "Brig Two Brothers Debit to cash advanced Shadrach Robinson for work 2.00," and April 13, "Brig Two Brothers debit to labour paid John Dodd .50." The difference in pay might reflect the number of days' work or a difference in the types of work or a difference in who performed the work. Two entries for women's work, possibly as domestic servants, indicate that they were paid by the week. An entry dated May 29, 1806, credits Betsy Foster by 64 2/7 weeks' help, and another, dated February 2, 1808, credits Olivia Blake by "19 weeks & 5 days services 15.00."[50]

The shift in John Watkinson's enterprises away from navigation created changes in these entries. Rather than noting the work on one of his ships, the entries detailed an increasing amount of work on his farm and in the care of his sheep. His ledger for 1813–1819 had a page for each person, itemizing and totaling entries for the transactions by the year. For example, the page for *Ziba Nash*, 1813–1814, shows debits including rent, cider, cash, beef, and rye; credits were entered by "potatoes, pumpkins, days of work, brot wood, chopping & earthing wood, carting manure, cleaned oats, carted gravel & timber, spread ashes in Hurlbut lot, carting beef, rolling stone." Under 1814–1815 entries show debits to cash, cider, and salt, and for credits by various types of work with an agreement to work for a year. The entries begin with a credit by work on the farm and continue, "agreed this day to work 12 Months beginning the 1 April 1815 and ending the 1 April 1816 for the sum of One hundred & ninety dollars, and further agreed to take good care of all the Stock, crops and tools etc and to receive for the same, house rent and the keep of one Cow 12 months." This ledger also included a list of transactions with "*Thomas Jones (a black man)*," containing entries for September 17 and 26, 1814, of debits to pork and cash. Credits were entered by work at "$10 pr month engaged for 12 months from this date"; another credit, dated September 26, specified "21 days work @33 cents 6.93."[51]

The problem of unsatisfactory work performance could be handled within this double-entry framework through debit. Thus, an entry consisting of credits to several laborers on the farm also includes a debit entered on July 3, 1813, for "John Pike to going home early & coming late 20 cents." Another entry details an interesting transaction. First, a long list of debits for Ele Harris, 1813–1814, includes "cash, 1 old cow, 3 days work for self, ½ day lost it being wet, pumpkins, 12 day lost it rained, homemade cloth, and credits by 1/4 amount wood sold, 1 wether sold, lambs, skins, by one quarter of 75 sheep the improvement of JRW flock as pr agreement values, by beef sold Ziba Nash, by keeping sheep 10 weeks." Then an unusual credit was entered: "by agreement not to drink spirits 10.00."[52]

Two other common forms of work agreements at this time were contracts signed by the crew of a ship and papers of indenture for apprentices. Both involved signing documents that set out the obligations of the employer and the responsibilities of the employee for a specified period of time, and both were backed with the force of law. Sailors' contracts were backed by an Act of Congress that enjoined obedience to the captain and diligent service for the duration of the voyage or as penalty the loss of all wages and any personal property on board ship. Apprenticeship papers were signed by a parent or legal guardian and stated that the apprentice was "to learn the art, trade, and mystery"—in this case, of spinning and weaving. The papers also specified the length of the apprenticeship and the employer's responsibility to supply clothing and board.

John Watkinson brought his old methods of bookkeeping to his new enterprise of running a textile factory. In the early years some of the tasks were performed by several women working in their homes on a putting-out system. The women were first debited to yarn they had agreed to spin or to wool that they would clean. When the work was completed, they were paid by the pound of work completed minus any wastage, and their accounts were so credited.[53]

Most of the labor, however, took place at the mill site, and most of the workers were paid by the week. The entries for these workers were grouped together as those for crews had been before a voyage.[54] The account books show weekly payments entered as credits for John Watkinson by cash paid out in wages for the workers. For example, an entry dated March 1, 1818, is titled "List of workmen at the Factory" and names 25 men, 9 women, 9 boys, and 2 girls. The work categories are: weavers, carders, ropers, spinners, dyers, finishers, fullers, pickers, a sorter, an overseer, and "1 man with the wagon," with each category assigned a monetary equivalent. These totaled $39.42. Wages were paid weekly but were calculated by the day, as shown by the entry "the 4 boys were overpaid 1 days cash," and one boy's pay was docked: "Edw Bohanning, July 25, deduct 10 cents for running away."[55]

The new aspect of the entries for the factory workers, however, was that they were made on a weekly basis, with each category detailed, and usually following the title "wages paid at factory" or "list of workmen at factory" or "factory wages." The heterogeneity of forms of hiring labor was giving way to the overwhelmingly single form of wage labor, and John Watkinson's

Saturday February 1ˢᵗ 1817

wages paid Weavers

,40	James Martin	#6...		
,30	James Furney	5...		
,29	Roman Perry	5...		
,60	Thomas Smith 2ⁿᵈ	5...	21...	

Spinners &c.

,45	Elijah Lucas	2.50	
,31	John Gallahor	3...	
,32	Roger Sykes	5...	
,78	John Williams 2ⁿᵈ a new Spinner	3...	
p?	Lucy Austin 5½ days	2.75	
p?	Sophia Hall	3...	
p?	John Bohanning	1.75	
p?	Albert Camp	1.75	
p?	Lumwell Camp	1.75	24.50

Finishers Dyers &c.

,33	Joseph Palmer	8...		
,34	Thomas Smith	5...		
,35	Stephen French	2.50		
,2	Seth Dart	2.50		
✓	Ruth Bills	...		
p?	Betsey Brainard	2.50		
,37	John Smith	7...	27.50	
p?	Oliver Bidwell	2...		
,38	John Williams	2...		
,40	Jane Wright for Wᵐ	12...		
p?	Abner Newton 1 Load Wood	4.20	20.20	93 20

3ᵈ

,54 Joseph Johnson Dr. to lost time ¼ day ,25
he began to sort wood

,79 Luke Haynes Cr. by work
began to sort wool this day

,16 Factory Dr. to 2 Loads wood of Fairchild 8...
1 dᵒ Abner Newton 4... 12...

A page from John Watkinson's Day Book, February 1, 1817. Watkinson, John Revel, business papers 1795–1833, in The Watkinson Library, Trinity College, Hartford, Connecticut.

small workforce expanded moderately over the years, from twenty-five to thirty-nine workers. Watkinson's factory produced fine broadcloth; cassimere, a softer fabric; and satinnet, an inexpensive cloth made of cotton and wool.

But the small and gradual changes in Watkinson's accounting practices barely reflected the far more fundamental change in his enterprise, which gradually but decisively had become one in which Watkinson's profits and survival were intimately tied to the work of the men and women in the textile plant. Watkinson's profits were inexorably linked to the necessity that the workers would willingly and regularly produce goods that he could sell for more than their wages. The old relationship of employer to hired laborer had been completely different.[56] The employer paid for a particular task or service but did not make a profit on the work done. His ship's sails were mended or his cows milked, the roof repaired or a dinner served. But in the new factories an entirely different connection between owners and workers was being forged. This relationship had occurred occasionally in various places in the United States, such as large commercial farms or small shoe workshops, but this was the beginning of its spread throughout the country. This was the transition to capitalism—this new relationship between owners and workers, whose partially conflicting goals, mutual dependency but unequal power demanded new ways of being and new forms of relating that are best described as class relations.

The year 1819 when Watkinson incorporated his Pameacha Manufacturing Company was an inauspicious year in many parts of the country, which had gone from postwar boom to a serious economic depression. Prices had dropped, farmers lost their land, thousands were unemployed, and bankruptcies were commonplace.[57] New England, however, had participated less fully in the boom and was spared the worst effects of the bust.[58] Nonetheless, the *Connecticut Courant,* edited by David's father-in-law, wrote in high moral tones of "our" failings, which had led to this crisis. "We have been unreasonably extravagant as a people; that while our expenses have been increasing for years, our productive labor has diminished; that the facility of credit...has encouraged a spirit of over-trading, and almost destroyed regular business by competition; that we became discontented with small gains and a steady, silent accumulation, and have involved ourselves in debt by wild and visionary speculations, in our haste to get rich."[59]

William was one of those who failed. He had remained in New York, faithfully following John's interests, despite chronic problems with his health. He married at last in 1823 but went bankrupt in 1826. None of his brothers, however, were seriously effected by the depression. John temporarily gave up his plans for expansion, writing to Gilbert Brewster, an inventor and manufacturer of textile machines, to hold off on bringing him a new spinning machine and the power looms he had thought to try, citing "the dullness of the times."[60] He added that he was planning a trip to several important factories, and a few notes in his handwriting indicate that he traveled through New York state the following year. As business picked up, John added new machinery to his factory, which continued to thrive, and in 1822 he began a new enterprise, Sanseer, manufacturing textile machinery.

In 1819 David took a new partner, Ezra Clark, into his wholesale hardware establishment with a contract specifying that David would take responsibility for banking but would engage in the business only when he wished; his partner would manage the wholesale store. David invested $11,000, his partner $1,100, and they were to share the profits.[61] This arrangement freed David to follow his numerous other investments and interests, which included the Hartford Bank, the Phoenix Bank, and the Hartford Fire Insurance Company. In addition, along with his brothers Edward and Robert, he incorporated a manufacturing company, the Union Manufacturing Company, to produce cotton cloth. Like John, David used the "dull times" to study manufacturing, traveling with his wife to England late in 1819 to visit the major industrial centers of Manchester, Liverpool, and London.

Within a decade some merchants had been transformed into industrial capitalists and would in turn reshape the market and the world to suit their interests. However, in these early decades of the nineteenth century only some 5 percent of the population was employed in factories(Lebergott 1961, 294). After the war ended and the bans on shipping were lifted, many merchants had once more invested in cargoes, and many captains had set forth from Middletown and other ports to take up navigation again. Captain Joseph Hubbard returned to the West Indies in 1815, Captain Enoch Hubbard was still sailing to St. Croix in 1822, Captain Daniel Hubbard entered Middletown from Martinique in 1821, and Captain John Loveland carried rum from Antigua in the spring of 1824. Farmers still farmed, but more and more they were producing for the market and risking some of their autonomy in the process. Artisans were still employed in their crafts, but an increasing number were unable to amass enough money to start their own shops and to become masters, remaining permanently in the dependent position of journeymen. Though relatively few in numbers, the investors in manufacturing and the workers who produced their profits had entered a class process that would shape all of their futures.

CHAPTER 5   The Collins Company

The decade from 1810 to 1820 saw the appearance of innumerable small firms, such as Watkinson's. It was a period marked by experimentation in forms of organization and in ways of combining household and factory production. While diverse forms of manufacturing continued to flourish, the next twenty years were to see a dynamic growth of factories that took over all the elements of production. The textile industries of New England are the best known examples of this dramatic development, but they were neither the only type of industry nor, necessarily, the most representative (McGraw 1987, 8). Each industry, region, entrepreneur, and workforce was in some ways unique, although what happened within each factory was effected by far more than the wishes or plans of a particular entrepreneur and the particular men or women who worked for him. Entrepreneurs learned from each other, even as they competed with one another. They read the books and papers that discussed both the technical and social issues arising from the new factory relations. Working people exchanged information and moved from factory to factory, comparing conditions. Though every factory had its own particular history, none, however remotely situated, was an isolated site.

The Collins Company, manufacturers of axes and other agricultural tools, was founded by John Watkinson's nephews Samuel Watkinson Collins and David Chittenden Collins. It grew from small beginnings in 1826 to a good-sized establishment by 1832. By Connecticut standards of the time its workforce was large; it employed three hundred men. As compared with the Hamilton Company in Lowell with its more than one thousand workers in 1836, it was small (Dublin 1979, 26). In contrast to the women and children employed in the textile industries, its workforce was composed of men. It was neither typical nor representative but it shared with every other enterprise of its time the difficult negotiations of the new capitalist relations between owners and workers.

John Watkinson's account books and letters revealed some of the decisions and problems facing an entrepreneur in the early years of industrialization, but they told very little about interactions within the factory or his thoughts as he dealt with his workers. However, his nephew, Samuel Watkinson Collins, left a mass of papers relating to the Collins Company, from which a vivid picture emerges of the process of establishing and running a factory in the early decades of industrial capitalism in the United States.

Collins's memoir, which he called "Memorandums," was written after his retirement, when he was in his sixties. It is a 352-page handwritten document which traces the company year by year from its founding in 1826 through 1867.[1] Although this document was shaped by the selective and partial nature of memory, by an imagined audience of future businessmen, and by the narrative form itself, much of the factual material has proved to be accurate. It also includes copies of speeches and notices that were written in the earlier years.

Some fifty of Samuel's letters remain from a daily business correspondence he wrote at the factory in Collinsville, twelve miles northwest of Hartford, and sent by a daily stagecoach to his brother, David, at the business office in Hartford. Like today's business calls or e-mails between close associates, they were done hurriedly, giving an unguarded view of his day-to-day concerns. The archive also contains contracts with workers over a five-year period, a copy of the company's rules, Samuel's correspondence in the 1860s with the new company president, and several other useful miscellaneous documents.

Samuel and David Collins were the sons of Elizabeth Watkinson and Alexander Collins, a Yale graduate, who practiced law in Middletown until he died unexpectedly in 1815 on a trip to Vermont when Samuel was fourteen and David, twelve. His widow, Eliza, moved from Middletown to Hartford with her children to be near her brothers David and Edward and her sister Ann Wells. The two boys were employed as clerks in their uncles' merchant establishments: Samuel at Edward's grocery store, where he later became a partner, David at David Watkinson's hardware store.[2]

In the early 1820s David set up a blacksmith shop in Hartford where men forged and tempered axes by hand from iron that was obtained from David

Watkinson's business.[3] The axes were then sent to the machine shop at John Watkinson's Sanseer factory in Middletown to be ground and polished and were returned to Watkinson's store, where they were sold.[4] This type of putting-out enterprise had by now become a common type of manufacturing (Henretta 1991, 285). It differed from the old craft or artisan shop, where the master craftsman found his own customers and his own supplies. Here the merchant not only took over the functions of supply and sale; he also collected a portion of the profits and exercised limited supervision over the work process. For David and Samuel Collins this became the first step in building their business.

Samuel described in "Memorandums" how in 1826 a partnership, Collins & Co., was formed between the two Collins brothers and their cousin William Wells of Hartford. The three young men invested $5,000 each in this new enterprise, a significant amount of money at the time. After some searching they located a favorable site, an old gristmill with a good supply of water power on the east bank of the Farmington River, twelve miles southwest of Hartford.[5] Although "Memorandums" is written in a straightforward and, for the most part, practical manner, it betrays a streak of romance by following a conventional narrative form in which the hero independently makes his way in the world. In this case, two heroes, the two Collins brothers, are portrayed as setting out on their own with "great expectations" to build an industry. "They were very young and inexperienced for such an undertaking. Though Samuel Watkinson Collins was 24 yrs of age and had been brought up to business, David Chittenden Collins was only just of age having served as a clerk in the iron business."[6]

Missing from the story are references to the family relationships that enabled them to found the company. Thus, neither David nor Edward Watkinson are ever identified as uncles, and though James Wells's name appears as an important financial backer and, later, as the crucial holder of their mortgage, he is not identified as an uncle. Likewise, their third partner, James's son William, is not referred to as a cousin. The importance of their family and the capital, connections, and experience they inherited is not part of such a story, yet it was clearly a vital part of creating the new factory. To their merchant uncles they owed training in business—in particular, David Watkinson's hardware business. To John Watkinson they owed their early education as to waterpower as well as the use of the factory in which David had axes ground and polished. Their cousin William Wells, eldest son of their aunt Ann Watkinson Wells, was asked to be their third partner because of his father's good bank connections.[7] From their grandfather Samuel Watkinson, they inherited some of their money and the family cultural expectations and knowledge of amassing capital.[8] Their enterprise developed far beyond the boundaries of family connections, but it was the family that gave them their start.

To someone outside their family, Charles Morgan, they owed much of their early success, which was based on their company's capacity to fashion a truly superior axe. During the first two years of the company's existence, the partners remained in Hartford while Morgan, a skilled blacksmith, was recruited from the nearby town of Somers to supervise eight men in the manufacture of axes at the factory (Wittmer 1977, 28). In 1869, some forty years later, Samuel Collins discussed Morgan's work in letters to William Wood, then president of the Collins Company. He was tracing the origins of the company's trademark, a topic that had arisen as the Collins Company was engaged in one of its innumerable lawsuits to prevent imitators from stealing its trademark.[9] He explained that the original axes had carried both Morgan's and Collins's names.

"There is no man living except myself who is conversant with our early history...except *Chas Morgan* of Somer. He resided here several years and was our first overseer....By grinding and polishing the Morgan axes my brother got up such a demand for them that we found it desirable to use both the name of Morgan and Collins on the axes for a year or so to show that they were the same."[10]

Another letter from Collins followed with more details as he recalled, perhaps with some guilt, the difficulty of persuading Charles Morgan to add the name Collins to the axes. "D[avid] C[hittenden] Collins first contracted with a blacksmith living in the town of Somers in this state...to devote his whole time to s[ai]d Collins making axes (forging and tempering) from stock furnished by s[ai]d Collins. We built a house for him here...and he moved here in 1827. The house was built according to his directions and he paid for it. His axes were stamped C. Morgan until he moved here in 1827...I remember about C. Morgan because he was very reluctant to have any name on his axes but C. Morgan."[11]

The transformation of a craftsman into worker, even a highly skilled worker such as Morgan, involved several changes that may appear small on paper but were large in life. As an independent blacksmith Morgan would have had many customers; now he became dependent on one. He had produced finished objects from start to finish; now he forged and tempered, while the grinding and polishing were done by others. He had followed his own will; now he was told what to do. He had proudly stamped his name on the axes he had crafted; now his work was claimed by Collins. Morgan was made a supervisor over a group of forgers, but he found the position to be a difficult one. "Charles Morgan goes away tomorrow to be gone to Somers 3 or 4 days—he complains of being sick, and thinks he has a good deal of trouble and Perplexity with the men."[12] Two years later he left the Collins Company and returned to Somers.[13] There is no record of whether he returned to his blacksmith shop. Morgan's experience would be repeated by many artisans and inventors at many other factories, where their skills were the source of the new technologies of production. In the early years of the industrial revolution some became partners of the entrepreneurs who provided the capital or members of the board of directors when the businesses incorporated, but such positions were almost invariably short-lived.[14]

From its beginnings with eight men in 1827—each man forging and tempering eight axes per day—the company by 1831 had grown to two hundred men producing two hundred thousand per year, with each man responsible for only one operation.[15] There were forgers and their assistants called "strikers," temperers, grinders, and polishers. For its time it was a remarkably advanced manufacturing operation, not only in its division of the work process but also in its adoption of innovative methods and new machines.[16] The partnership had begun with an investment of $15,000. Six years later, in 1832, the company employed three hundred men and reported a capital investment of $250,000 (U.S. Treasury Department, 1969 [1833]). New buildings were constructed for the factory, and a steadily increasing number of houses were built for workers. The factory-village was named "Collinsville," and in years to come it would boast a library, a school, and three churches.

Five years after the company was founded, David Watkinson wrote to William Meeking with pride about David's nephews' new enterprise, describing first, however, the untimely death of their third partner.[17] "Wells has lost his eldest son, of the consumption, which proceeded from a neglected cold, and was of short duration he was 26 years old, possessed of fine Talants, and had about 3 years since engaged with his two cousins, sons of my Sister Collins, in the manufacturing of axes, a business which bids fair to be very successful. These three young men were very capable and enterprising, and would probably have done equally well, in any other business they might have taken hold of."

Their choice of axes, however, had been a fortunate one; when they began manufacturing them, the only axes on the market were inferior ones crafted in ordinary blacksmith shops or cheap imports from England which the purchaser had to grind himself. "They have built up a village in a retired spot, about 15 miles from Hartford, where there was a great and unimproved water power and are now employing more than 200 men, in the making, grinding, and polishing axes which are of a quality for strength, beauty of shape, and finish, far surpassing anything before made and do command almost double the price of any English axe brought to this country. They are making...two hundred thousand pr year which sell easily... and are in great demand—this is the largest business done by any one Company in this state."[18]

During these years vast new lands were being cleared in the interior of the country, and the demand for axes was considerable. Canals had sped transportation and cut the costs of shipping wheat and other agricultural produce from the North and West and cotton from the South. General Jackson had forced Indians from their homelands, opening new lands to farmers and planters. For farmers the Collins axes eased the arduous task of turning "wilderness" into cultivated fields.[19] However, many found that producing enough crops to pay back the money borrowed for equipment and survival took too long. They sold their improved land to speculators and moved back or moved to newer, cheaper land to repeat the process. For planters, driving large gangs of slaves, the axes sped the process of clearing the fresh new lands to plant cotton for sale to British and Northern textile mills.

The company developed numerous styles of axes with names that suggested the region and use for which they were designed. David Collins, who was in charge of the company's sales, assessed the markets carefully and urged Samuel to modify some of their axes for use by slaves. Samuel was somewhat resistant to making an inferior axe even though, as his letter implies, he too believed that a slave could not be expected to take the care necessary for a fine tool. Writing from the factory at Collinsville to the Hartford office, he debated his brother's contention that axes should not be ground as thin for slaves as for freemen.

"D[avid C[ollins] has often urged upon me the necessity of grinding axes thinner for freemen than for slaves.... You would not of course send plain axes among slaves but the Pennsylvania pattern is used by both slaves and freemen. There is however a certain thickness that is right for chopping and will not break if carefully used, and I think *myself* that we ought never to have an axe thicker than that standard, but it be understood that our axes are a nice article and require careful usage."[20]

Their first axes had been lightweight Yankee broad axes, followed by a heavier Kentucky axe, which was preferred by the South; additional patterns and products followed rapidly so that merchants and agents sent in their orders for fifty dozen or seventy-five dozen Yankee, Georgia, Ohio, Pennsylvania, or Kentucky axes and adzes "suitable for Mississippi and Missouri."[21] The company shipped to merchants in Boston, Philadelphia, and New Orleans and sent its own agents to the West and South. Within only a few years the Collins Company joined the growing number of New England's enterprises that had become full-scale industrial manufacturers with a national distribution. Demand for the products was strong, and distribution was uneven but relatively successful; the most critical and challenging problem in running the new factories was finding, keeping, and controlling a workforce.

A number of historians have debunked the myth that in the United States the process of industrialization was smooth and painless.[22] They have documented workers' dissatisfaction with the new factory environments and their fervent efforts to have a say in their hours, pay, and the work process itself. Samuel Collins's memoir and letters give a view from the top of how this played out on an everyday basis within the factory. He wrote about constructing and maintaining the dams and wheels that brought power into the factory. He wrote of ice slowing the flow of water, the problems of purchasing good-quality steel, the effectiveness of new machinery, the difficulty of dealing with the banks, and the greed of merchants, who swallowed up the profits on the axes. Above all, he described over and over again the difficulties of shaping artisans and farmers' sons into a reliable, productive workforce.

Collins wrote that when the company began, only unskilled workers were available, which made it necessary to spend time in training them. The company instigated a practice, therefore, of having men sign long contracts and withholding part of their wages, "thus binding them as apprentices learning a trade."[23] "As there was but a few axe makers in the country we was obliged to take common blacksmiths and learn them to make axes, as they would utterly spoil some of the iron and steel and make a large quantity of poor work that could not receive our stamp and must be sold cheap we bound them to work for several years paying but once a year and then retaining a part of their wages until an equal amount was earned in the following year."[24]

A group of twenty-eight letters written between August and December of 1830 by Samuel to David provides an entry into the tense scene of contention between workers resistant to control and an owner who believed authority must be imposed. It was a contest waged within the factory over hours and behaviors, quality and discipline. The letters describe the scene through the eyes of the owner. Though the view is, therefore, partial, it provides a glimpse at the other side of the encounter as well.

A recurring theme in these letters was the problem of training unskilled men and then keeping them out of the clutches of competitors. The success of the Collins Company in manufacturing axes had encouraged others to imitate them. Daniel Simmons of Berne, New York, and Warren Hunt of Douglass Axes, Massachusetts, were their main competitors. "It takes half my time to watch axe makers who are hovering round here," wrote Collins. He had found two competitors in the shop, who pretended at first that they manufactured forks rather than axes. "I told them...that we are real pirates and hold no communion with any axe maker that we intend to run them all off the ground or sink them."[25]

He continued to describe this event in a second letter that same day: "Hunt had considerable conversation with Marvin Gages at noon and told him that they wishes to hire workmen etc. Simmons said to me 'I find you have hired Winslow and Wingate for 3 years,' he expressed much surprise that they should let themselves for so long a time, he seemed to have considerable to say to Wingate." The threat was serious, and it placed Collins in an awkward position where he felt compelled to keep several men on who were not satisfactory workers rather than see them hired by Hunt.

Marble's time is out and I am quite at a loss whether to keep him or not, he wants to stay and work at our piece prices (which he has never done heretofore considering them too low) but I have steadier better men among my night grinders, men more attentive to directions and better every way, *do more and do it better* but Marble poor as he is will be an acquisition to Simmons, Hunt, or any other axe concern, because he has seen good work and his ideas of work are raised—Wm Brainerd's time is out in October and I ought not to keep him without it is, from such motive as keeping him away from other folks—he is a mischief maker and not a profitable man he does not earn his wages.[26]

Another young man was planning to leave, but Samuel threatened to withhold the wages he had already earned and thereby persuaded him to sign apprenticeship papers, binding himself for five years.

I told Marsh I never would pay a farthing for the 6 mo. work he had done if he left me now—and we finally came to an understanding & put it in writing for five years. The only writing I want from his guardian is something to the following import. "Whereas I am Guardian over this Albert Marsh who had let himself with my consent & approbation to Collins & Co for five years at blacksmithing, this is to signify that I shall not make any claim for wages which A. Marsh may earn extra. [That is, above the agreed upon yearly amount he was to be paid, and the demand he was apparently making]

Collins continued, "You may apply the above verbatim and have him sign it the first time he is in town and I think I shall not have any more difficulty with the boy."[27]

The story continued a couple of weeks later. "Simmons made offers to Wingate and Winslow,... Marvin Gages has applied for a discharge, says Hunt of Douglass have offered him $600 per year and the privilege of forging axes @ 1/- each.... Cornwall stays away unaccountably, he went home convalescent, and I have strong suspicions that he is off—M. Gages got leave of absence for a fortnight before he applied for a discharge. I assured him that I would prosecute him for damages as long as he lived if he broke his contract and he said he should not think of leaving unless we agreed to it." Collins went on to quote Gages as suggesting that he had assumed from Collins's criticisms of his work that he would not be held to his contract. "I had found much fault with his work & that I might be willing to part with him. I told him I would continue to find fault unless his work is done well."[28] As this letter suggests, men left not only for better wages but also when they felt dissatisfied or, perhaps, unjustly criticized. Collins, however, felt he had gone to the trouble and expense of training men whose skills might now benefit one of his competitors.

He wrote gleefully in October that, "I got one piece of information... that was news to me—viz that *any person* who attempts to hire our workmen is liable to prosecution."[29] The plot thickened: "I am getting further information of Hunt's secret emissaries—Marble is empowered to hire 10 of our foremen," and a pencilled note added, "Hunt's emissary hired one of Morgan's foremen."[30] He prepared to act. "Have you ascertained when Hunt was here from my letters written at the time? I expect him here again soon and must have a writ ready for him."[31]

By law, workers could not regain their pay if they left before their contracts ended.[32] By law, competitors were guilty of "enticement" of another's property when they hired Collins's men. It was law made by judges, who freely interpreted the old common law inherited from England and who strenuously laid down precedents that almost invariably supported employers. Educated men, judges tended to associate and to sympathize with men of property.[33] Their picture of how the public good might best be served was that of an orderly society in which those with power and capital should lead and those without should work and follow. However, their law and their ideal were far from the reality of the workplace.[34]

Despite contracts and threats, men did leave before fulfilling their contracts, even though it meant sacrificing their pay. And despite promises and coaxing, they frequently left at the end of those contracts. "Nothing but some decided step on our part (that will give an impression that we are determined to prevent men from leaving us) will prevent a number of our best men doing it when this year expires."[35] As long as jobs were readily available, one of the workers' strongest defenses against the demands and discipline of management was their ability to leave and find another job (Prude 1983, 144).

Collins, of course, deplored this state of affairs. "I want very much to see more applicants for employment in every department that I may make some changes for I think it would have a salutary influence on some (even on those who wish to leave)."[36] He tried various strategies to keep his workers. "I am very glad you are going to bring C. S. Hubbard out here. Depend upon it we ought to bring every man out here and pay him all the attention in our power (lay him under some obligation, if possible) that we wish to have engage in our article in *earnest*."[37] And: "I was occupied most of the day on Saturday in bargaining with Robinson and Horner for another year and finally accomplished it and put it in writing tolerably to my satisfaction."[38] The company housing at Collinsville was an inducement both to come to Collinsville and to remain, particularly for men with families. "It is considerable of a job for them to pull up stakes and move elsewhere and having a family to support they are not willing to be discharged and take their chance of finding another place."[39]

In addition to the problems of keeping men at the company was the difficulty of producing axes in quantity while maintaining the high quality that was the basis of the company's success. This involved far more than simply teaching technical skills. The problems that Collins and other manufacturers faced were embedded in the new relation of worker to product. Dividing production into small tasks dramatically increased speed and quantity, but it diminished any sense of craft, of pride in the product—the pride that Charles Morgan had had in his axes. Collins found that criticism of someone's work could backfire. "I have some difficulty with this boy. No. 1 he has grown careless and overheats his axes and upon my finding fault with him he quit work and has been laying around for a day or two."[40]

Collins was frequently dissatisfied not only with the quality of workmanship but also with the quantity produced. He recalled having paid a premium for two years "to the best men in each branch of the business" but that "it proved a failure. It did not pay."[41] He later tried piece rates to raise the quantity, paying a low monthly rate of $12 or $14, to which the amount earned through piecework was added. "I can fill our shops with good men @$12 and $14 per month and these men at our piece prices can make one dollar per day besides their board if they work hard." In contrast, the men who were simply paid $1 per day were less productive. "Spencer polishes 65 to 70 axes per day/ while our $12 men next to him get off 80 to 90 and do them as well as *he* can (I would observe that we polish much more.... If I was rid of all my dollar per day men I never would have another unless he earnd it by the piece—indeed I think I shall never renew with Brainerd or Spencer unless it is at our piece prices."[42]

The "rationalization" of labor—that is, the division of production into ever smaller and simpler tasks—demanded steady, predictable work, so that the different tasks could be integrated. This necessity was contrary to any previous work experience. Farmers' schedules alternated between spurts of exceedingly hard, long hours of work and periods of light, easy chores. Artisans' work was task oriented so that the end result was what mattered, however long it took. Factory work was not always more difficult or time-consuming or intrinsically more unpleasant than the work of farmers and artisans, but its only rewards were monetary, and its only satisfaction lay in receiving approval for producing more, faster than someone else. The schools that would model later generations of children to these specifications were not yet in existence, and Collins was hard put to find ways to maintain steady production while insisting on high quality.

He was faced with a difficult and complex set of problems. When men were paid by the day, the quantity of work frequently fell; however, when they were paid by the piece, they had an incentive to produce quantity at the expense of quality. If the axes they had produced were discarded upon inspection, their rate of pay fell, and they were disgruntled and angry. Since there was a division of labor, the poor work of one branch affected the production of another, leading to discord among the men themselves as well as dissatisfaction with the company. Collins described with concern a day when, returning to the factory after a brief absence, he came upon a scene of dissension and chaos. The foremen, who were the men responsible for forging, were complaining about their assistants, the strikers, while the strikers claimed to be working as hard as the grinders and for less pay; in addition, there had been anonymous threats against the temperers, who had been discarding poorly forged work.

I returned from Salisbury last evening and I find some things here rather unsettled several men petitioning to be released—Smead had quit and cleared out without permission (this morning). The strikers [assistant forgers] have entered into a combination not to work by the piece without their price is raised and the foremen have some of them quit working by the piece and make only 6 or 8 per day / after having made 14 to 16 per day/—other foremen say they must quit working by the piece unless their strikers are more animated and attentive—The strikers say that the grinders are making one dollar per day and work no harder than they do—our strikers have no difficulty in making $16 per mo. and some have made $18 by the piece. In addition to all this, anonymous communications have been addressed to the temperers threatening them to ride them on a rail etc. etc. if they continue to throw out bad work as they have done.[43]

He continued his description by complaining that the quality of workmanship was suffering from the men's dissatisfaction. He blamed the entire situation on the lures of other axe makers and felt that his only course of action was to threaten the men with a loss of wages. "We have had more bad work and more steel overheat lately than we have had before for many months—all this I attribute to other axe makers having been here to hire workmen. I have not made a practice lately of detailing my troubles to you but things at this moment seem to wear rather a serious aspect, and although I do not see but one course for me to pursue, vis. to threaten them with the loss of their wages, and make some examples of them, still it may produce serious trouble and inconvenience if there should be any stoppage."[44]

By the following day he had calmed down and assured his partner that the situation was in hand. "I do not apprehend however that I shall have any *very serious* difficulty to encounter, that will amount to an open and *general* rebellion." He emphasized the necessity for continuous supervision of the workers. "I attribute this declension in the quality of work (from which this trouble has all emanated) chiefly to a want of constant personal attention on *my* part *every* day to *every* man and *every* axe."[45]

In addition to increasing supervision, he proposed to change the way in which the strikers were paid. "I think I shall raise the price by the piece for strikers and have them lose the poor work the same as the foremen do, heretofore strikers have been paid on all they made (half what the foremen have) very much depends on the strikers and it is very desirable to stimulate them."[46] The problems, however, continued, and competition from other axe manufacturers increased Collins's concerns about quality. "I consider that the competition the ensuing year will render it absolutely necessary that our grinding and finishing should be done better than it has been.... we cannot do this without either lessening the quantity of the forging or increasing the number of the grindstones—when we insist on nice work, it checks the quantity about half."[47]

Scheduling men to work a late shift into the night was another source of conflict. In 1829 Collins had reduced the working day from twelve to ten hours, finding that the men accomplished just as much and burned less coal.[48] But adding a shift so as to run the factory at night would increase production and make good use of water power at times when the river was high. The workers proved unwilling and resistant, however. In the late fall of 1830 he wrote about the need for night workmen. "There will be a surplus of 1500 axes in the tempering room unless I get some night men to pressing [grinding] which I intend to do as soon as I can find the right men! I find that this can be done better in the night than any thing else, but my present set of hands will not work nights any longer—pretend to be sick, work sometimes half the night and sometimes not at all."[49] In his next letter he continued to outline the difficulty. "The grinders feel cross and take this opportunity to be sick many of them...I am hiring men to grind nights as the only alternative *raw hands* ...it is very difficult to get men to grind nights."[50]

He persisted in his search for a solution, considering the workers' reluctance to be an expression of dissatisfaction as well as a response to the difficulty of working at nights in bad weather. "I am enlisting men for night grinding they commenced last night (5 men) but will not begin to do anything for several nights.... This falling off in the grinding is attributable to several causes—firstly they have for some times worked very hard and steadily by the piece, and were about ready to think of a respite—when our refusing to accept the axes, in connexion with the bad weather which made it very dark, and occasioned some colds, turned the scale, and they are sick and missing and what are left might almost as well be."[51] The men's resistance was successful, and Collins conceded defeat in a letter a month later.

"I think we shall have to build another grinding shop, for men will not work nights for any length of time and never do their work as well or do as much of it, as by day."[52]

By law the employer had the right to exert total authority within the workplace. Within the first decades of the nineteenth century the common law had been freshly interpreted to represent the relationship between employer and worker as that of master and servant. Formerly in the United States a person hired for a day's work or a week or two of work had not been considered to be a servant. In the first edition of a book titled *System of the Laws of the State of Connecticut* by Zephaniah Swift, published in 1795, Swift stated "that in Connecticut neither 'labourers' nor indeed any person 'hired by the day's work, or any longer time' were 'by our law, or in common speech, considered as servants'" (quoted in Tomlins 1993, 263). In his second edition, published in 1822, he found "it necessary to add for the first time that 'yet while employed, the relative duties and liabilities of master and servant, subsist between them and their employers'" (263). The law was a powerful weapon for employers, but, as Collins well knew, as long as labor was scarce, the workers could contravene his attempts at domination.

A notice that Collins posted in the factory itemized in tones of great reproach all of the ways in which the men had disobeyed and disregarded the company's rules. "Our rules have not been enforced. We were willing to see how men would act if left to themselves. The experiment has been tried and the question settled. From small infringements our workmen have gone on to large, until our patience is exhausted, and we cannot suffer the evil to exist any longer." He continued with a list of their misdeeds. "It has even come to this, that great numbers of our men have gone home to maying, and harvesting without leave, and we have not men enough left to carry on with our business. Some men commence work fifteen or twenty minutes, and even half an hour after bell ringing; and some leave their work during bell hours for that length of time and even leave the shops and go up to the houses and stores."

The penalties for specific misdeeds followed:

We do therefore give notice to all men in our employment, that none of these things will hereafter be tolerated. No man in our employment will have credit for a day's work, unless he goes to work at bell ringing, or calls on the overseer of the shop where he works, and give a satisfactory excuse, and every man who washes up before bell ringing without leave, and leaves the shops during working hours without leave, will be considered as breaking our rules, and will be treated accordingly in our settlement with him. Also every man who leaves off work for more than one day without reporting himself to his overseer as sick, or giving some other good reason. And every man who is absent from the village for more than one day without leave, will be considered as breaking our rules, and will be treated at time of settlement accordingly.

In a tone of benevolent authority he noted that good, responsible men would be in complete accord with the regulations. "In justice to some few men in our employment, we will say that such rules for them are wholly unnecessary and superfluous—with them we have no fault to find, and we are sorry that the conduct of the majority renders such rules necessary—such men, however, see the necessity and importance, of regulations in such an establishment, and will be the last to complain."[53]

From Collins's point of view these were wholly reasonable rules, to which any sensible man would agree. From the workers' side they were an oppressive set of authoritarian rules over their time, their bodies, and their needs. In this conflict of desires and interests Collins always did his best to underplay his dependence on the workforce. In his efforts to deal with the workplace turmoil he had encountered in recent months, Collins had concluded that he would have to raise the piece rates of the strikers, the foremen's assistants. However, he had postponed actually doing so to avoid any possibility that the workers might see his move as a concession. "I shall wait however and endeavor to avoid any appearance of yielding to their demands."[54]

On the one hand, Collins did everything within his power—including cajoling and threatening—to prevent a skilled worker from leaving. On the other hand, he felt that letting any worker believe that he was irreplaceable was disastrous. "If Goodrich *will* leave I would not have him come back for you can make his place good for less money—and he will if he comes back think you cannot do without him which will impair any man's usefulness."[55] He refused to give a raise to an excellent worker, letting him go rather than allowing him to feel essential. "I have parted with Wm King who blacked our Axes—He '*struck*' (as it is called) for higher wages, & of course we parted, though I could have 'better spared a better man'—Wm will handle more axes in a given time than any man I know of, & and if he should apply to you and your present King does not answer your expectations you had better take this one & he will answer your purposes *well* until he takes it into his head that nobody can fill the place but himself & then you can satisfy him to the contrary as I have done."[56]

The first organized confrontation between all of the workers and Collins occurred in 1833, when the men formed a "combination," an association, to protest a decrease in wages for piece work, which Collins claimed was necessary because of poor business conditions brought on by a cholera epidemic. Collins credited the fact that the men had not previously joined together to refuse to work on his wisdom in employing only Americans and in selecting them with care, so that the village had been "a pattern of order and sobriety."[57] The implicit contrast was with foreigners—English, Scotsmen, or Irish—who were viewed as intemperate and potential radicals.

Workers had been forming combinations from the early 1800s throughout the New England and Mid-Atlantic regions. Many employers appealed to the law to combat them, and in almost every case prior to the 1840s the courts interpreted the common law to convict the workers on the basis that such associations in and of themselves were criminal conspiracies against the public good.[58] The workers were usually fined between a day's and a week's pay.[59] The prosecutors and judges who sought convictions did so in the name of protecting republican institutions from groups formed to serve private interests, while the workers defended their associations in the name of revolutionary republicanism, the right of free men and free women to join together against tyrannical, self-seeking employers (Tomlins 1993, 125). They spoke the same language, "republicanism," a language that resonated with Revolutionary faith that all white men were equals, that all shared the privileges and responsibilities of citizenship, however unequal they might be in property or position. The judges and the workers they convicted shared a language; they differed in how they applied it to their interpretations of the social scene.[60]

When the workers confronted Collins with a petition signed by their combination, he did not appeal to the courts; he responded directly to the men with a speech couched in republican rhetoric, which he claimed to have "written off hand in a short time while the men who brought the petition…were waiting for my reply." His speech and the workers' reply to it were copied into "Memorandums."

"I have received through your highly respectable Committee a very respectful remonstrance against our alteration of piece prices, and I am particularly pleased with the *candid, manly,* course which you have pursued at this crisis, it is worthy of *yourselves* and the high character you have always sustained as a community. It is creditable to you as American citizens and speaks well for Universal Suffrage and the prospects of our Republic."[61]

He continued this speech by pointing out how correct he had been in his policy of employing only Americans, "believing them to be not only more ingenious and industrious than foreigners, but more enlightened and consequently more rational and reasonable." He pointed out how much better manufacturing communities were in the United States than elsewhere, even when faced with a test such as this dispute over wages.

"Instead of such disorderly and disgraceful conduct as we hear of in manufacturing communities in other countries on similar occasions and which has prejudiced some against manufacturing in this country, and to question the policy and expediency of allowing them the rights of freemen at the polls we find here assembling quietly by hundreds not at a tavern to heat their blood and warp their judgements with grog but in the cool open air in front of a temperance store where pen ink and paper can be procured and business conducted in a truly *republican town meeting style.*"

A refusal to adjust wages was transmuted into a flowing discourse on community, nationality, citizenship, suffrage, and the republic. He addressed them as "fellow citizens" and attempted to minimize their differences by stating that "rich and poor will meet together the Lord who made them all."

He went on at some length to deny the truth of statements that had described him as an "*avaricious hard-hearted* man, selfish and unreasonable without patriotism and public spirit and caring for nothing but [his] own selfish gratifications."[62] In fact, he sought to assure the workers that he had their interests at heart. "If there is a favorite object of pursuit with me it is the welfare and happiness of the inhabitants of this village and that can only be promoted effectually and permanently by such prudent and judicious management of our business as will enable us to meet all our engagements."

He emphasized the personal nature of his relationship with the men. "I have addressed you personally instead of using the name of our Comp[an]y that I might address you more familiarly," and on the basis of his "character for veracity" asked the men to believe that "we *cannot afford* to pay such prices as we have paid."[63] He continued by tracing the history of their employment and wages, assuring them that they would be free to go when their "time of settlement" arrived, and he ended by writing, "If you think you can commence work under the new tariff with better courage after a holiday and a game of ball you can take next Monday and enjoy yourselves," and signed it, "Respf, your friend, Saml W. Collins."

The workers not only accepted the pay cut but also sought to impress Collins with their acceptance and friendliness, emulating his style in their response. "The Committee to whom your communication was addressed respecting reduction of wages are directed by the *unanimous vote* of the meeting before whom it was read to express to you their entire satisfaction with the views therein contained, and their resolution to go on cheerfully in the discharge of their duties." They assured him of their trust. "We have no doubt of the correctness of the statements in your communication and our entire confidence in our employer will not allow the supposition that he would wish any thing unreasonable."

Their reply ended with sentiments of republican patriotism. "In the welfare of our village and in the prosperity of the manufacturing interest of our country we as residents here and as American citizens feel a deep interest and hope to do all in our power to promote our common welfare."[64] This almost scripted play of words in a shared discourse may have expressed a hope of what both Collins and the workers knew to be an illusion. Still, these attempts to convince themselves and each other that they had mutual goals limited, if only for the moment, the terms of the struggle to shape the workplace.

There is no record of how the workers spoke about Collins in other contexts, beyond, perhaps, the accusation that he was avaricious and selfish. However, letters from Samuel Collins to his brother demonstrate that the language in which he spoke or wrote *about* the workers was very different from the one he used in speaking *to* them. An extremely vivid and significant metaphor surfaces in a few of the letters in which he described his troubles with the men. In a letter of September 10, 1830, in which he detailed the need for constant supervision of the workers, he wrote, "They wax fat and kick unless they are bridled and spurred *every* day."[65] It appeared again in his statement, "I find married men the most docile and manageable."[66] The metaphor resurfaced in a letter several years later: "Benjamin I have no doubt is a smart, *spirited* fellow. I think he would require kind treatment. I do not believe he would require urging, & I do not think he would bear discipline."[67]

The metaphor provides a striking image of the form of authority and cooperation, mutual dependency, and, above all, control that capitalist production demanded. Not the mindless obedience of slaves or oxen, what was required was physical strength, limited intelligence, willingness to accept direction, and energetic participation. The day-to-day operations of the workplace involved a relationship that Collins symbolized as one of rider and horse, a relationship between two distinct species, a remarkably apt image of class.

Yet this was a symbolic representation of class relations at a particular moment. Contemptuous though it was, it described two creatures of flesh and blood, man and horse, dependent on each other, the one for locomotion, the other for care and food. It symbolized not only a relationship of dominance, but also one of mutuality rather than opposition. Within the next ten years the ensuing struggles within and beyond the workplace would rapidly erase the clarity of that image of mutual dependence.

CHAPTER 6   Breaking Community,
Building Class

The growing impact of the new industrial form of manufacturing shattered many of the old, familiar ways of organizing thought and action and led to the creation of new ones. New divisions broke apart old unities, and old enmities were smoothed over as their separate components merged into integrated wholes, all rapidly taking on a cultural patina of naturalness. The idea of the factory was separated from that of the community, economy from society, worker from citizen. Entrepreneurs joined with stockholders and bankers to become a powerful upper class confronting a disorganized, unruly working class. As this new upper class attempted in every way to mold the workers into a disciplined, compliant labor force, it collided with their resistance to the transformation of work into a commodity to be bought and sold rather than an activity engaging whole human beings.

As factories became the major sites of manufacturing, the splitting off of work from home became not only a physical but a social separation. The law had deemed the factory a private realm free from interference by elected officials, wherein an employer was granted dominion as a master over servants. Home, by contrast, was within the community, the public realm in which all free white men were equal. Marking the dividing line between the factory as an economic realm distinct from the moral domain of community was a contested and difficult process. Who should have access to water? Who should pay taxes? Who should educate workers' children? In every community these and similar conflicts consumed town meetings and courts and enriched lawyers. Samuel Collins kept a lawyer occupied for years in the state capital petitioning for a change in boundaries so that Collinsville would be located in a different township, which he felt was less greedy for taxes. He failed to change the boundaries, but finally succeeded in getting the company's taxes lowered.[1]

These ongoing changes had been set in motion by the actions of the new industrialists, yet the changes were not part of an intentional plan. Many factory owners, like Collins, desired to be part of a small, harmonious, rural industrial village. They knew of and shared American fears of replicating the wretchedness of Great Britain's industrial cities and were determined that their factories would not create these terrible conditions. Samuel Collins declaimed: "It has been said that our manufacturing villages have a demoralizing tendency. I wish to show there can be an exception. I would rather not make one cent than to have men go away from here worse than they came."[2] He built workers' houses and a Congregational church, and his domain extended even into the households and over workers' wives. The company provided housing at very low rents, but families were required to take in boarders, and women were expected to cook for such single men. In the early years Collins clearly conceptualized both factory and village as part of a single community over which he exercised a benevolent paternalistic authority.[3] In the speeches of both Collins and his workers at the time of the 1833 combination, this vision of factory and community as an integrated whole could still be discerned, and the struggle for power within the workplace appeared as a discordant and therefore unnatural element. Between the combination of 1833 and a second one in 1846 both vision and actuality drastically changed.

The Collins Company had begun in the form of a partnership. But its 1834 reorganization into a corporation had significant ramifications. In September 1833 the partnership had been forced into bankruptcy as the Hartford Bank precipitously demanded immediate payment of all of its notes. The company's sales were good, its plant expanding, the Collins trademark so well regarded that unscrupulous competitors put the name "Collins" on their own axes, but the Collinses could not quickly put their hands on sufficient cash to meet the bank's demands. In "Memorandums" Collins blamed the unjust and untimely cutting off of credit on a change of directors of the bank, as their friend General Terry was replaced by former Governor Trumbull as bank president.[4] But Collins's memory seems to have been faulty. The change in directors he referred to had taken place some five years earlier. Oddly enough and unmentioned by Collins, two of his uncles, David and Robert Watkinson, were directors, as was a more distant connection, Barzillai Hudson, father-in-law of David and Edward Watkinson.[5] Further, Uncle

James Wells held their mortgage, and after him David Watkinson's firm was the company's major creditor (Wittmer 1977, 42).

The directors may have had hidden motives underlying their decisions, but Collins & Company was not the only enterprise cut off from credit in the fall of 1833. National forces were at work as state banks throughout the country cut back their loans in response to the closing of credit by the Second Bank of the United States in Philadelphia. The president of the Philadelphia bank, Nicholas Biddle, was attempting to spread financial havoc throughout the country in order to force President Jackson to approve a recharter of the bank and to leave large federal deposits there.[6]

Collins made no mention of this political battle, instead explaining to future readers of "Memorandums" his view of the reasons for the company's shortage of cash at this time. He first blamed it on the fact that a large portion of their sales went to merchants who sold on credit to Southern planters. These planters paid off their debts in cotton after the harvest, and only then would the merchants pay Collins & Company, after skimming off a healthy profit of their own. Collins would have preferred to sell directly to the planters and to keep the full amount. Collins's second reason for the company's lack of cash on hand was his favorite complaint: the problem of training and keeping good workmen, while competitors forced wages up and prices down.

In hopes of increasing production and profits, he had borrowed money to enlarge the axe works and to buy new machinery, counting on the Hartford Bank's usual leniency. Unfortunately the new machines did not arrive in time to stave off bankruptcy. Put to use soon after the company was in receivership, however, these machines quickly proved their effectiveness, earning more than what was needed to pay the creditors.[7]

Whatever the causes may have been, the result was that the company was put under the trusteeship of the largest creditor, James H. Wells. In May 1834 the company was incorporated under the name of the Collins Manufacturing Company[8] with a capitalization of $100,000, and stock was distributed among the creditors to settle accounts. One of the company's largest customers, George Handy, a wealthy hardware merchant from Philadelphia, was made president, and Thomas C. Perkins of Hartford, one of the incorporators, secretary. David Collins was appointed as agent and treasurer, essentially continuing to carry out his previous responsibilities, and Samuel Collins was given the title of superintendent, continuing to run the plant at Collinsville. They contracted to serve the corporation for five years for a salary of $1,500 per year. A separate arrangement was made to secure the

Collins & Co. trademark to the new corporation. In exchange for their transferring exclusive rights to its use, Samuel and David Collins received $25,000 each in stock; so they as well as the other stockholders benefitted from the immediate jump in the value of stock that followed this transaction. In this way, the Collins brothers were forced into, even as they were compensated for, incorporation of their business. Such incorporation was becoming the order of the day.[9] While Collins made it clear that he and his brother had not been financially hurt by the incorporation, he wrote about it with some poignancy. "Collins & Co. gave up every dollar of property they possessed and with it of course went all their 'great expectations', but they had the satisfaction of paying their debts in full and receiving an honorable discharge from every creditor."[10]

But despite Collins's sentimental attachment to his old partnership, even without the bankruptcy a manufacturer as large as the Collins Company probably would not have remained untouched by the new and increasingly dominant form of business organization (Gilje 1997, 4–5). Not only were corporations able to raise more capital with less liability for the entrepreneur; they also provided investors the means to expand their capital from the profits of many factories and to gain a portion of control without the commitment to one particular factory.

As a partnership, Collins & Co. had been managed by the two brothers, with Samuel carrying the heavier responsibility. They borrowed from the bank and their relatives to construct buildings and to purchase machinery, and they repaid these debts, with interest, from their profits. Their primary goal was to develop and to maintain a successful business venture in a highly competitive world. When the company was transformed into a corporation, however, a different set of relationships was initiated. The financing of improvements and expansion was now handled through issuing stock, with profits distributed in the form of dividends decided on by a board of directors, who had their own agendas. They were concerned with keeping dividends high to keep their stock rising in value. They had an interest in the company's success, but only as it affected their holdings.

When times were good and profits high, no problems arose; but when times were bad, Collins found himself placed in a difficult position, trying to satisfy the stockholders' demands, the needs of the company, and those of the workers. The "times" were dependent on the vagaries of the market, where swings between boom and bust increased in intensity as industrial capitalism spread through the country. There were several good years after the Collins Company became a corporation—demand for axes was high, sales were good—and in 1836 a generous dividend was distributed to the stockholders, with enough of a surplus remaining to build a small Congregational church in Collinsville. A year later, however, economic disaster struck the country. Four to five years of unbridled speculation and a glut of goods brought on the Panic of 1837. A run on the banks occurred, with the banks closing down and suspending payments, cutting off access to cash or credit; the panic marked the beginning of a five-to-six year depression.

The company found itself in a serious predicament, "having large stocks of raw material on hand and with large contracts for iron to be delivered. We had notes to pay and not much to pay with, our sales were small and we had very little cash capital." The company attempted to raise cash by creating and selling new stock, but times were poor for selling; the stocks went for a lower price than company officials had expected. Samuel Collins bemoaned the fact that the year before, when times were good, they had paid out large dividends. "It now became painfully evident that we had made a great mistake the previous year in paying such large dividends to stockholders as we now needed the funds to sustain the concern." The large stockholders and directors, who resided in New York and Philadelphia, followed their own interests, ignoring the needs of the company. "They made large dividends and sold out when the stock brought high prices."[11]

Although the situation appeared to be critical and the board was called together daily, "debating financial expedients and trying to negotiate with some of the Banks for aid," Collins assumed that the depression would not last and proceeded to make large structural improvements, suspending work in order to build a large new dam, which greatly increased the amount of waterpower available and expanded production.[12] While eventually his expenditures would prove worthwhile, his optimism at this time was unfounded as the hard times continued and the company's financial condition went from bad to worse.

In April of 1838 Collins posted a notice stating that men would be let go as their contracts ran out and that the company would close in July for the summer. The notice promised employment in the fall for those who applied, whether or not business improved. Men with families could remain in their houses without paying rent. The notice ended with a strong condemnation of the governing Democrats, whom Collins blamed for the depression. He urged the men to vote against Jackson's and Van Buren's Democratic Party in favor of the conservative Whigs.[13]

"I cannot close this notice without expressing my extreme regret and mortification that we are obliged thus to disappoint the reasonable expectations of so many nor can I refrain from throwing the blame where I think it belongs, vis. on our *National Government*. I seldom say much about *politics* but on this occasion must remark that I hold it to be the duty of every citizen to go to the *polls* and vote *conscientiously** and having done so, submit quietly to the decision of the majority and to the laws enacted by them." The asterisk referred to a footnote at the end of the notice: "That is vote the *Whig ticket*." The notice went on to characterize those in power as "*vicious, tyrannical and oppressive* of the character I deem the late *acts* of our *General Government* and were it a monarchy I would appeal to the *Sword* as it is a representative government I appeal to common sense and the ballot box."[14]

This political note was a rare occurrence in Collins's writings, and it aligned him with curious bedfellows—in particular, the financial interests that strongly opposed the Jacksonian Democrats' efforts to regulate the banks. Collins had always regarded banks and bankers as difficult and hostile forces which had to be handled carefully. Banks supplied money when times were good and called it back when it was most needed. "My experience with Banks has led me to the conclusion that although in their petitions for a charter they generally if not invariably claim that it is to accommodate the *Public*. In practice no regard whatever is had to that in distributing their favors...If you are very urgent they will suspect you are weak and perhaps unsound and not worthy of credit. They will insist on shorter paper and more premiums and if your urgent need continues they will probably cut you off *entirely*."

He went on with advice as to how to deal with bank directors. "The best way is to keep very still, calm and quiet, saying but little and appearing indifferent. This inspires confidence in your position and your ability to manage affairs. It shows that you have confidence in yourself, of course one should be good natured and complaisant making friends with the Directors especially with the Bank officers. It is not well to attract much attention to your case or attempt to make explanations, it leads them to surmise and criticise. Their loans in hard times are very much a matter of favoritism."[15]

In 1839 the company's troubles increased as the Hartford Bank cut back its credit even further. The company treasurer went from bank to bank and was finally able to cajole small assistance from the Connecticut River Bank and the Exchange Bank. The value of the company's stocks fell, and the stockholders, hoping to shore up the price of shares, declared a dividend, only to find that they could not pay it. Looking back at these times from his vantage point of 1866, when the company was prospering, Collins still believed that the company had been better off as a partnership than a corporation; he reiterated the idea that individuals in a partnership may accumulate profits against a possible crisis, whereas a corporation pays its profits out to the stockholders. "The individual sometimes accumulates profits enough to sustain him when the crisis comes, but as the corporation divide their profits they are pretty sure to *break* when the crisis comes unless they have an adequate capital paid in, and when they have that they seldom get the benefit of such services as a man gives to a business of his own that he has built up himself."[16]

He pointed out to his imagined audience of fellow managers that the partnership of Collins & Co. had been criticized when it failed for "the folly of attempting to do business on *borrowed capital,* that they should not have contracted for so much *raw material* and *owed so much money,* especially to *workmen.*" He then named the members of the board of directors of the corporation in the late 1830s and noted, "There was not at that time in the City of Hartford seven men with as much wealth as these above named, and yet at this time the concern was in as bad a condition as Collins & Co. were when they failed."[17] As the wealthy stockholders offered no assistance, the treasurer, Alfred Smith, suggested that the company hold back the workers' pay. According to Collins, Smith had "discussed the question of paying the workmen only once in six months which if adopted would have made us largely indebted to them without the same excuse that Collins & Co had of *binding* them to fulfill their engagements."[18]

These passages from "Memorandums" contrast the dedication and responsibility of men like himself, who built a business and struggled to keep it afloat, with the mentality of stockholders, who looked for quick profits from the company but felt no obligation to it. In his letters of the late 1860s to the president of the company, William Wood, he gave practical advice on a wide range of topics, including the careful handling of boards of directors. He suggested submitting a written report at the semiannual meeting of directors, "but I would not advise you to go much into *details,* I tried that and gave it up, and I found it often led to useless discussion on matters of minor importance to the neglect of more vital point. Some of the Directors have other important engagements and after looking at our *figures* and *footings* they begin to look at their watches and are off before we are half through and when we come to voting we have not a quorum."[19]

Such dilettante behavior contrasted strongly with Samuel Collins's lifelong passionate interest in every facet of production and sales. In multiple ways his abilities, his knowledge, and his daily work contrasted with those of the stockholders. He designed the complex construction of dam and race that provided waterpower.[20] He purchased and experimented with coal and charcoal, iron and steel. He understood how steel might best be smelted, knew the correct thickness of each type of axe, and hired and supervised the workers. The stockholders, by contrast, knew the price of stocks and the amount of their dividends and gambled on their predictions of an uncertain market.

In much of his writings Collins seemed to place himself on a boundary line of class between the workers and the stockholders, sympathetic to those who labored, antagonistic to those who did nothing but demand profits. But while this was how he presented himself and, quite possibly, perceived himself, objectively he was on the stockholders' side. The necessity to produce a dividend had become an additional factor in his calculations, and it exerted a persistent pressure to intensify production. "The quantity of those articles that 1 foreman with his striker will turn out in a year will pay us a profit of $800 per annum.... Unless we look out sharp we shall find all our profits this year and every year (unless we get *hog fat*) locked up in Axes and grindstones and coal and scrap iron etc. so that we never should have any thing to pay a dividend with."[21]

The necessity to raise profits through increasing production provided a powerful incentive to improve and to invent machines. Even before incorporation Collins had sought to mechanize the factory. The first machines to be installed had been the trip-hammers; the next, in 1834, were Hinman's machines for shaping and welding axe polls (heads), which had been ordered before the company was incorporated and which speedily proved themselves. After incorporation the company further encouraged innovations in manufacture and made use of the work of several technicians, including a first-rate inventor, Elijah Root, who provided three new types of machines. The first two mimicked hand techniques, while increasing their speed and accuracy; the third completely reoriented the way in which axes were manufactured.[22]

Technological innovation was the result of mechanical genius and a culture receptive to some kinds of change, but the machines that were invented were not the only machines that could have been invented. Employers invested in those that not only speeded production but also gave them a strategic advantage with which to counter the prime weapon of labor—its scarcity. Technology was thus shaped by at least three quite different though interrelated elements. Obviously first was the effort to speed production by machines that could work faster than men. The second was the particular location of the inventor, whose experiences and perceptions were influenced strongly by the community in which he—and at this time it was invariably "he"—worked.[23] The third and frequently most important was the owner's need to control, to avoid being dependent on a skilled, trained worker, who, as Collins so frequently complained, could take his knowledge elsewhere and easily find work. As the machines became smarter, less training needed to be expended on men, and men became more easily replaced.[24]

The depression that lasted from 1837 to 1843 proved in the long run to be a benefit to employers, though certainly not one of their own making. Many businesses failed in this period, but in those that survived, such as the Collins Company, the employers gained power. As the demand for labor lessened and workers experienced the threat of unemployment, employers could pick and choose and impose more stringent regulations and terms more advantageous to themselves. Even when the market began to show signs of improving in early 1843, a surfeit of labor remained, and Collins was able to cut wages. He posted a notice on January 17, 1843: "Having frequent applications for work, and some offers to work for *less* than we now pay, we have concluded to receive proposals for forging bitts of Axes, and also for hammering off the heads for this year ensuing. As we are not willing to contract for a larger quantity than we are now making, those who are now at work will do well to put in proposals unless they are willing to lose their places."[25]

As times improved, however, the balance shifted again, and the quality of work fell. Collins noted that the work done when jobs were scarce was of a finer quality than that done after August of 1843, when business began to revive and jobs once again became more plentiful. "We had made but few axes for several years and had a choice of workmen, we had reduced the cost to 18 per doz, which is as low as we ever got the cost, we had greatly improved the quality, but we lost it all before long by...bad shaving, bad heating and bad management."[26] Despite his complaints, however, the company showed a considerable profit and in 1844 was once again able to issue a dividend of ten percent to its stockholders, the first dividend in five years. Profits continued, new buildings were constructed, and dividends remained high, but once again Collins bemoaned the loss of good workers to competitors. "The demand for axes the past year or two has quickened the competition and many of our men having been bribed to leave us we advertised in 40 newspapers in different sections of the country for workmen to fill our new stone building."[27]

In this seesaw of the struggle for power between employers and workers a powerful weapon for the capitalist side was the momentous influx of immigrants, especially the hundreds of thousands of Irish Catholics fleeing the famines of Ireland (Palmer 1984, 247). The census for three small townships in south-central Massachusetts showed that by the 1850s 70 percent of the workers in local textile mills were recent immigrants from Ireland and Canada (Prude, 190). In Lowell, immigrants replaced the famously independent mill girls, and the corporation soon reduced the ladylike boardinghouses to just another set of workers' tenements (Sellers 1991, 289). While American capitalists could not take credit for driving the immigrants from their countries, they could claim with justice that they eagerly put them to work and that it had been their support of technological development that made it possible to put unskilled peasants to work at factory machines. Although Collins had bragged in 1833 that he hired only Yankees, ten years later, like other employers, he saw the Irish as a solution to some of his labor problems.

The intensification of production created new and dangerous conditions in every factory. As employers sought to lower costs and to increase productivity, industrial accidents involving workers proliferated (Tomlins 1993, 296). At the Collins Company, the danger was not only from accidents but also from the process of grinding, which released particles of stone dust into the air. As long as the grinding was housed along with other parts of the process in relatively well-ventilated shops and men worked at a variety of tasks, the effects were minor. Once rows of grinding stones were set up within a single shop and men worked at them continuously, however, the workers would, over a period of approximately ten to fifteen years, begin to sicken and eventually die from the destruction of lung tissue caused by silicosis.[28]

It is difficult to gauge when Collins first became aware of the human costs of grinding. It was well-known in the cutlery factories of Sheffield, England, where it was called "grinders' asthma," a name that minimized the terminal nature of silicosis. In the earliest years of the Collins Company the danger may have been unknown, though Collins was well-informed about the technical processes involved in producing axes. However, a letter written from Samuel to David Collins as early as the 1830s suggests an awareness of this danger. "Encourage stout men to come on, I want to see our gang improved in muscle—I want to hire 3 stout fellows to grind nights as long as they live we have only 120."[29]

Certainly over the years the serious consequences of breathing stone dust became clear to Collins as well as to the workers. It is very possible that some of Collins's difficulties with getting men to grind at night had been due to their knowing or suspecting that the stone dust was harmful. By the

1840s they definitely knew, and Collins wrote, "There had been so many deaths among the grinders that no Yankee would grind." He was soon faced with a shortage of grinders that slowed down production. "We averaged only 673 tools per day this year because we could not get them ground, and yet our facilities for grinding were equal to 1000 axes per day with good grinders but they were not to be had." Collins had hired Irishmen to substitute for the Yankees, but "the Irish were so awkward and stupid that we did not get the quantity needed even by having extra men working at night."[30] It is possible that the Irish "stupidity" was a form of resistance, since as a more vulnerable workforce they could not simply refuse the work as did the more economically secure Yankees.[31]

A new technique for shaving the axes was tried, but it was developed to preserve the machinery, not the men; the "awkwardness" of the Irish limited production and "the effect of running our grinding with green Irishmen became visible by the increased 'wear and tear' of machinery."[32] The new method, however, was not completely effective and was utilized as an addition rather than as a replacement for the continued use of the grinding stones.

This discussion of the problems of grinding was written in "Memorandums" and conveyed no sense of responsibility or remorse for the men who had died in Collins's employ. His assumption, which was undoubtedly correct, was that other men in his position did and would do the same. He expected businessmen, the anticipated audience for his remembrances, to accept his point of view. Yet to anyone else it is a shocking and callous statement from a man who considered himself to be a moral and decent human being. The separation of economy from society, workplace from community, and market from morality had clearly become an internal or psychological reality, not merely a physical or geographic fact.

The law had helped conceptualize the divorce of these realms. It absolved the employer of responsibility or liability for illnesses or accidents caused by whatever might be defined as the usual conditions of industrial work. The discourse of law—again developed by judges interpreting the common law—viewed workers as free agents who had freely contracted to carry out a particular job. Since the dangers of grinding occurred in any factory where grinding was part of the industrial process, the work conditions were interpreted as normal. Just as workers signed contracts which meant that they accepted the rules of the workplace regardless of whether the rules were understood, so they by law accepted the perils as well, understood or not.[33] There are no indications that either judges or employers were disturbed by the contradiction between the law of master and servant, which placed workers as subordinates to their employers, and the assumption of equality in contract.

Collins's reaction to the grinders' deaths was, therefore, legally and morally sanctioned. Relations in the workplace were set by the rules of the market at the discretion of the employer.[34] Intercourse within the community was ruled by the laws of the government and by the moral rules of Christianity, as symbolized by the Congregational church built in Collinsville. Within Samuel Collins's mind the separation, which had been only a small fence in the 1830s, was now a towering wall. In 1845 he physically separated himself as well, first moving to Hartford as treasurer and then president-treasurer, while Root acted as superintendent of the works. Collins returned to Collinsville several years later when the Hartford office, with David Collins in charge, was relocated to New York City. On his return he built a new house on the outskirts of Collinsville.

In the 1820s and 1830s many factory owners had lived within their company's village, in a bigger house but close to the houses of their workers. By the 1840s, in contrast, most of them had moved farther away as the contradiction between an owner's position as employer and his status of fellow citizen became more glaring and more uncomfortable.[35] Though differences in wealth had always existed in American towns—in the past a fine house might have stood next to a shanty—now the wealth might too easily be perceived as due to the labor and subordination of a fellow citizen. A farmer might envy a merchant's large house and luxurious coach or laugh at his pretensions of superiority, but, unlike a factory worker eyeing his employer's mansion, he had no reason to believe that it was his own hard work that had created this elegant lifestyle.[36] Collins claimed that he had moved to the outskirts of Collinsville because of the noise and smoke of the new railroad and the new shops, and these may indeed have influenced him, but far more important, there was no longer a need or place for the appearance of neighborliness, and he probably felt more comfortable at a distance.[37]

The physical distance eased the contradictions embedded in the complex relationship between capitalist and workers that was simultaneously increasing in intimacy and distance. The intimacy was in gaining one's own wealth through buying and selling the energy and hours of another's life. The distance came by treating that energy and time as objects with no other connotations, with no human ties of responsibility and obligation. The emerging class relationship could no longer be encapsulated in the metaphor of horse and rider. Instead, the idiom of the market served as a mode of activating, understanding, and rationalizing this relationship. It dominated a speech that Collins made in 1846 as he left behind most of his old republican discourse for the language of the marketplace. He kept the speech and copied it into "Memorandums," believing that "it contains some ideas that may aid some future manager."[38]

The occasion was another combination by the workers, who presented a petition for a raise in wages that Collins had no intention of granting. The differences between this speech and the one he had given in 1833 revealed the extent of the changes that had taken place in the class relationship along with some remnants of the past. In his 1833 speech Collins had emphasized the shared citizenship between himself and the men, addressing them as "fellow citizens." In 1846, however, he addressed them as "gentlemen" and referred to them as "laboring men." He began with a statement of "my own feelings and views lest you should misunderstand and misapprehend me" and continued by saying, "The most unpleasant feature of my situation here is that I am in the midst of a community who think I am getting rich from the proceeds of their labors without allowing them a fair compensation for it."

He suggested that the reason for this mistaken perception was that, having seen the company make a large investment in new construction, workers had assumed that considerable profits were on hand. In an argument that may have been original to Collins but which has been stated and restated in myriad clashes between labor and management ever since, he patiently explained the capitalist's view of the difference between capital and profits. "It is perhaps natural that you should supose just at this time that the large and expensive addition that we are making to our establishment is not only an indication of the prosperity of the business but also is proof that we have accumulated a large amount of profits to be able to expend so much money but the *fact* is we have not accumulated *any* profits but are spending our original capital paid in by the stockholders, and we are *borrowing,* looking to future profits to refund it."

Improving business and economizing were necessary in order to pay the stockholders a fair return on their money, he said. "Neither is the business very *profitable,* on the contrary competition is so close and the price of axes constantly falling that we are obliged to enlarge our business and make a *nimble ninepence* of it. In looking at the future we feel compelled to do more business and economise the cost as much as *possible* in order to save for our stockholders fair interest on their money invested here." He expected the men to understand and to accept the stockholders' rights and expectations. "I presume that no laboring man would expect that those who have money and lend it to furnish him with stock and tools to work with [would do so] for less than 6 to 7 pr ct."[39]

He continued with a long explanation of the different rates of interest in Connecticut and New York, where some of the stockholders resided, and the risks that investors faced of losing their money—"by *fire* and by *flood,* by *bad* debts and *bad management* and by deterioration in value from *wear* and *tear* and natural decay." The stockholders had averaged only 7 percent interest over the years that the company had done business, and he claimed, "They are not getting *rich.*" Collins also assured the men that he himself was not profiting from the company: "I have not added a dollar to my property during the last ten years." He admitted that he could economize more and suggested that habits of economy were more important than "the amount that a man *receives.*" His speech was steeped in the logic or rationale of the capitalist class; in his view, only a misguided person would question whether Collins's investments in the company and, therefore, his personal worth might not be more than it had been ten years earlier, or whether the workers' possibilities of economizing might not be equivalent to his, or how stockholders earned that 7 percent.

These questions may have been in the back of Collins's mind as well, and a curious statement that followed with overtones of classic republicanism suggests that he was not completely convinced by his own rhetoric. "I wish myself that property was more equally distributed than it is, and that all might be obliged to labor in some way, it would be for the best good of all and I would favor any course of legislation that would have a tendency gradually to equalize property without destroying the inducements to industry and enterprise."[40]

After discussing why money does not buy happiness, he turned to consider the rights of the workers, juxtaposing their rights against those of the stockholders and situating himself in the position of an impartial judge. "I fancy that in this case I can see the truth clearly and render impartial judgment. It is written in Scripture that "*the laborer is worthy of his hire,*" and were it not written there *common sense* would teach it to us. That you should have a *living* is of more consequence than that the capitalist should get interest on his money and your wages are paid to you *monthly* in good times and bad times, whether the Company are making or losing money your wages are paid *first,* that is *all* as it *should* be, *so far.*[41] A living is the basis of your rights—Six pr ct the base of his, (after he has paid you enough to live on)." He moved to the question of how any surplus should be handled and argued that it had been fairly divided between the workers and the investors: "They have received a little more than simple interest for the use of their money, and the workmen in this establishment have on the long run received a little *more* than a *living*."[42]

These musings on rights and fairness were quickly abandoned as his speech addressed the truths of the market, supply and demand. Comparing farm workers and industrial workers, he said, "The *farming* interest of this country is the great paramount laboring interest and must ever on the long run regulate the price of what is called common labor." Farm laborers averaged $12 per month—more in summer, less in winter—plus their board, a wage that "the most feeble man in our employ can earn...easier than he can do it at farming if he will take the same number of hours to do it." However, he pointed out, many men at the Collins Company left work early "by ½ past 2, or by 3 o'clock, and they have plenty of time and strength left for a game of ball, and I am glad to see it, but they ought not to expect us to pay for time spent at play." As to farmers, "they are too *tired* and *exhausted* to feel like *play*."[43] He had referred to playing ball in the 1833 speech as well, but in a far more expansive mood.

Next he compared the skills needed by farmers and by axe makers, and his conclusion displayed the dramatic effects of technological change in diminishing the need for skills and training. In the early years he had consistently complained of the time it took to train farmers' sons or common blacksmiths to make axes. In this speech, made less than twenty years later, he argued that, "The fact is that axe-making has become so simplified that any Yankee farmer boy of average ingenuity and strength can as soon as he is of age and starts for himself soon get hold of any branch of the business with very little practice. It followed that given the abundant supply of potential workers, therefore, the laws of the marketplace dictated that no raise in pay would be forthcoming. "As New England is full of such young men who desire to avail themselves of such advantages where they can work the year and have a chance to work by the piece and by a little extra exertion earn more than they can on a farm that I cannot see any probability of wages advancing here unless farm wages advance."[44]

Again a note of discomfort broke into his speech: "I thank God that the demand for labor is such in this country that we employers cannot do you any great wrong if we were disposed to."[45] This statement acknowledged the inequality and intrinsic conflict between employers and workers yet placed Collins firmly on the side of the employers. The men did not receive their raise, and the following year the Collins Company distributed dividends of 10 percent to the stockholders.

Collins compared the speech he had made in 1833, "which was written off hand in a short time while the men who brought the petition and those who signed it were waiting for my reply," to the more carefully composed second one. "I must confess however that the first one though less argumentative was the most effective, but the circumstances and the men were different. At this time though the men continued at work they were not satisfied and before long one and another left."[46] No record of the men's reply exists, but Collins was no longer speaking their language. In fact, the circumstances, the men, and Collins himself had changed considerably in the thirteen years that separated 1833 from 1846. The change in their relationship was succinctly expressed in the closing of each speech. In 1833 Collins had ended on a personal note, signing, "Your friend." In 1846 his peroration ended with the impersonal "Yours Respect."[47]

Collins's 1846 speech was indicative of the partial but not complete victory of capitalist class relations. Collins was a transitional figure still caught up in the old dream of a cooperative and harmonious rural industrial village while acting within a tawdry, unfeeling, and competitive marketplace. He addressed "Memorandums" to fellow businessmen, but he regarded other axe makers as competitors and unscrupulous enemies. He had friends and relatives who were bank directors, but bankers were dubious allies, to be handled with cunning. He defended the rights of stockholders in his speech to the workers, but he considered the stockholders two-faced opportunists. Nonetheless, despite all that he did *not* share with these other capitalists, the critical relationship was the class relationship of capitalist to workers, the one he *did* share with them.

There is no specific moment, day, or year when one can situate the appearance of a capitalist class and a working class in New England.[48] It did not happen in 1820 or 1830; it was a continuous process but in no way a smooth evolution. It built on what had come before at the same time that it tore down the past. Many of the diverse elements that combined in a new and lasting relationship of class had been present in New England for decades, even centuries. Foremost among these were inequality of property ownership and differential access to political power, which in turn were associated with marked differences in education, access to credit, and ways of life. However, in the past none of these had either led to or depended on lasting structures or institutions that implemented the domination of richer over poorer.[49] In the second and third decades of the nineteenth century capitalists began to construct such institutions, weaving complex webs of meaning around their usurpation of power over the private sphere of the workplace, shoring up their domain, expanding its boundaries, and extending their hegemony to the public sphere of the community.

CHAPTER 7

For Their Own Good

A visitor to Hartford, Connecticut, today would find it hard to imagine that this city had ever been the center of a prosperous regional economy and the site of a budding ruling class. But in the early decades of the nineteenth century some fifty prosperous white men and their gracious wives and sisters actively created connections and institutions that secured their dominant roles and positions of power within Hartford and its environs. The men were directors of banks, industrial corporations, insurance companies, and rail-roads, who frequently discussed the implementation of plans for the philan-thropic and cultural progress of their city, plans that actively engaged many of the women as well. David Watkinson and Olivia, his wife, were among them.

From his earliest years in Hartford, where he had settled in 1798 after his brothers' deaths in New York City, David Watkinson had invested in a number of enterprises. Like many other successful merchants he kept only a small part of his capital tied up in "store goods." The rest was invested in Hartford real estate, a Connecticut River wharf, and bank stocks, as well as in insurance, navigation, and manufacturing companies. Many of his earlier investments had been in companies related to the mercantile trade, such as those making river improvements to ease navigation as well as canals and turnpikes to speed country goods to the river ports; his newer investments were in textile mills, his nephews' axe factory, railroads, gas companies, and speculation in Western lands, reflecting the shifting economic opportuni-ties of the times.

His financial abilities had quickly brought him recognition in Hartford, where in 1814, at the age of thirty-six, he was made one of the directors of the new Phoenix Bank. In 1818 he was one of the incorporators of the Connecticut Steamboat Company, along with several other merchants (Martin 1939, 196). In 1819 he incorporated the Union Manufacturing Company with his brothers Edward and Robert, was made a director of the Union Company, which had been organized in 1800 by prominent merchants to improve the river below Hartford, and became a director of the long established Hartford Bank (Martin, 190, 208).

He was already a wealthy man. He and his wife, Olivia, lived in a fine house with Grecian pillars on Prospect Street in one of Hartford's best neighborhoods. His brother, Edward, married to Olivia's sister, Lavinia, had moved next door. David and Olivia had no children of their own, but their nephews and nieces were continually in and out of their house. David and Edward's sister Ann Watkinson Wells and her husband, James, lived across the street. Elizabeth Watkinson Collins had moved nearby with her children soon after her husband, Alexander, died in 1815. In less than twenty years David had established himself as a respected member of Hartford's social elite, while Olivia herself was from an important and prosperous family. As fit their position and interests, they had become active in Hartford's new benevolent institutions—David as one of the board of directors of the American Asylum for the Deaf and Dumb, and Olivia as an organizer and manager of the Beneficent Society for Orphan Girls (Clarke 1966, 5).

Like other Hartford business leaders, Watkinson served on the boards of numerous enterprises. He was on the same boards as at least sixteen other men, fourteen of whom were merchants and the other two lawyers. In all, membership on boards of directors and positions as officers of banks, insurance companies, and corporations rotated among some forty or fifty of these leading men of Hartford (Martin, 214–17).

Their control of industries through boards of directors, banks, and stockholding removed them from the gritty actualities of the factories that produced their profits. While their demands for dividends and rising stock values forced superintendents or managers to find means to induce men or women to work long hours at increasingly monotonous and frequently dangerous tasks, they could and usually did remain distant from the factories. Nevertheless, they were directly concerned on a daily basis with the increase of their capital. Superficially their involvement in industrial capitalism was no different from their ventures in mercantile capitalism. Others constructed and managed the factories, just as others had sailed the ships and faced the perils of weather and politics. However, this new industrial form of organization offered both a new possibility and a new necessity to control the sites where the interest on investments was generated.

Their shared concerns and numerous encounters appear to have smoothed over many of their past and present differences. The religious divide, which had formerly been significant, had been bridged, and Congregationalists and Episcopalians cooperated in business and philanthropy. The removal of the Congregational Church's privileged status as the official, tax-supported church of Connecticut in 1818 had opened the way to an easier relationship between former religious rivals. Watkinson, for example, became a director of both the Phoenix and Hartford banks, which had been formerly Episcopalian and Congregationalist, respectively. He served on these and many other boards with Charles Sigourney, a leading Episcopalian businessman, formerly a hardware merchant like Watkinson, whose wife, Lydia, a nationally known poet, had converted to the Episcopal Church at the time of her marriage. Political differences had also receded with the failure of the Federalist opposition to the War of 1812 and the American victory. The fervor of Jeffersonian Republicanism had faded, and the emerging upper class shared a fear and hatred of Jackson and his populist appeal.

These men, who served together on numerous boards of industrial corporations, were the same men who, along with their wives, attended meetings of the boards of the new charitable and cultural institutions. They addressed each other in their letters as "Esquire," an honorific of English origin, and considered themselves gentlemen to be accorded the respect due to their positions of wealth and power. As the dominant and leading group in Hartford they felt a responsibility to mold their city into a moral and orderly place, and there were many problems to claim their attention.

The eighteenth-century solution to caring for the sick, insane, poor, or indigent had been for the family to provide the necessary aid and support. When the family was unable to assume this responsibility, funds were provided by the village or town to some other family who would undertake whatever services were deemed appropriate. By the nineteenth century, however, as land in the eastern states grew scarcer and the market economy grew ever more dominant, the number of people unable to be self-supporting had swelled beyond the capacity of families to provide for them. The possibility that the state and/or the federal governments might take on these responsibilities was not an obvious or congenial thought to Hartford's elite. So, as the unquestioned leaders of the community—at least in their own minds— they took on this arduous Christian burden.[1]

Their efforts to improve the lot of the poor and unfortunate were sincere. They were not merely motivated by material self-interest, yet their understanding of the causes of social unrest or poverty could not help but be powerfully shaped by their own experiences and concerns. They sought causes that pointed away from the upheavals of the market and the impact of industrialism and repudiated the discourse of critics who held that the wretchedness of England's manufacturing cities was the inevitable price of industrial capitalism. They studied English technology and copied English fashions, but they were determined to construct a society free from what they perceived as the Old World's decadence and misery, results of the Crown and aristocracy, which were institutions totally foreign to the republican heritage of the United States.[2]

David Watkinson fully shared these beliefs. His family had emigrated to escape just such arbitrary aristocratic rule. When, in 1819, David and Olivia undertook a year's visit to Great Britain, they carried with them the full set of New England expectations and values. Their itinerary took them through the most industrialized regions of England and Scotland: Liverpool, Manchester, and Glasgow. Olivia kept a journal of their travels, describing "pleasant situations," including a stay in London and a visit to Watkinson's birthplace in Suffolk, as well as visits to numerous factories. A perceptive observer with a gift for description, she wrote about their landing in Liverpool and a visit to the Duke of Bridgewater Canal "and the immense piles of flint, sand and clay, that was to be transported to the different factories, in boats through the locks." She described their trip by canal boat to Manchester: "I thought it a pleasant mode of sailing, the boat is drawn by two horses which trot by the side of the canal. We passed many beautiful situations. As we approach Manchester the water is black with the dies that come from the factories. We pass under the Dukes canal while boats are passing over us loaded with goods drawn in the same way by horses."[3]

In Manchester they went "to different parts of the town, to see the printing of calico, the cutting of fustian [a fabric woven of cotton and flax]." From Manchester, she wrote, "we went to Mr Devonports Poterys...the forman, politely shoed us every part of the process of making china and glass."[4] The glassworks of Wolverhampton provided an unusual spectacle. "A most curious place, it has the appearance in the night of a town that has been burned down, nothing remaining but the chimneys, fire issuing from them and innumerable heaps which proved to be glass works, there appeared to be but one street through the town, each side of which were large coal pits and hundreds of people at work in them."[5]

She found the Scottish highlands "enchanting," but also noted, as they traveled along the Clyde near Dumbarton Castle, the place "where a few days before several persons had been killed by the soldiers that were called upon by the inhabitants to quiet the disaffected labourers." She also noted that at the nearby manufacturing town of Paisley "a great number of soldiers were stationed there to keep the people quiet."[6] The Watkinsons traveled to the counties of North and West Yorkshire, passing through several textile manufacturing towns, which she characterized by the fabrics produced in each: Leeds, Bradford, Halifax, woolen cloths, bombasts, coarse cotton goods.[7]

Their sightseeing was not limited to factories. It included a visit to a "celebrated watering place," Blenheim Palace. They attended the theater and the opera, saw the crown jewels at the Tower of London, saw the Bank of England—"an immense and very extensive stone building it is said it covers several acres of land it employs 1100 clerks."[8] They visited some of the British institutions that, like theirs at home, sought to aid the unfortunate and to correct or punish the undeserving. They spent time at a Deaf and Dumb Asylum and a Hospital for the Insane, "two melancholy yet interesting visits. I feel that we had great cause for gratitude that we had been spaired from both afflictions."[9] The Hospital for the Insane impressed her as comfortable and well-ordered, while at the Women's Prison she was struck "with horror, not that there are any cruelties inflicted, but the height and thickness of the surrounding wall and gates, excited such feeling in me as I never had in visiting any place."[10]

Throughout her journal she contrasted her New England simplicity and piety—recording how she and Mr. Watkinson, as she referred to him, observed each Sabbath and noting the sermons they attended—with the pretensions and decadence of the English aristocracy. She described women who, after dancing all evening in low evening gowns then nursing themselves for two or three weeks so that they could attend another ball, died of consumption. "I am glad," she wrote, "not to be so tempted." She disapproved of the prince regent: "I have not heard of any generous acts . . . but a thousand extravagances to gratify his pride, one that he has at his Pavilion at Briton 6 hundred wax candles burning every night if he is there or not, and the poor that scarcely have enough to eat, are taxed, . . . in every way to pay for it." As to "the higher Order of people . . . there is no real happiness among them it is all envy, strife, jealousy, and dissipation, 3 o'clock is the usual for retiring 12 for rising."[11] She observed that both wealth and poverty were more extreme than in the United States. "Thursday . . . very severe weather, every paper has accounts of the sufferings of the poor…the poor in America are very well off in comparison with this country where there is much greater wealth and much greater poverty."[12]

David did not leave a journal, and only a few of his letters written during this trip remain; however, his letters also convey a sense of the social and moral superiority of New England. In a letter written from London to an old friend of the family's, the Reverend Ward of Stowmarket, England, he voiced his disapproval of the Anglican established religion, "as God needs not the aid of human laws to compel his creatures to worship him." He argued that the requirement of paying for the church was added to an already heavy burden of taxes, which he blamed on "the extravagant management of those at the head of affairs and the great national debt." The taxes had a demoralizing effect on those with only a little property, rendering it "almost impossible for those individuals of small property to suport a family without devoting too much care and time for this object and leaves them too little leisure with their families and useful meditation and reflection."

The situation of poor people was even more serious: "The poor are still worse off I mean not only as respects themselves but as to the rest of the community in what a degraded state must this numerous part of the community be and how can they respect themselves when they are under the necessity of begging for part of their maintenance from the parish. I will not attempt to prove that from this source the great profligacy amongst this class arises from want of self respect; probably many other causes tend to produce the numerous instances of intemperance, robberies, murders and suicides etc. which occupy so great a part of the daily newspapers of this country.…The profligacy of the high taxes must be felt through every rank."

He continued by addressing the differences between the two countries that he believed to be at the root of the miseries of the English poor: entailed estates, which restricted inheritance of land to a single heir, limited representation in elections, and the game laws, which proscribed the former customary right of commoners to hunt on the estates of the landed aristocracy.[13] He was expressing the typical New England view that the main causes of English poverty, and possibly even of crime, lay in the tyrannical and aristocratic system.

While both David and Olivia were troubled by the poverty they observed in their travels, their sympathy was intermingled with doubts as to whether the poor merited assistance or restraint. As David pointed out, there were "probably many other causes" for the high incidence of crime and intemperance among them. This question of deserving versus undeserving poor appeared vividly in Olivia's description of an incident that occurred one day while she was walking in London. She passed a young woman, who was searching the ground and weeping. Finding a sixpence on the walk, Olivia handed it to her. "Seeing the money the woman dropped upon her knees exclaiming with a most expressive face, God bless Maddam, this shows the value of money with the poor, and never do I walk out without meeting with some of the most distressing, and disgusting, objects, it is very difficult to know from their appearance if they are worthy or not, in some instances I am told if I were to take out my purse when charity is asked they would snatch it and run off."[14]

This was an immediate and practical question, but on a deeper level one of larger social import, which was to preoccupy the Watkinsons and other New Englanders of the owning class for the next decades. The issue was especially troublesome since what they believed to be the social causes for poverty in England were not present in America, where the people had a say in the government and labor was scarce and relatively well paid. Therefore, poverty and the social ills at home could only be due to individual misfortune, such as being orphaned or afflicted by deafness, disease or insanity, or to individual shortcomings, foremost of which was intemperance (Rothman 1971, 163).

Their trip to England reaffirmed their belief that they, along with other members of Hartford's elite, had an important role to play in promoting the social as well as the financial well-being of their city, and the Watkinsons returned to Hartford to take their place in both the commercial and benevolent activities of their emergent social class. David expanded his holdings to include the Enfield Canal Improvement Company, the Del Hudson Canal Company, the Connecticut River Valley Steam-Boat Company, and the Providence, Hartford & Fishkill Railroad Company. He became president of the New Haven & Springfield Railroad, a director and president of the Hartford Manufacturing Company, a director of Hartford Fire Insurance, and a major stockholder of Mutual Life & Trust. He was a trustee of the Hartford Savings Society and, along with a group of other wealthy Hartford men, invested in land in Indiana and Illinois, which promised to return more than 100 percent on their investment.[15] He continued to serve as a director of the American Asylum for the Deaf and Dumb and became an incorporator and financial benefactor of the Hartford Hospital; he also became the treasurer and director of the new Connecticut Retreat for the Insane.

He took an active role in promoting the missionary efforts of religious revivals and the temperance movement that had developed from them. In the early decades of the nineteenth century the religious revivalism of the Second Great Awakening swept through the country in a series of waves that peaked in 1807–1808, 1812, 1815–1816, 1820–1821, and 1825–1826 (Keller 1968). The causes and meanings of the revivals were complex; the movement has been attributed by scholars to various factors: to the "market revolution," to the "transportation revolution," to the separation of work from home, and to a growing sense of class as artisan masters moved away from their workshops and lost control over their journeymen. The revivals resulted from middling folks' fear of losing their farms and their patriarchal way of life or from the clergy's missionary activities in the face of skepticism, "infidelity," and foreign ideas of "rationalism."[16] These waves of religious fervor, which varied in intensity and duration, expressed the fears or insecurities of many types of people in different social situations facing the increasing destruction of community ties and the building of new and firmer class boundaries.[17]

New England's emerging capitalist classes in Hartford, Boston, and elsewhere accepted a version of Christian thought that validated their own righteousness as proven by their worldly success and their support of Bible, missionary, and temperance societies. They viewed religion as a way to spread morality and self-control to the undisciplined and disorderly population, especially to the stream of new immigrants whose baggage included corrupt European political ideas.

In one of Watkinson's letters to an English cousin, he described the positive results of encouraging religious practices throughout the country. "The state of society in this extensive country may be said generally to be improving, although in the new settlements where the population is always much scattered, and too thin to support the expense of a regular preaching society it is in a deplorable state made up from immigrants from various parts of the world, yet in the developed parts of the country an unusual attention to religion prevails."[18]

Ten years later he wrote to William Meeking about the salutary effects of the religious revivals. "The moral and religious state of the community is also improving. Revivals of Religion are taking place to a greater extent through this country than was ever before experienced, particularly amongst the Orthodox Societies of the Congregationalists, Presbyterians, Baptists, and Methodists, and of course greater exertions will hereafter be made in behalf of Missionary, Tract, Bible, and other benevolent societies."[19] Watkinson frequently mailed parcels of religious tracts to the Reverend Ward in Stowmarket, who in turn reprinted and distributed them throughout his surroundings.[20]

Closely allied with the Second Great Awakening was the temperance movement. The problems of poverty, crime, and disorder were blamed on the use of "ardent spirits." Even though intemperance was known to affect those of higher social standing—for many years the Watkinsons worried about Jane Gill's eldest son, until finally he was cured by a minister friend—the main goal of the movement was to improve the character and habits of the working population.[21] Throughout the eighteenth century as before, drink had been part of the rituals of every working day. Farm laborers expected to celebrate planting, harvest, lunch, and supper. Workers in craft shops expected to drink with their employer during several breaks a day. The temperance societies easily convinced employers that temperance would increase production and improve the health of their employees. Convincing the workers was more difficult.

Some manufacturers, Collins among them, included a statement forbidding alcohol in the workplace and limiting its use in the village in the contracts that each worker had to sign: "no man will be retained ... who is guilty of disorderly conduct, or carries spirituous liquors to the shops, or drinks them daily and habitually elsewhere."[22] Collins bought and closed the local tavern and fired several men who did not fulfill the standards of the contract.[23]

David and John Watkinson both had built their capital on the sale of rum and had freely partaken of alcoholic beverages in their youth,[24] but by the 1830s both men were active in the American Temperance Society. Captain Charles March, Reverend Ward's son-in-law, had visited them in Connecticut and had been converted by the American Temperance Society and by John's example to give up "the habitual use of ardent Spirit." Continuing on his voyage to Georgia and points south, he wrote to thank them for their inspiration and guidance and extolled the glories of temperance in extravagant prose, describing his successful attempt to enforce sobriety on his ship and crew. "This is the first attempt made I believe by any ship out of Great Britain. So far good has resulted from it—but the trial I anticipate [will be] in Port."[25]

Over the years, however, the temperance movement was only a partial success. Even within the elite circles of business owners it met with resistance, especially among those who owned distilleries or traded in strong liquors. It was successful in the important struggle against employers supplying the traditional alcohol within the workplace, and it succeeded even more in spreading the underlying message that the cure for poverty, crime, and disorder lay in reforming the individual. Just as evangelical religion taught that salvation lay within the actions of each individual, so temperance focused attention away from social change and onto individuals, who could and should be taught to take the responsibility to cure themselves.

It was believed that individuals who had not been properly trained by their families were easily led into drink, madness, or vice by the corrupting and disorderly elements of society. Such individuals could be rehabilitated by removing them from society and putting them into a controlled and ordered environment, where they could be taught self-discipline and responsibility.[26] As Hartford's business leaders sought to mold their community into a productive, profitable, and ordered society, this ideology shaped their thoughts about the kinds of institutions that would serve their purposes. The businessmen themselves were neither inventors nor theoreticians, but they gave their financial and political backing to the creators and purveyors of these new ideas of social reform.

This was the theory underlying the construction in Hartford of the Retreat for the Insane. It was organized in 1824 by Dr. Eli Todd, the son of a wealthy merchant, who sought the support of Hartford's business leaders to found a new institution. Like many other experts in this period he believed that the incidence of insanity was increasing, due to the fluid and even chaotic state of the society in which sons did not follow in the footsteps of their fathers but strove for more than they could gain. In so doing, it was thought, they strained their minds and became insane (Rothman 1971, 133). Todd patterned the new Hartford asylum after the Quakers' York Retreat in England (Grant [n.d.], 176). Chains and restraints were eliminated, gentle persuasion was used to shape obedience to benevolent authority, and a rigid daily schedule was imposed, the most important part of which was the periods of regulated work. Each segment of the day was signalled by bells, and patients were expected to learn proper habits through regimentation and steady labor (Rothman, 144).

The day-to-day running of the Retreat and similar institutions was the responsibility of professionals such as Todd, but it was men such as Watkinson who chose which institutions and which policies would receive funds. In 1827 he received a tribute for his efforts on behalf of the Retreat: "At the annual meeting of the Directors of the Retreat for the Insane, 14th May 1827. Resolved unanimously; that the thanks of this board be tendered to David W Esq. for the useful services he has gratuitously rendered the Institution as Treasurer of the same."[27] Watkinson was not merely a social figurehead or donor; he was deeply involved in supporting and shaping this and the other philanthropic institutions with which he was associated. "We have with us in America a large field for usefulness," he had written to William

Meeking on a second trip to England, "and I was actively engaged just before leaving home in procuring funds for the establishment of some interesting institutions in the town in which I reside for the benefit of the rising generation."[28]

He shared with Olivia a particularly strong interest in the Beneficent Society for Orphan Girls.[29] The name was not truly accurate, as most of the children were not orphaned but, as he described to Meeking, were "taken from families of the most vicious habits from 4 to 8 years of age." They were "bound to the society, who after giving them some education and correcting their bad habits, bind them out into pious families (at the age of 8 to 10 years untill 18 years old), some of whom have since settled well in the world, and several have become subscribers to the funds of the society."[30]

The "vicious habits" were unspecified, but they would have included intemperance, sloth, and uncleanliness, possibly even crime, and, certainly, poverty. The children's "bad habits" were not specified, but they could be corrected by hard work and religion. These girls not only "settled well" but also understood and appreciated that the change had been for their own good, as their donations to the society proved. Some years later Watkinson helped to establish a school for indigent boys on the same model.

These institutions embodied several new elements: they removed the needy or unfortunate from the care of the family and from the disorder of the community, they provided a form of professional supervision, and they were based on the proposition that rehabilitation would be attained through the practice of obedience to authority and a regimen of scheduled labor. These rehabilitative efforts were considered successful when the patient or child gratefully incorporated these practices as part of a new self.[31] These same elements became components of a blueprint for new prisons.[32] Unlike the philanthropic undertakings, the penal institutions were solely state supported, but the state legislature included many of Hartford's business leaders or men from closely related families. In the past, deviants and criminals had been punished, frequently severely, or even hanged; the punishments included shaming, whipping, or, in the case of outsiders, "warning off"—that is, being sent out of town. Jails had been for temporary storage until a case was tried or for debtors until they had paid off their debts. Now prisons were built for the purpose of incarceration as part of the process of rehabilitation.

The appeal of this paradigm to a nineteenth-century New England upper class was the formulation that regulated, disciplined work had the potential to rehabilitate. It was a belief that resonated deeply in the social psyches of Hartford's businessmen. Unlike the temperance movement and the Bible societies, which had been part of a conscious effort to train and to control an unruly workforce of independent-minded Yankees and wrong-thinking immigrants, these institutions appealed on a different level to the need of the upper class to see the factories that generated their wealth as engines of a moral world.[33]

Within the collection of David Watkinson's correspondence are two long letters, the first written in 1827 to the Reverend Ward, the second in 1831 to Meeking, describing Connecticut's state-of-the art new prison, built in the 1820s in Wethersfield, a few miles from Hartford. Though the prison was not a part of his philanthropic endeavors, it followed the same principles of rehabilitation, and he was "much pleased" and fascinated by it, as is evidenced in the details of his letters.[34] He first described the old prison in which the inmates "were at night all shut into one Room or so lodged that they had free communication with each other," thus becoming further steeped in crime. They plotted together and made frequent attempts to escape, "which in defeats they were loaded with chains." In contrast, in the new prison the criminals were "treated kindly and their chains have all been taken off as they gave proof of good behaviors."

Training at various skills was an important part of transforming the undeserving into moral and employable men. "I went through their work shops which consisted of Blacksmiths, Waggon builders, Coopers, joiners, Shoemakers, Nail Makers, and in the summer and autumn many of them are employed in making of brick and in consequence all are brought some mechanical art whereby they may readily get a living when discharged without having recourse to their old tricks."

The prisoners' only social communion was prayers; their only reading material, the Bible. "They sleep and take their meals in separate cells although they are together in the shops during the day they are not allowed to speak to each other after the day's work is over a lamp is placed opposite to show an overseer of their cells for the purpose of enabling of them to read their bibles with which each one is furnished... the captain who is a pious man [reads] the scriptures and prays with them and I have been informed within a few days a very deep interest in religion has been excited in most of these poor wretches."

There were critics of this system of silence, which was practiced at the other new prisons as well, but Watkinson apparently did not have a sense that the prisoners were men like him. He expressed nothing but gratification at the moral work that was being carried out and at its success in instilling a moral sense so that the prisoners themselves understood that they deserved the treatment they received. "The captain whom I frequently see at my counting Room says there is a great improvement in their conduct and many of them are perfectly reconciled to the justice of their punishment." Like the indigent girls who eventually become subscribers to the institution that had placed them in servitude in good homes, the prisoners accepted that their treatment was for their own good.

Watkinson praised the rehabilitative effects of temperance and work. "A very great proportion of those placed in this institution have been in habits of intemperance: on entering the walls they are at once deprived of all drink except water, and although for some days they undoubtedly feel a great want of it yet there is no sickness in consequence of this deprivation; but on the contrary many who are brought there much emaciated from their vicious habits are restored to good health by temperance and regular work."

After four years the prison had proved itself financially as well as morally profitable. The salary of a "Pious chaplain," who provided "daily religious and moral instruction," as well as "the salaries of the Governor, the Guard, and overseers of the workshops and their own support is paid by the labour of the Prisoners, and the State last year received about six thousand dollars profits above every other expense attending their government and support."[35]

American prisons were a model for Europe, and Watkinson mentioned in his second letter about the prison that French government agents had been extremely impressed with the regulations at the Wethersfield prison.[36] Twenty years later, however, both the prisons and the insane asylums were overcrowded, and any serious attempt at rehabilitation had fallen by the wayside; even so, the state legislature continued to support them. Incarceration had become a "natural" or accepted way of dealing with these problems, whether it cured or corrected. The prisons and insane asylums had proven to be successful in other ways. They had established important and pervasive social categories in which "normal" and "sane" were defined as comprising not only the capacity and willingness to obey authorities but also the self-discipline to work diligently and soberly at whatever task was set.

Watkinson's beliefs and philanthropies were more than affectation or strategy. The practices and values he sought to inculcate in the community were those he practiced in his private life. Within his large family he played a role similar to the one he played on the public stage, exemplifying the highest moral and cultural virtues, assuming responsibility, and assisting when necessary. The David Watkinson archive includes a sheaf of letters to him beginning "Dear Uncle" or "Dear Brother," which request advice, express deep gratitude for his help, and reflect back upon him the image of the ideal virtuous gentleman. After his father's death, he had been named as one of the executors of his father's estate along with John and Robert, but he was the one the family most frequently turned to for assistance. He handled the affairs of his widowed sisters Sarah Pledger and Jane Gill and had taken Eliza's son David Collins into his firm. He became the guardian of Edward's three youngest children after Edward's death at the age of 58 in 1841. David himself lived to the age of 79.

He took these familial responsibilities very seriously. While his charges were of school age he concerned himself with their education, inquiring of their tutors what progress they were making in their studies and in their character development. When they were older he helped them get a start. He provided his nephews Elias Pledger and Elias Gill with advice and money for their commercial ventures, while they acted in part as his agents in various enterprises. He brought his nephew Alfred Gill into the hardware store as a junior partner. He corresponded with his young namesake, nephew David Blair Watkinson, Edward's son, during his years at Yale and performed the sad office of caring for him when he became sick, probably of pneumonia, and burying him when he died at the age of twenty.[37]

His benevolence to his brother William and to William's children also followed the same moral precepts that guided his public philanthropies. Forced into bankruptcy in 1826, William had remained in New York City with his wife and children, struggling to make ends meet despite poor health and a compromised business reputation. A letter to David in 1834 indicated that Sanford, William's oldest child, had been put in the care of David and Olivia in Hartford. "Dear Brother I duly received your favor [letter] . . . with one from our dear Sanford, who appears to be realizing all the benefits in their full extent, that were anticipated by any one of us."[38] When Sanford paid a return visit home two years later, William found his son even more improved. "My dear boy arrived safe this morning to our great delight, in excellent health, and very perceptibly improved in all respects; thanks, inexpressible thanks to you and your good wife who under Providence are entitled to all the praise."[39] The letters make clear that Sanford had been in need of moral guidance and a suitable education as well as physical care, and William was grateful for "the course adopted for the improvement of my son in his health and mind and morals. . . . It is only a subject of regret to me that the excellent course pursued necessarily involve such a heavy expense and so much of your and Olive's care."[40]

In December of 1836 William's older daughter, Jane, was also put into the care of David and Olivia. Apparently there had been widespread family concern as to the children's upbringing, as another member of the Watkinson family, Jane Watkinson Gill, commented in a letter to David that she was glad to hear of "Sanford and Jane's improvement."[41] William himself waxed eloquent in his gratitude to David and Olivia for their care of his children. "I thank you…especially regarding our dear children who will have cause thro' life, and God grant it may be Thro' eternity too, to bless the memory of their earthly benefactors."[42]

True to the principles of rehabilitation and training, the children had been taken from an unsuitable family, which had not properly raised them to avoid the temptations and corruption of society. Jane was sent to a boarding school and Sanford was sent to board and to work with E. G. Hubbard, a family connection in Middletown. David visited the boy, paid for his board, and followed his progress. An excerpt from a letter written to David by Hubbard describes the kinds of behavior that were considered to be problematic and the methods by which Hubbard was trying to instill good habits in the boy.

> I wish it were in my power to state that he has been uniformly attentive and industrious but although I cannot say as much yet I do think he has somewhat improved in his habits and has been more useful to me since the time you called here than he was before. I have kept Sanford pretty constantly employed thinking it to be necessary in order to prepare him for future usefulness But it has required considerable attention on my part to accomplish this. He has been regularly to church and to the sabbath school and has recited the lesson there to the satisfaction generally of his teacher but does not appear to take any special interest in the subject of religion.[43]

Industriousness, promptness, responsibility, piety—these were the traits to be inculcated, and these were the essentials missing from the education the children had received at home.

William's wife was surely to blame. She was rarely mentioned in the family correspondence, although she and William were married in 1823, and these few references employ her name or refer to "William's wife." She was never called "sister," a term applied to every other sister-in-law. It is not clear why she was not welcomed into the family circle, but by this time William and his family believed that she had failed to provide the proper setting for the children's development.[44]

William wrote about his wife's response to a long-awaited letter from their son. "The first direct tidings of him since he has been at Middletown (I believe the only tidings of him) and they afforded relief to her troubled mind which all I could say would not do. Her feelings are strong in whatever bent is given to them and she had become exceedingly restless." In another culture or another time, describing someone as passionate and animated might be a favorable portrayal, but in this culture at this time these were the signs of a disturbed and inferior sort of person, usually a female. He ended this letter with a reference to their domestic problems: "Accept for yourself and Olive our (now) united love."[45]

The unity, however, did not endure, and shortly afterwards with David's encouragement, William left his wife and New York, traveling first to the South, hoping to evade his creditors and to regain his health, and then to Hartford. He returned to New York close to a year later and took up cheap lodgings of his own. His children were once again residing with their mother, who, to William's angry surprise, listed herself as a widow in the city directory. William still worried about their corrupted environment, suspecting that Sanford might occasionally drink cider or beer and that under their mother's influence they were not attending church. Emotionality, intemperance, and atheism were clearly associated in his and his family's minds, and such flaws inevitably led to financial and moral ruin.

However, William's children remained on the virtuous path where David and Olivia had set them. A letter from Sanford to his uncle demonstrated the success of David and Olive's guidance in instilling a properly dutiful and industrious attitude. "Dear Uncle Sir/ I received your kind letter enclosed in one to Mother from Aunt. I sincerely thank you for your kind advice and shall endeavour to follow it. I get along very well in my new place and endevour to please the Mr Hyslops they are very pleasant indeed to me and so are the other clerks. I have managed so far very well to get down to the store about seven o'clock and we shut up the store a little after six o'clock and then I go strait home or stop and see Father."[46] Sanford advanced in his work over the years in the employ of several merchants. In 1848 (the date of his last letter in the archive) he was working for a Mr. Moen, a business connection of the Collinses', in a position of some responsibility, though still in need of a loan.[47]

A few years earlier Jane had thanked David for the money in her account, reported that she had three pupils studying piano, and mentioned that sister Mary and her mother needed new coats.[48] Another letter thanked him for his gift of $300 to buy a new piano. David contributed money to William for his own support and his children's and sent a small allowance to William's wife after their separation. William died in 1852, living his last years in David's house in Hartford, where, a month before his death, his daughter Jane was married to her cousin Elias Gill.[49]

David and Olivia Watkinson were clearly generous, responsible, and benevolent people, as were many of the other Hartford philanthropists.[50] They sincerely desired to make their community a peaceful and orderly place, but they never questioned that it would be a place in which they were the ones to make the decisions and to implement the practices that would maintain their privileged position. Philanthropy in the family or in the community clearly defined who gave and who received. In the community it united those who gave as a class and it identified them as a moral and superior group, whose wealth was a sign not of greed but of virtue.[51]

Not everyone, of course, shared their belief that they, the elite, knew what was best for the region, for business, or for the people around them. Combinations were formed and protests were organized against the moneyed interests; on the personal level as well, their assumption of the moral high ground could be trying to lesser men and women. At times David Watkinson appeared pompous, and Olivia hinted at this quality in a letter to England: "Mr. Wat would have added to the letter but he is too busy being president of the Railroad from New Haven to Springfield, through Hartford."[52]

On at least one occasion Watkinson's power to control and his certainty that he knew best infuriated his younger brother Robert. As manager of a textile factory, Robert had presented a plan to increase production and profits; he had developed the plan after long and arduous work. David, a member of the board of directors, not only voted against Robert's proposal but also persuaded his fellow directors to dismiss it. In a long letter, unusual in that anger seeps through the politeness, Robert expressed his frustration and outrage: "Your want of consideration for me shews itself by a forgetfulness that *I* am (or ought to be) *the* Person who best knows the interests of the manufacturing concern and not the Directors, if they were a hundred in number." He continued by describing how it would be if their roles were reversed and he and other stockholders of David's railroad always blocked or delayed required improvements. He asked what would happen if Robert were a silent partner in David's iron trade and, knowing nothing of the business, interfered in its management, "pretending to know better than you" even after David had managed it through difficult years.

He went on for several pages, finally attacking what could only be David's own words.

And, here, let me say, *is* where, in doing *your duty* as you have supposed, you have repeatedly done what I have deemed to be contrary to your duty—in so much, as, to have disregarded the better knowledge of the Agent and to have conceived that you knew by intuition better than he could know by experience. I do not question your good judgment where fair or equal opportunity is afforded you to form an opinion, and, Providence has made me to respect my own general talent equally with yours— it then follows (if this is correct) that *your* judgment is best in your Iron business or Rail Road and that it is *my duty* as a silent partner to endeavor to accord with you *therein* and scarcely to insist that you are wrong in your views thereupon, altho differing from mine. and so it appears to me to have been *your duty* in the cotton concerns, to have *endeavord* to think, that I knew best the interests of the Manufacturing Cos.

What was particularly infuriating was David's absolute conviction that under any circumstances his judgment would be superior to Robert's (and anyone else's). The letter ends angrily. "Hoping that I have now made this matter sufficiently explicit to be understood by you, or any to whom it may be in part stated. If I have failed so to do, it seems to me that I must ever fail, as before I have done."[53] David's reply is not in the archive, but one can imagine with what patience and forbearance he responded to his brother's shortsightedness and irrational anger, his failure to appreciate that what had been done was for his own and others' good.

William's wife, Elizabeth, must have had similar unworthy feelings aroused by the calm and generous munificence of her brother- and sister-in-law, who encouraged her husband to leave her and reformed her children. The dissimilarity between Olivia's position and her own was extreme. Olivia's descriptions of her greenhouse (with "almost a thousand plants, many of them in full bloom") and the grounds of her house ("the garden which is pretty extensive, in one part of it is a rise of ground from the top of which you have a prospect that would make a beautiful picture") express vividly her setting of wealth and refinement.[54] Elizabeth, by contrast, had been left a single woman with no income of her own, dependent on the generosity of a brother-in-law who considered her a poor influence on husband and children.

She attempted once to direct the course of her daughter Jane's education, an act that William strongly criticized in a letter to David, describing the situation.

> One or two expressions in Jane's letter to Mrs W made no doubt under the evil dictation of her mother, had better been omitted, and leads me to explain the facts of the case, which are that at our last quarrel, she, in great anger threatened an immediate separation, and said the children might go, and she would then go herself and sew for some milliner, but it was *on condition only* that they were sent to some first rate boarding school and not such as Jane was doomed to before and that I had better write you at once about it.... I told her I would write you *no such impudence,* and she must do it herself or get Jane to do it, etc. etc.etc. I am glad to perceive by Janes letter that there *is a subdued tone.*[55]

As a poor supplicant, however, Elizabeth could not make demands and had no choice but to represent herself as a deserving recipient of charity, expressing only gratitude to David and Olivia. "I feel under great indebtedness to your brother for his kind allowance of $2 per week, and to Mrs W for her offer of taking care of the children who I hope and trust will give her full satisfaction."[56] She wrote to Olivia, addressing her as "sister," and conveyed a picture of humility, penury, and gratitude in a single paragraph: "Dear Sister, I have been anxious to write to you for a long time, but not knowing how to send by private hand, and fearing that a letter from me would not compensate for the expense of postage I deferred until today when I received a few lines from your husband inclosing me $16 for two months for which I am very much obliged to him, and also for that which he sent in November. I told Joseph [Sanford] when I wrote to him to tell his uncle and thank him for it."[57] As the argument about Jane's education demonstrated and other letters indicated, Elizabeth was not in agreement with her benefactors. Like the workers who formed combinations and the outspoken political supporters of Jackson, the lower orders were not always appreciative of what was done for them.

David wrote a will in 1849, adding codicils each year until his death in 1857, with bequests to all of the family members, including his wife's family, plus a large array of charitable organizations. His bequest to William was left in trust with two of his nephews, with the instruction to give the interest to William during his lifetime to use for his own and his children's support. His estate was valued at half a million dollars (Clarke 1966, 6), a considerable fortune at this time.[58] At a memorial ceremony at The Connecticut Historical Society two months after his death, an eminent educator, Henry Barnard, executor of Watkinson's philanthropic legacies, claimed that Watkinson's generous bequests to "various humane and literary institutions, make him the largest pecuniary benefactor to such objects, that Connecticut has yet known" (Barnard 1858, 89).

In the seventh codicil to his will, written in 1852, Watkinson increased his bequest to the institution for orphans and indigent children and gave clear expression to his creed, the justification of business by philanthropy. "It has been an occasion of regret with some of my best friends, that so much of my attention has been given in advanced age to business pursuits. However worthy the object in view, and the motive which influenced me, it may well be doubted what course my duty as a Christian enjoined on me; but if greatly increased means of doing good have flowed from my persevering attention to business, I am slow to review my course with regret."[59]

This codicil must have been addressed to that future audience of close friends or relatives who would be present at the reading of his last will and testament. Perhaps he was speaking in particular to those who felt he should retire from his active engagement with business concerns, making clear to them the inherent relationship between commerce and virtue. His words were part of an important discourse, shared by most, if not all, of Hartford's upper class, who had begun to have even more in common than wealth, acquaintance, and ownership of the means of production. Through their practices and their language they had transformed a struggle for control into a reigning capitalist culture that continually rationalized itself as one of benevolence and morality.

Conclusion: Distancing Production

In a small way the Watkinsons have taken the reader into their confidence. They have introduced Samuel Sr., the patriarch and country gentleman; Sarah, his quiet wife and companion; John, the busy merchant; Samuel Jr. and Richard, toiling at desks as merchants' clerks, while sisters Mary and Elizabeth dutifully sewed their shirts, and Jane carefully composed letters to her older brother. Samuel Collins shared his perceptions of the factory, the workers, and the stockholders. Olivia gave her views on British society. David demonstrated his financial acumen and his benevolence to his unfortunate brother, sister-in-law, and their children, as well as his philanthropic efforts on behalf of his community. The family has provided a close, albeit limited, look at what it was like to experience life first as members of an elite network of merchant families at the turn of the eighteenth to nineteenth century and then, in the ensuing decades, as part of an emerging regional upper class. They were a varied group of complex individuals, part of a unique family with its own history, but they were deeply marked by thoughts, beliefs, and actions that adhered to their involvement in the changing processes of class construction and class culture.

As merchants, men had focused upon the everyday work of organizing a cargo of country produce, maintaining the ships, advising their captains, selling the sugars and rums, and carefully keeping their accounts. For the most part they followed a set pattern of trade, counting on established networks. These networks were based on trust—trust that payment was forthcoming, that notes were redeemable, that partners and business associates would be honest in their dealings. Family ties through kinship or marriage were the best guarantee, and women played a major role in the work of maintaining them. Visiting, writing, entertaining, and caring for sick relatives were important elements of women's daily lives. Kinship terms were extended to relatives through marriage, and the term "friend" applied to kin and close non-kin alike, suggesting the reciprocity in which women especially exerted themselves. Family was the only form of security in an unpredictable world, and success was not considered a matter of individual skill or luck, but of one's social connections. When, for example, David Watkinson spoke of brother William's difficulties, he did not point to personal failings but rather to William's misfortunes in his business and marital associations.

Merchants learned to represent themselves as frank and sincere, their books and their countenances open to scrutiny. Yet these balanced accounts concealed more than they revealed. In this early form of market mythology debits and credits neatly evened out. Merchants' location along the networks of trade but outside the sites of production made it appear easy to ignore the relationship that produced their profits. The West Indian plantations were out of sight, and the topic of slavery was unspoken. But the very silence suggests that considerable cultural efforts were expended in smoothing over the contradictions inherent in celebrating New England's freedoms while profiting from the West Indies' slavery.[1] This cultural accomplishment met a new challenge as merchants turned to industrial manufacturing. Here was a very different situation in which their workforce was not only visible but, at the beginning, made up of fellow white New Englanders.

Of course, merchants, such as John Watkinson and later his nephews, Samuel and David Collins, had no foreknowledge that they were active agents involved in changing their world. John's early factory accounts demonstrate a continuity in his dealings with his small workforce. His method of giving out wool to be "picked" and then returned for pay seemed remarkably similar to that of his father's wool-combing establishment back in Suffolk, which had cloaked exploitation with a paternalistic relationship.[2]

Both John's textile mill and the Collins brothers' axe company rapidly evolved from putting-out operations, yet paternalistic relations of authority were continued in various forms, such as the apprenticeships at the Collins Company and the contracts that held back pay for three or six months. In the factory Collins promulgated rules and reproaches and appealed in his speeches to the personal relationship and commonalities between him and his workers.

But neither a reality nor a pretense of common cause could withstand the pressures of the capitalist industrial scene. The new factories placed new demands on the workers, demands that were stubbornly opposed. Workers did not readily accept the loss of their ability to allot their own time or to decide how best to carry a task to completion. Only gradually would these new constraints become accepted as "natural." As Collins's letters explicitly stated, his major problem was to get workers to do what he needed to have done without letting them believe that they were essential. The complicated strategies involved in this vying for control took place in every factory and formed a basic component of class formation.

Owners found the means of consolidating their command over the workplace despite the ongoing resistance of workers. The interpretation of the common law of master and servant to include all who worked for hire had sanctioned an employer's authority and workers' obedience within the factory. Technological innovations helped to reduce the dependence on and the autonomy of skilled workers and made it possible to employ unskilled workers without investing heavily in their training. The long depression between 1837 and 1843, combined with an influx of Irish and French Canadian immigrants, began to end the situation of labor scarcity, which had previously provided workers with their most powerful weapon—the ability to leave when the conditions of work in one factory became too onerous and to easily find another job. Collins and other New England factory owners replaced many of their independent, skilled Yankees with the more vulnerable immigrants.

The Collins Company was one of the early corporations to be chartered as a purely private organization. Samuel Collins had only grudgingly accepted the corporate form when it was forced upon him, and throughout his life he questioned the legitimacy of shareholders' rights and powers, even suggesting in one of his speeches to his workers that those who did not work should not be entitled to their wealth. Of course, he did not act upon this, and though he may have been hypocritical it is still noteworthy that these words could not only be thought but also said. In later years they would become unthinkable.

Collins would have agreed with sociologist William Roy's argument that corporations were neither more productive nor more efficient than partnerships. He perceived the stockholders' concerns for immediate profits as detrimental to long-term productivity, as dividends and share values took precedence over investments in construction or improvements in machinery. Corporate directors, such as David Watkinson, could enforce decisions that at times went against the interests of those who were directly involved in management. Then as now, managers found themselves forced to shape their actions to meet the short-term accounting demands of the annual report.

Corporations had originally been chartered by Connecticut and other New England states as public institutions; corporations were envisioned as a way to build turnpikes and bridges in lieu of raising taxes. The privatization of corporations transferred power and privilege from public into private hands and gave wealthy stockholders the ability to hold controlling shares in many corporations. In Hartford, and elsewhere, this shared power contributed to the emergence of a regional upper class.[3]

In the process of consolidating their structural dominance, most owners physically moved their homes far from the workplace; more important, however, was the ability of this owning class to find powerful cultural means of increasing the distance between themselves and their workers. Collins's early speech had referred to his employees as "fellow citizens," but in the 1840s he spoke in the language of the market, which had spread far beyond the merchants' account books. The hegemony of the market discourse dissolved alternate understandings of the domination of one class over another through a displacement of human agency onto impersonal natural forces. In the symbolic language of the market, labor had become a commodity, the value of which was dependent on supply and demand and the disposition of which was conceptualized as divorced from the person. The perception of worker as distinct from fellow human had progressed to a point where Collins felt comfortable in writing of the deaths of the grinders merely as an incovenience. This separation of worker as "costs of labor" from worker as fellow citizen was then, as it is now, strongly contested, forming the baseline for every "combination" and strike as workers struggled not only for so-called economic benefits but also for respect for their full humanity.

For the owning class the factory and workers were part of a domain they related to only in terms of the market. The community and the home were part of a different domain where they could demonstrate compassion, civic virtue, and sentiment.

Distant from the gritty reality of the factory floors and the day-to-day overseeing of workers, Watkinson and his fellow corporate directors supported philanthropic and penal institutions in which the therapeutic paradigms had been abstracted from the new relations of production. Self-control, obedience to authority, and scheduled work distinguished the normal from the abnormal, the good from the deviant, and the deserving from the undeserving. In acts of philanthropy Hartford's upper class defined itself through its Christian authority, its definitions of appropriate behavior, and its benevolence.

Expansive in their dominance as a regional ruling class and following the example of their Boston counterparts,[4] David Watkinson and his elite circle created new institutions of culture and learning, such as Trinity College, the Wadsworth Atheneum (an art museum), and The Connecticut Historical Society. In these establishments, Hartford's elite displayed their appreciation and appropriation of the insignias that had marked a leisured aristocracy, even though, with the exception of Atheneum founder Daniel Wadsworth, who had inherited a fortune from his merchant father, the subscribers and directors of these institutions were businessmen like David Watkinson.[5] They were a new kind of aristocracy.

Landed aristocrats would certainly regard these newly risen men and women as middle-class—manufacturers, tainted by their commercial interests. In Great Britain and parts of Europe, the landed gentry continued to hold sway after the appearance of successful industrialists. But, in early-nineteenth-century New England, such aristocrats were few and far between, and neither in economic nor political power was their position superior to that of these new industrial and financial capitalists. Culturally, however, elites such as Hartford's emulated cultural forms of the gentry despite the contradictory pull of republican beliefs inequality and simplicity (Bushman 1992). David and Olivia's criticisms of Britain's despotic and decadent aristocracy were typical New England responses, but so were their manners and fine house and garden typical of New England's adaptations of the accouterments of a former English and colonial aristocracy.

Many of this Hartford group found the old Congregational church too plain and too uninhibited in its emphasis on revivalistic conversion (Bushman 1992, 327). They converted to Episcopalianism or moved to Hartford's new and fashionable North Congregational Church, welcomed by its minister, the Reverend Horace Bushnell, whose reading of the Scriptures was in perfect accord with their interests and beliefs. He taught that "Religion should not intrude upon business. The law of self-interest prohibited charity in trade. . . . During the hours of business, merchants were to act 'under the laws of trade,' reserving their charities . . . for a separate chapter of life" (quoted in Cross 1958, 46). It was a perfect expression and validation of the separate moral worlds distancing production from society. Most of David Watkinson's friends and associates joined Bushnell's church or became Episcopalians, but he and Olivia remained members of the old, strict, and plain

First Congregational Church, where he had worshiped ever since he first settled in Hartford,[6] Likewise, to the end of his life he retained an old-fashioned
belief that business activities were justified by good works rather than completely "separate chapters" of his life. Nonetheless, he and Olivia were certainly members of that elite, whose aesthetic "good taste," their creation of
beauty in gardens and homes and their appreciation of art, Reverend Bushnell
equated with God's own creation of the world (Bushman, 330).

This upper-class culture comprised gendered domains, so that women
were associated more closely with the cultivation of ties of friendship and
kinship, while the realm of the market and public power came to define the
roles of men. In philanthropic endeavors, men tended to be more active on
the boards of directors; women, in relating directly to those who were the
objects of charity.[7] Such charitable work fell easily within the feminine
sphere of sentiment and nurture so that women were "naturally" suited to
it. in addition, as Cott has suggested for women's active participation in religious endeavors, it was an opportunity for women to enjoy "the community of their peers" (1977, 141). Olivia's thoughts on the subject are not available. It is truly unfortunate that Olivia and her "sisters," with whom she
undoubtedly corresponded, left so few letters. The only commentary on her
philanthropic efforts comes from David, who wrote, "In humble imitation
of her Saviors example she literally went about doing good."[8] And it had
been Olivia who took on the physical care of William's children, while
David directed their futures. Both men and women demonstrated and
justified their superior social position through their concern for and generosity to the poor and unfortunate and, in so doing, helped to obscure the
relations of class, which were culturally out of sight and mind.

Upper-class language and culture empowered certain possibilities and restricted others. To be upper class was not only to act in certain ways and to
refrain from others, but also to see and feel only socially approved perceptions and socially acceptable emotions. To transgress against these ways was
not impossible, but it was to risk feeling ridiculous and disloyal to one's
family and friends. Was it conceivable, for example, that John Watkinson
should or could have refused to enter the West Indian trade because its
profits were evil, as many of the Watkinsons' English friends believed? Had
he drawn back, appalled at the exploitation from which his modest fortune
grew or had Samuel Collins raised the costs of manufacturing by eliminat-
ing the grinding wheels or shared his profits more equitably with his workers, they might have been better men but they would have been thought
mad and radical—and both assumptions might well have been true. Ques-

tioning the basic principles of upper-class culture by suggesting that upper-class wealth was dependent on lower-class work and an unjust division of rewards threatened the hard-won distance on which upper-class culture and identity rested.

This conundrum lies at the very heart of the conjoined processes of capitalist class and culture. Industrial capitalism sets up an intimate bond of mutual dependency between owners and workers, but for the owning class to profit, it must obfuscate this relation in order to establish and maintain control. This denial becomes a critical underpinning of capitalist culture. When Collins's workers called him "avaricious," implying that he was gaining wealth through their hard work without making a fair return, they struck a nerve.[9] Upper-class repudiation of this mutual relationship and its inherent imbalance was and is achieved by distancing the owners from the facts of production. This dynamic of denial makes use of many modes of distancing—physical, legal, moral, and, even, psychic—to separate in actuality and symbolically those who produce and those who own, those who work with their heads and those who work with their hands, factory and community, workplace and household, even individual and family. These numerous bounded domains and oppositions form the structure of capitalist culture, which incorporated cultural elements of the past while shaping them to new purposes. Caught up in this dynamic, Hartford's elite were both similar to and distinct from their former merchant selves.

Many components of upper-class culture were appropriated by middle-class folk, who copied the mental as well as the household furnishings of their betters.[10] Respectability and refinement marked professionals and white-collar workers, marginalizing those who did manual labor or casual labor or could not or would not accept the coin of cultural hegemony. These norms of behavior and belief were inculcated in household and school so that future generations were raised to accept as "natural" and American the practices and discourses of this capitalist culture. The myth of individual success through self-discipline, temperance, obedience to authority, and hard work was one more form of distancing, separating in practice and belief the individual from family, fellow workers, and community. For some, in fact, in an expanding economy it provided hope and proved that the status of family background was not a limiting condition. For others, less fortunate, it brought the conviction that failure was due to personal deficiencies rather than to unlucky family circumstances and the organization of society.

In telling his story of the Collins Company, Collins's memoir acknowledged his brother's importance, but this narrative of their success through hard work and perseverance depicted two young men on their own in an impersonal world of stockholders, buyers, sellers, and workers, rather than acknowledging the training and financial support of their numerous uncles. This story of the hero (and currently, also, the heroine) who succeeds on his or her own merits has become a familiar myth of our culture.

As an autonomous group who could shape and control their region, Hartford's ruling class was short-lived. Like the better-known but similar Boston Associates they were outdone by the wealth of New York and became a locally elite group of wealthy families, only some of whom became a part of the national upper class, which was forming between the end of the Civil War and the turn of the century.[11] The legacy, however, of practices and meanings formed in the early years of the nineteenth century became the foundation of the continuing processes of class and culture. It was by no means a passive handing down of unchanging traditions, but part of the social context with which future generations would contend.

The search for less expensive and more docile workers who are or who appear to be easy to control continues earlier strategies on an expanded scale—hiring foreigners, legal and illegal immigrants for specific kinds of work, assigning jobs by race and gender, moving factories offshore, and employing "flexible" or part-time workers.[12] This differentiation of the workforce has strengthened the hand of the owning class by making it far more difficult for labor to organize and to demand a more equitable reciprocity.

Today, distancing from the community has been extended to an almost complete abrogation of the social contract.[13] Where intense disputes once concerned whether a company owed not only taxes but also other responsibilities to the community and region in which it was located, now they occur only in particular situations—who should pay for pollution or workmen's compensation cases, for example—but not in principle. When corporations relocate factories offshore, they destroy towns, social ties, and local cultures that have taken generations to construct. The justification for such actions is worded as the necessity of "remaining competitive," an appeal to the market that is perceived as a force beyond the desires or plans of the owners.[14] As Nash has pointed out, the hegemony of this belief system is such that the very workers who lost their jobs when General Electric downsized its plant at Pittsfield defended the company, saying its officials "could not let any commitment to a community interfere with their decision to remain in production" (1995, 200). Corporate owners and managers accept no responsibility for making reparations for their destruction of home communities or for contributing to the foreign communities whose workers they employ, asserting that simply by offering employment, however low the wage level, they are contributing to the recipient nation.[15] Instead, many of them support their own large foundations that aid the deserving—countries or individuals—while extending their control and sustaining their positions of power.

In the discourse of present-day capitalist culture the market is not only a force but also a benevolent one. Institutions and practices that are not open to market regulation are suspect. That which does not make a profit for a group of owners is not worth doing and/or is of dubious morality. This triumph of the private corporation over public institutions transfers more and more elements of social life from the domain of morality and responsibility to the domain of hierarchy and opportunism; a domain that is characterized by the short-term accountability of expediently constructed year-end statements and the illusion-making of corporate public relations and annual reports.[16]

The discourses that surround capitalism with an aura of goodness and naturalness have become deeply ensconced in the cultures of great numbers of people around the world. Class processes are currently transcending national borders as they once surmounted regional boundaries, and cultural practices and beliefs continue to deny mutual connections that now encircle the globe. These are not the only critical social forces shaping today and the future, but to ignore them is to accept the categories of capitalist culture as the only accurate representations of reality and to close off alternative modes of thought and action. To simply dismiss capitalist culture as unreal, however, is to risk underestimating the power of class and the strength of culture.

Abbreviations

PERSONS

DC	David Collins
DW	David Watkinson
EW	Elizabeth (Eliza) Watkinson
JW	John Watkinson
MW	Mary Watkinson
OW	Olivia (Hudson) Watkinson
RW	Richard Watkinson
SWC	Samuel Watkinson Collins
SW Jr.	Samuel Watkinson Jr.
SW Sr.	Samuel Watkinson Sr.
WW	William Watkinson

LOCATIONS

CCA	Collins, Samuel Watkinson, Letters, and Collins Company Papers in the Canton Historical Society
CCH	Collins & Company Papers in the Connecticut Historical Society
DWC	David Watkinson Collection in the Connecticut Historical Society
DWP	Watkinson, David, business and personal papers, in WFP
JAC	Watkinson, John Revel, account books, in Connecticut State Library
JAO	Watkinson, John R. & Co., account books and letters in Olin Library, Wesleyan University
JBW	Watkinson, John Revel, business papers and correspondence in WFP
RWL	Watkinson, Richard, letterbook, cash book, and letters received in WFP
SJA	Journal kept by Samuel Watkinson Jr., 1795–1798, in DWC
SJP	Watkinson, Samuel Jr., personal and business papers in WFP
SSA	Watkinson, Samuel Sr., personal and business papers in WFP
WFP	Watkinson Family Papers in the Watkinson Library, Trinity College
WWL	Watkinson, William, in Miscellaneous Watkinson Family Papers, 19th c., in WFP

MANUSCRIPT DOCUMENTS

MR Diary	Mary Russell diary, typescript in the Connecticut Historical Society
OW Journal	Olivia Watkinson travel journal 1819, 1820, typescript in DWP
SC Memo	Collins Company 1826–1867, 1 vol. "Memorandums," catalogued as "Memoranda," in CCH

Notes

INTRODUCTION

1. Crossing the disciplinary boundaries between history and anthropology in either direction is no longer unusual, and the precise naming of a category is somewhat arbitrary. See: Comaroffs 1992; Kalb, Marks, and Tak 1996; and O'Brien and Roseberry 1991.

2. See Sellers 1991, 1996. Farmers had always set aside some small portion of their crop to exchange for essential goods with the local merchant, and those close to the coast or to riverine arteries of trade had raised livestock and crops for sale; however, the "transportation revolution" had instigated a more widespread connection to the market. An interesting argument over the timing and significance of commercial farming is summarized in Kulikoff 1989 and debated by Rothenberg 1992.

3. See Pessen 1973 for a description of the distribution of wealth in antebellum America and Daniels 1988 for stratification in New England.

4. See Johnson 1993, Keller 1942, and Cross 1950.

5. See Jeremy 1981 for a detailed study of the complex process of bringing British textile technology to the postrevolutionary United States.

6. Needless to say, there are many other definitions of these two concepts. My usage here rests on the work of many scholars who have followed Edward P. Thompson's lead 1966 [1963] and 1978 in defining class as a process and as a relationship, in grounding class in a system of production composed of antagonistic groups, and in emphasizing the importance of culture. For extensive discussions of this approach, see Kalb 1997; Steinberg 1999.

The concept of culture is endlessly debated in anthropology, but in recent years there has been some consensus that culture should not be considered as a homogeneous whole with a set of traditions handed down through generations to which something might be added or from which some elements might be lost. Now culture is understood as a dynamic force, engendering meanings that are frequently saturated with the relations of power intrinsic to everyday practices. See, for example, Sider 1996, 132, and Wolf 1999, 287–89.

7. Over the past two decades a number of social historians have studied the making of the bourgeoisies of England, France, and Germany. See, for example: England—Davidoff and Hall 1987 and Koditschek 1990, France—Friedman 1991 and Garrioch 1996, Germany—Blackbourn 1991 and Geary 1991. Although, as Koditschek points out, these studies are limited in their descriptions of bourgeois culture, they clearly demonstrate that there is no generic capitalist class, strictly determined by a mode of production. The particulars of each country's setting of the state, other classes, the abundance or scarcity of labor, and its cultural history are distinct, and none resembles the context in which such classes developed in the United States.

8. These sources are cited throughout the book.

9. Outstanding examples are Dawley 1976; Prude 1983; and Wilenz 1984.

10. See Farrell 1993; Hall 1982; and Story 1980.

11. Beckert's (2001) important study of New York City's bourgeoisie is a critical resource not only for its historical work in tracing the formation of New York's upper class at the end of the nineteenth century, but for its theoretical approach. He addresses on a national scale what is attempted here on a far smaller regional scale.

12. Raymond Williams pointed out how the "separation of the social from the personal" always conveys a sense of "fixed explicit forms" (1977, 128). A study that communicates a sense of immediacy is Joy Day Buel and Richard Buel Jr. 1984, *The Way of Duty: A Woman and Her Family in Revolutionary America,* which provides a remarkable description of eighteenth-century New England through the correspondence of Mary Fish.

13. The Connecticut Historical Society and the Watkinson Library at Trinity College.

14. These are in the Special Collections and Archives of Olin Library at Wesleyan University, Middletown, the Archives of the Connecticut State Library in Hartford, and the Watkinson Library.

15. In the collections of the Canton Historical Society, Canton, Connecticut, and in the Connecticut Historical Society.

16. Although the women, like their brothers, were all educated, none of them showed that engagement with the intellectual life that is revealed in the letters and journals of the upper-class women described in Wallace 1972.

17. Grizel Blair and David Blair, Mount Steward, Scotland, to Sarah Blair, Lavenham, Nov. 11, 1768; Blair Family in WFP, Genealogy.

18. SW Sr. to Mr. John Webb, England, Jan. 31, 1801, in SSA.

19. DW to Wm. Meeking, Nov. 16, 1831, in DWP.

20. MR Diary, 9–10.

21. OW Journal, 92–93.

22. Reverend William Ward, Stowmarket, to DW, Hartford, Oct. 1831, in DWP.

23. SWC to DC, Aug. 11, 1830, in CCH.

24. OW Journal, 20.

CHAPTER ONE: THE VOYAGE

1. Sarah Blair Watkinson's birth date is given both as 1744 and as 1743 in genealogies in WFP.

2. SW Jr. to Wm. Meeking, ca. May 1, 1795 (n.d.), in SJP. His full name was William Meeking Jr. but the "Jr." will be dropped in notes as he, not his father, was the Watkinsons' correspondent.

3. Watkinson paid £126 sterling for his party of 9 plus £70 for "finding his family in Provisions to Boston," (Receipt, in SSA).

4. Useful sources for the description of England's political climate in this period are Dickinson 1985; Duffy 1997; Jones 1983; and Tilly 1995. An interesting description of the flight of some of the radical leaders to the United States and their subsequent involvement in the Jeffersonian party is told by Twomey 1989.

5. The Taylors were a family of artists and writers, well enough known that the family's correspondence, publications, and memoirs have been carefully archived. Today the most familiar of their writings is Jane Taylor's poem, "Twinkle, Twinkle, Little Star." For this study it is pure serendipity that this family knew and described Lavenham and the Watkinsons.

Davidoff and Hall in *Family Fortunes* discuss the Taylors' lives at length but imply that their Lavenham acquaintances were of little importance or social standing. The

Taylors, however, in all of their references to Lavenham refer to the Watkinsons with great respect and friendship.

6. See Heard 1970 and the National Trust 1975.

7. His account book shows holdings in Sierra Leone and what he referred to as "British 4 percent stock," in SSA.

8. Edward P. Thompson might almost have been writing of the Watkinsons and their friends when he spoke of "humiliations and its impediments to the career open to talents," which in eighteenth-century England "the aspirant professional man or tradesman" remedied by emigration (1978, 143).

9. SW Sr., Accounts, in SSA.

10. January 1795, Congregational Church of Christ, Book 2, "Transactions. . . ." in Suffolk Records.

11. SW Jr. to Wm. Meeking, July 8, 1795, in SJP.

12. WW, off Deal, to Wm. Meeking, July 20, 1795, in WWL.

13. SW Jr. to Sarah Watkinson (mother), Oct. 13, 1795, in SJP.

14. The Lavenham census of 1778 listed 1,741 people in 395 houses. In 1784, when Middletown was incorporated as a city, "The dwelling houses in the city, 299 in number" (Field 1819, 40) Field The censuses of 1790 and 1800 enumerated the population of the township of Middletown at 5,375 and 5,001, but did not distinguish the city from the township. The 1810 census gave 5,332 for the township and 2,014 for the city (Martin 1939, 11).

15. Martin points out that Middletown and Hartford were almost entirely commercial centers. Her data relate to Hartford, for which more information was available, but she states that Middletown's commerce was only slightly smaller. In 1795, Hartford, with a population of 5,000, had nearly ninety merchants (1939, 13).

16. The two most important sources for Connecticut's mercantile trade are Martin 1939 and Saladino 1964.

17. A description of this rich material culture can be found in St. George 1985.

18. The best descriptions of eighteenth-century Connecticut's towns are Daniels 1988 and Mann 1987.

19. Hall 1981 describes the destructiveness of this political battle in Middletown. Samuel Watkinson Sr. at first regarded this political strife with only a distant interest. He wrote back to England shortly after Jefferson's inauguration in 1801, commenting coolly on the political passions he saw around him. Democrats were Jeffersonians. "In this country party has run high but those stiled Democrat, vis those who were opposed to a standing army, a land tax and the Alien and Sedition Bills are now the majority—and the business is reported to be settled Jefferson for president and Burr Vice president the Votes were equal" (SW Sr. to John Webb, Jan. 31, 1801, in SSA).

Ten years later, however, when these political wars threatened the possible loss of his shares in the Bank of the United States, as the Democrats were refusing to renew its charter, Watkinson became more concerned with American politics. "But the Democratic Party which is dominant increases and rages against any institution where Federalists may be at the head and Englishmen have any influence spurred on as it appears to me by a foreign agency. It is the apparent determination of the party to put it down that they may trample all under their feet that had any connection with it" (SW Sr. to John Webb, Feb. 1, 1811, in SSA).

20. SW Jr., Aug. 5, 1795, in SJP.

21. SW Jr., Marblehead, to Wm. Meeking, July 16, 1795, in SJP.

22. SW Jr. to Wm. Meeking, Aug. 1, 1795, in SJP.

23. SW Jr. to Mr. Phillips, Suffolk, April 1, 1796, in SJP.

24. SW Jr. to Wm. Meeking, July 4, 1796, in SJP.

25. MR Diary, p.26.

26. MR Diary, pp.65–66. Russell's observations are supported by the work of Dudden 1983. The Russells were extremely critical of slavery, so the "black boy" was probably indentured or hired rather than a slave.

27. SW Sr. to Wm. Meeking, after April 7, 1796 (n.d.), in SSA. Both Mary Russell's and Samuel Watkinson's comments on the lack of deference shown by their inferiors were typical English responses. According to Nevins, "All travellers in America, from 1780 to the present day have been impressed by the manliness of carriage and address evident among social groups which in other lands would be obsequious" (1923:6).

28. SW Jr. to Wm. Meeking, July 4, 1796, in SJP.

29. SW Jr. to Mr. W. D. Bedingfield, Neadham Market, Suffolk, April 1, 1796, in SJP.

30. SW Jr. to Mr. Sam Warwood, Battiford Hall, Suffolk, April 1, 1796, in SJP.

31. SW Sr. to Wm. Meeking, April 7, 1796, in SSA.

32. Ibid.

33. SW Jr., July 1795, in SJP.

34. This may have been Samuel Slater's pioneering textile mill.

35. SW Jr. to Mr. Pledger, Boston, Sept. 19, 1795, in SJP.

36. Two historians of this period, Nash 1979 and Henretta 1991, suggest that class structures were nebulous. A valuable summary of discussions about class in America at this time can be found in Henretta's essay "Wealth and Social Structure." He concludes that "a definitive synthesis is as impossible as it is unwise" (1991, 188–89).

37. SW Sr. to Wm. Meeking, April 7, 1796, in SSA.

38. This description is based on the author's visit to Lavenham in 1997.

39. Watkinson watched its construction over the next few years with proprietary pleasure. "We have been very busy of late in building a very large meeting house with a *high steeple* to it within 100 yards of my house" (SW Sr. to Wm. Meeking, Aug. 21, 1798, in SSA).

40. SW Jr. to Mr. Phillips, Suffolk, April 1, 1796, in SJP.

41. SW Sr. to Wm. Meeking, soon after April 7, 1796 (n.d.), in SSA.

42. Ibid.

43. SW Jr. to Wm. Meeking, July 31, 1797, in SJP.

44. MR Diary, 11.

45. MR Diary, 22.

46. SW Sr. to Wm. Meeking, April 10, 1797, in SSA.

CHAPTER TWO: CAPITAL, KIN, AND CONNECTIONS

1. The most comprehensive study of merchants for the period after Bailyn's classic, *The New England Merchants in the Seventeenth Century,* is Thomas Doerflinger's, *A Vigorous Spirit of Enterprise.*

2. While individual (men's) names stand out in historical narratives of successful merchants, such men were almost without exception backed up by family connections or capital. Wadsworth, for example, had been adopted and trained by his merchant uncle, Matthew Talbott, while Elijah Hubbard came from a prominent family, long established in Middletown.

3. See Farrell 1993; Hall 1972 and 1982.

4. See Hall 1972.

5. Marilyn Strathern's insight about similarities in the symbolic representations of lineage and class have been extremely helpful in considering capital as the corporate property of this family (Strathern 1982).

6. SW Sr. to Wm. Meeking, Lavenham, England, April 7, 1796, in SSA.

7. Apparently Elijah Hubbard did not have any associations with merchants in Boston who would take the Watkinsons on as clerks.

8. JW to RW, Nov. 27, 1796, in RWL; RW to JW, Nov. 11, Dec. 9, 1796; RW to JW, Feb. 26, 1797, in RWL.

9. JW to RW, Nov. 27, 1796, in RWL.

10. As Richard described it: "Brother Samuel and myself have purchased beer from Middletown brewery and will bottle it and try to sell it, partly 'giving the proprietors a little encouragement' and for profit, brother David seems to have drunk all his" (RW to WW, May 12, 1797, in RWL).

11. SW Jr. to SW Sr., Dec. 18, 1795, in SJP.

12. "Eighteenth-century court records similarly indicate that the terms *servant* and *apprentice* were used interchangeably" (Tomlins 1993, 246).

13. SW Jr. to SW Sr., Dec. 28, 1795, in SJP.

14. SW Jr. to Wm. Meeking, July 4, 1796, in SJP.

15. SW Jr., April 27, 1796, in SJA.

16. In the large cities, however, even though apprenticeship remained common and tradition still held, a growing trend saw clerks hired with no expectation of advancement to partnership. An influx of young men from the countryside, who were willing or forced to accept employment on these terms, was a relatively new and unsettling element in New York (Smith-Rosenberg 1985, 80–81).

17. SW Jr. to SW Sr., Dec. 8, 1976, in SJP.

18. RW to MW, Oct. 30, 1796, in RWL.

19. RW to JW, Dec. 26, 1796, in RWL.

20. RW to JW, Dec. 9, 1796, in RWL; a note at the end of the page reads, "This Letter was not Sent."

21. RW to SW Sr., Jan. 26, 1797, in RWL.

22. It is difficult to appraise Samuel's criticism of Richard's handwriting, as the letters quoted here are from Richard's letterbook. How much he corrected or did not correct in the actual letter he sent remains unknown.

23. SW Sr. to RW, Feb. 1, 1797, in RWL.

24. SW Jr. to RW, Jan. 18, 1796, in SJP.

25. See Ditz 2000.

26. In a letter quoted in chapter 7, it is an indication of Robert Watkinson's extreme anger at his brother David that he did not correct the errors in his letter and copy it over.

27. RW to WW, March 15, 1797, in RWL.

28. RW to WW, May 12, 1797, in RWL.

29. SW Jr., Sept. 20, 1797, in SJA; SW Jr. Invoice, Dec. 13, 1797, in SJP; RW to SW Sr., Nov. 3, 1797, in RWL; RW cash book in RWL.

30. RW to SW Sr., February 1798, in RWL.

31. SW Sr. to RW, Feb. 1798, in RWL.

32. Agnew 1986 presents a fascinating discussion of how the theater provided a way in which the economic and instrumental relationships might be conceptualized. Ditz 2000 discusses at length the efforts and difficulties of merchants' portraying themselves as trustworthy men.

33. RW to MW, May 28, 1797, in RWL.

34. SW Jr. to RW, Dec. 2, 1795, in SJP; SW Jr. to SW Sr., Dec. 18, 1795, in SJP; SW Jr., Dec. 21, 1795, in SJA.

35. SW Jr. to WW, Dec. 5, 1796, in SJP.

36. SW Jr., in SJA.

37. SW Jr. to Wm. Meeking, July 31, 1797, in SJP.

38. SW Jr. to WW, Jan. 15, 1797, in SJP.

39. SW Jr. to Wm. Meeking, Feb. 11, 1797, in SJP.

40. RW to WW, Dec. 5, 1796, in RWL.

41. RW to WW, May 12, 1797, in RWL.

42. RW to MW, Nov. 26, 1797; RW to EW, April 1798, in RWL.

In his study of New York City during this time, Blumin states: "The hours of business for merchants…were variable and seldom long.…[C]lerks worked longer hours, but they were not always at their desks, or even at the store." Clerks were able to enliven their time by taking off at midday for lunch and for a walk with a friend (Blumin 1989, 21–22).

43. SW Jr. to Wm. Meeking, July 4, 1796, in SJP.

44. RW to EW, April 29, 1797, in RWL.

45. See Davidoff and Hall 1987, 348.

46. Although this letter is addressed merely to "Miss Watkinson," Mary was the likely recipient, since she was the one with whom he regularly corresponded.

47. SW Jr. to MW, April 26, 1797, in SJP.

48. SW Jr. to MW, Dec. 8, 1796, in SJP.

49. RW to EW, April 29, 1797; RW to EW, April 1798; RW to EW, May 1797; in RWL.

50. RW to Jane W., Dec. 27, 1796, in RWL.

51. RW to Jane W., Oct. 3, 1797, in RWL.

52. RW to Jane W., Nov. 1797, in RWL.

53. As in any society in which kinship is a major organizing system, continuing acts of reciprocity are the glue that holds the society together. While late eighteenth-century New England had many other overlapping institutions—polity, religion, and law—kinship was still a basic structuring principle.

54. RW to MW, Aug. 1, 1797, in RWL.

55. RW to MW, Nov. 1797 (n.d.), in RWL.

56. RW to Sarah Pledger, in late 1797 (n.d.), in RWL.

57. JW to RW, June 30, 1796, in RWL.

58. It is also quite probable that John used a false name, knowing that Richard would recognize the person, in case the letter was opened by someone else.

59. JW to RW, July 25, 1796, in RWL.

60. Some twelve years later, some of those who had been excluded started a rival set of balls, charging 50 cents more for admission to each event ($3.00 to the others' $2.50). "The new balls were so expertly conducted that many subscribers of the City Assembly bolted and joined the enemy camp" (Batterberry 1973, 40).

61. RW to WW, March 15, 1797, in RWL.

62. RW to EW, Dec. 26, 1796, in RWL.

63. RW to MW, Nov. 26, 1797, in RWL; "Lanham" was probably a reference to Lavenham.

64. Samuel Sr. wrote to one of his old friends in Suffolk, "to congratulate you on the very valuable connexion you have formed for Cousn Eliza may every blessing attend them, and their posterity and bocking and baize flourish for ever together" (Jan. 31, 1801, to Mr. John Webb, in SSA). Bocking and baize were two kinds of wool, and this marriage was bringing together two families in the wool trade.

65. This is a topic that Ditz 2000 deals with at length.

66. DW to Samuel Meeking, Lavenham, April 21, 1842, DWP; Samuel was the son of William Meeking, who had recently died.

67. SW Sr. to Robert Watkinson (England), Jan. 14, 1799, in SSA.

68. SW Jr. to Wm. Meeking, June 20, 1798, in SJP.

CHAPTER THREE: BALANCING THE BOOKS

1. On some of the islands where there was land unsuitable for sugar cultivation, generally hilly slopes, slaves might be given a half day off during the week to raise provisions for themselves and to sell any excess (Stinchcombe 1995, 53). It was, however, necessary to import most provisions as well as any essential manufactured items.

2. For an overview of this history see: Bailyn 1984 [1955]; Daniels 1988; Doerflinger 1986; and McCusker & Menard 1985.

3. See Edward P. Thompson 1978, "Eighteenth-Century English Society," for his comments on the merchants' profits from massing together producers' small surpluses.

4. As mentioned in the first chapter, Wadsworth became one of the wealthiest men in the country. Elijah Hubbard of Middletown, who had been appointed commissary and superintendent of stores for the Continental troops in Connecticut, prospered on a smaller but still impressive scale. Wadsworth is described by many sources, Hubbard by a few. See Saladino 1964.

5. SW Sr. to Wm. Meeking, April 7, 1796, in SSA.

6. A valuable guide to sources for this chapter has been a remarkable undergraduate honor's thesis by Jennifer Ellen Young, 1979, "John Revell Watkinson: 1772–1836: A Study in Early Industrial Development, Middletown, Connecticut." Wesleyan University.

7. Watkinson and his partners (first Elijah, and then Joseph, Hubbard) owned, bought, sold, and invested in several ships during the years 1795–1812 in which John was involved in navigation. These included *Brig Caroline, Brig Samuel, Brig Two Brothers, Schooner Sally, Schooner Hannah, Sloop Industry* and *Sloop Leopard*.

8. Hogsheads were the large wooden casks in which rum, molasses, or sugar were shipped. They held approximately 63 gallons or 6.77 bushels (Shepherd and Walton 1972, 172). Since these were average equivalents and a hogshead of rum might hold more than 100 gallons or less than 5 bushels, merchants priced by the gallon and bushel.

9. See Ditz 2000.

10. See, for example, Winjum 1972.

11. Vol. 2 in JAC.

12. Ibid.

13. In JAO.

14. Merchants at times resorted to illegal maneuvers to avoid a particularly oppressive tariff or to transport proscribed goods. A letter from John Watkinson to his captain indicates that he was willing to bend the law. The letter was written January 27, 1812, as war with England was about to break out and Congress was considering a law prohibiting "the importation of any distilled spirits." Watkinson wrote to Captain Joseph Hubbard in the West Indies, advising him what to do if this law was passed before he returned to Middletown.

> You had better have the cargo consigned to yourself in the bills of lading and leave out the consigned name and place of destination in your manifest, the Brig had better be cleared out for Lisbon and as we shall calculate to meet you at Montague

Point Light house or have a letter there for you if the times are difficult you will be very particular and let us know as accurately as you can the time of your sailing from the West Indies. Of course whatever cargo you have you must lay off Montague with the Brig and come on shore with the boat, and if you find no orders there you will come into New London harbour and let us know in six or eight hours after you arrive that we may be there and get her away within the forty eight hours if it is necessary to some Foreign or other port—if the Revenue cutter should be out you had better if possible keep out of her way till you have seen or heard from us, should the cutter board you then you must fill up your manifest bound to Lisbon and consigned to yourself [JRW to Capt. Joseph Hubbard on board the *Brig Lambert* at St. Bartholemews, Jan. 27, 1812, in JAO].

15. In JAO.

16. Elijah Hubbard Account Book for 1801–1806, in Middlesex Historical Society Library.

17. *Middlesex Gazette,* June 15, 1804.

18. In Yale Shipping Collection.

19. Certificate of Drawback, Middletown Shipping Records, in National Archives.

20. Noah Talcott to JW, April 28, 1806, in JBW.

21. N. Talcott to Watkinson & Hubbard, July 26 and Aug. 18, 1806, in JBW.

22. N. Talcott to JW, Nov. 12, 1806, in JBW.

23. Coit & Edwards to JW, Feb. 18, 1807, in JBW.

24. Watkinson's partner was now a different Hubbard. His original partner, Elijah Hubbard, died in 1808, and Captain Joseph Hubbard, a distant relative of Watkinson's wife, became his partner in navigation. Watkinson had also taken on a new partner in his dry-goods store, a son of William Johnson, a fellow English immigrant.

25. Meigs & Talcott to Watkinson & Hubbard, Jan. 13, 1810, in JBW.

26. JW to Messrs. Hall Hull & Co., New York City, March 5, 1810; Watkinson & Hubbard to Capt. John Loveland, n.d. but almost definitely March 29 or 30, 1810, in JAO.

27. Watkinson & Hubbard to Sylvester Pulcifer & Co., March 5, 1810, in JAO.

28. S. Pulcifer & Co. to Watkinson & Hubbard, March 10, 1810, in JBW.

29. Vol. 2 in JAC.

30. Watkinson & Hubbard to S. Pulcifer & Co., March 29, 1810, in JAO.

31. Vol. 2 in JAC. A "barrel," like a hogshead, was both a physical entity and a standard measure, equaling 31 1/2 gallons or 3.38 bushels.

32. Watkinson & Hubbard to S. Pulcifer & Co., April 30, 1810, in JAO.

33. In JBW.

34. S. Pulcifer & Co. to Watkinson & Hubbard, May 13, 1810, in JBW.

35. Watkinson & Hubbard to S. Pulcifer & Co., May 18, 1810, in JAO.

36. Several entries for March, April, and May, vol. 2, in JAC.

37. Watkinson & Hubbard to Sumner's, May 25, 1810, in JAO.

38. Entry, May 31, 1810, *S Hannah,* vol. 2, in JAC.

39. In JBW.

40. Vol. 2 in JAC.

41. Ibid.

42. Watkinson & Hubbard to Capt. Daniel Hubbard, June 6, 1810, in JAO.

43. Watkinson & Hubbard to Capt. John Loveland, May 28, 1810, in JAO.

44. Vol. 2 in JAC.

45. Entry, June 28, 1810, vol. 2, in JAC.

46. Watkinson & Hubbard to Capt. John Loveland, ca. June 6, 1810, in JAO

47. Vol. 2 in JAC.

48. In JAO.

49. Several entries for June and July 1810, vol. 2, in JAC.

50. In an earlier letter to Loveland, Watkinson had reproached him for not writing—"Dr Sr Your letter from Petersburg dated 23 Inst 6 days after your arrival there we were happy to receive but as we are not afraid of the expense of postage we shall expect in future that you will write at least once as soon as you arrive in port" (March or April, [n.d.] 1810, in JAO).

51. Sylvester Mather to Thomas Mather and Watkinson & Hubbard, Aug. 12, 1810, in JBW.

52. Capt. J. Loveland to Watkinson & Hubbard, Aug. 17, 1810, vol. 2, in JAO.

53. Joseph Frith Jr. (Turks Island) to Watkinson & Hubbard, Sept. 1, 1810, in JBW.

54. Record of Impost duties paid 1799–1818, Middletown Shipping Records, in National Archives.

55. Vol. 2 in JAC.

56. Ibid.

57. Entry, Oct. 24, 1810, vol. 2 in JAC.

58. Entries, Oct. 8, 1810, and Jan. 10, 1811, vol. 2 in JAC. Of course, interest was charged on the notes.

59. Entry, Dec. 29, 1810, vol. 2 in JAC.

60. Entry, Oct. 19, 1810, vol. 2 in JAC.

61. Entry, Jan. 10, 1811, vol. 2 in JAC.

62. Vol. 2, pp. 97–98 (double pages), in JAC.

63. JW to WW, Dec. 8, 1810, in JAO.

64. Capt. Joseph Hubbard to Watkinson & Hubbard, Jan. 4, 1811, in JBW.

65. Record of Impost duties paid 1799–1818, Middletown Shipping Records, in National Archives.

66. In JBW.

67. Watkinson & Hubbard to R. Montgomery, Jan. 16, 1812, in JAO.

68. Thus prices are given in the letter from Sylvester Mather to Thomas Mather in St. John's, Antigua, quoted earlier in chapter 3; a similar letter from another merchant, Thomas Sandford, in Barbados, addressed to Elijah Hubbard, Watkinson's first partner, described his efforts to get a good price for a shipment of horses, beef, and staves. He wrote that he had "landed the horses and sold 14 which average about $105 each. I am in hopes I shall be able to bring the average to $100." On August 19 he added that he had sold more horses, "the average of what sold is above $100...part of the staves are delivered the other will be as soon as possible." The letter continued, "the beef is now on hand are in hope to get $10" and went on to recommend that they send "10 to 20 hogsheads of tobacco" on their next vessel (Aug. 15 and 16, 1806, to Elijah Hubbard, in JBW).

69. Current accounting methods divulge more information as they strike a year-end balance of assets, which merchants rarely did, but they, too, follow arbitrary conventions and fit their methods to corporate goals.

This characteristic of accounting results from the fact that none of the basic categories of economic analysis—profit, loss, revenues, and so forth—have a transparent meaning in a complex economy. Whether or not a particular firm is profitable in a given quarter or a given year is not just a matter of whether it took in more money than it paid out; it depends, for example, on how one counts certain expenditures, since capital investments are treated differently from current expenses. The precise determination as to whether a particular cost falls into one category or the other depends upon the accounting rules in effect at the time. The seemingly objective economic facts of contemporary life are themselves shaped by accounting conventions. (Block 1990, 32)

70. Vol. 2 in JAC. Determining an exact estimate is difficult, as his notes are scattered and some entries are ambiguous. Young estimated his fortune at $53,700, including the property his wife had inherited from her father's estate, valued at $7,500 (Young 1979, 27–28). Unfortunately the source for this is no longer known.

71. The house is now part of the National Guard Armory. The archaeological excavations were undertaken by Wesleyan University. The findings are discussed in Brenda Gray's 1978 undergraduate honors thesis.

72. According to Chatfield, "Eighteenth century businessmen had no clear concept of capital as 'wealth for profit' seeking a maximum return.... Worse, they failed to see that capital produced income.... Income was considered the businessman's reward for risk taking, ingenuity, or sheer luck, not for investing *per se*" (1977, 106–07). Chatfield was referring not only to merchants but even to early industrialists who still maintained the partnership form of organization.

In her study of the account books of Berkshire paper mills, McGaw noted that early industrialists' adoption of conventional double-entry bookkeeping from merchants gave them very little information about either fixed or working capital. "Judging from their books, paper makers did not misrepresent the facts when they reported to Treasury Department investigators in 1831 that their rate of profit was 'altogether uncertain, and unknown'" (1987, 151).

73. The benefits of the West Indian trade to New England's farmers and the degree to which they were enmeshed in the network of trade was thrown into sharp relief during the Embargo Act of 1807–1809, which effectively shut down the trade. "The prices of imported goods rose greatly while those of domestic agricultural produce, lacking a market, declined in like measure" (Martin 1939, 66).

CHAPTER FOUR: CONTINUITY AND CHANGE

1. SW Sr. to John Webb, Jan. 31, 1801, in SSA; Barnard 1858, 88.

2. SW Sr. to John Webb, Jan. 31, 1801, in SSA.

3. SW Sr. to WW, Jan. 15, 1801, in SSA.

4. WW to Wm. Meeking, June 1, 1803, in WWL.

5. SW Sr. to Wm. Meeking, Feb. 27, 1805, in SSA.

6. Feb. 6, 1805, notice in *Connecticut Courant;* SW Sr. to Wm. Barhard, Feb. 27, 1805, in SSA.

7. WW to Wm. Meeking, June 1, 1803, in WWL.

8. SW Sr. to John Webb, Jan. 17, 1806, in SSA.

9. SW Sr. to Robert Watkinson, England, Jan. 25, 1810, in SSA. This may have been the precipitating factor that caused John and his wife, Hannah, to confirm their full membership in Middletown's Congregational Church in 1809.

10. Ibid.

11. SW Sr. to Wm. Hickman, Lavenham, Jan. 25, 1810, in SSA.

12. All of the advertisements that follow in this chapter are from the *Connecticut Courant,* which at this time was a weekly newspaper.

13. SW Sr. to Wm. Meeking, Jan. 25, 1810, in SSA.

14. WW to JW, March 26, 1810, in WWL.

15. This seems to be due to more than the chance of what is found in the archives since several letters exchanged between John and David during this time can be found in the archives.

16. WW to JW, May 3, 1810, in WWL. His new business was located on a street of importers and shipping brokers (Albion 1961, 260).

17. WW to JW, May 18, 1810, in WWL.

18. WW to Wm. Meeking, Nov. 1, 1810, in WWL.

19. Ibid.

20. SW Sr. to John Webb, Feb. 1, 1811, in SSA.

21. The discussion here rests mainly on Charles Sellers, whose formulation of a market revolution has integrated an extraordinary amount of historical data. His 1991 book, *The Market Revolution: Jacksonian America, 1815–1846,* and some of the discussions of his position in Stokes and Conway, 1996, provide rewarding entries into this period.

A very interesting analysis by Rothenberg 1992 traces the expansion of market involvement in Massachusetts through the increasing homogeneity of farmers' prices as their production more and more responded to market demand.

22. See Merrill 1977.

23. Two major sources on this time period and on the social and political context of the refusal to renew the charter of the Bank of the United States are Sellers 1991, especially pages 59–63, and Hammond 1957, pages 210–20. Sellers wrote a particularly deft phrase that sums up American politics then and now: "Under the Republican banner of equal rights a recurrent paradigm of American politics emerged, as a democratic majority asserting equality empowered an aspiring elite asserting opportunity" (38).

24. SW Sr. to John Webb, Feb. 1, 1811, in SSA.

25. Fortunately, within a few years the shares were transferred to the state banks. The shareholders' capital was secured and only the interest lost (Hammond, 225).

26. JW, "Copy of my letter to William Feby 18th, 1811 in answer to his to his Father," in JBW.

27. Ibid.

28. Ibid.

29. WW to Wm. Meeking, May 25, 1811, in WWL.

30. The Watkinsons were tied to England by commerce, family, and friends, but even Samuel had described these efforts of the British government to destroy American trade as "disgusting" (Jan. 25, 1810, to Wm. Meeking, in SSA).

31. Public response to their ill-timed speeches to this effect at the Hartford Convention of 1815 sealed the fate of the Federalist Party. The Treaty of Ghent, which ended the war, had already been signed as they postured.

32. An excellent summary of the Republican/Federalist feuding in Middletown is in Hall 1981, 13–17.

33. In 1795 Washington's administration signed the Jay Treaty, which specifically approved the continuance of commercial ties with Great Britain (Tomlins 1993, 90).

34. U.S. Bureau of the Census, 1960, quoted by Lebergott 1961, 216.

35. JW to WW, April 1812 (n.d.), in JAO.

36. SW Sr. to Wm. Meeking, Jan 25, 1810, in SSA.

37. See Porter and Livesay 1971.

38. Interesting summaries of the discussions of whether the market revolution signals the transition to capitalism in the United States can be found in Johnson 1993 and Clark 1996. Earlier arguments concerning when capitalism began in the United States and what this transition consisted of are summed up in Kulikoff 1989.

39. JW to WW, April 10, 1812, in JAO.

40. The first American attempt at wool manufacture had been the Hartford Woolen Manufactory Company, begun in 1788 by Jeremiah Wadsworth. At first carding (combing and paralleling fibers prior to spinning) and fulling (cleansing and thickening the cloth) were carried out in the factory while spinning was put out to neighboring households. The company then became the first American wool manufactory to utilize power machinery for spinning wool and to bring spinning out of the household and into the factory. Neither Wadsworth nor his partner knew anything about wool manufacture, so they hired English deserters or former prisoners of war in order to gain the necessary skills (Jeremy 1981, 118).

The Connecticut state government subsidized their efforts, exempting all buildings from tax for five years and all workers from poll taxes for two. Washington visited the factory and had a suit made of its cloth. Hamilton commented favorably upon it, but there were difficulties in getting machinery, workers, materials and capital. The cloths they produced were of poor quality to a public accustomed to fine British woolens, and the factory closed in 1794, paying its one and only dividend in the form of cloths. The most useful sources for this topic are Arthur Cole's, 1926, *The American Wool Manufacturers,* David Jeremy's, 1981, *Transatlantic Industrial Revolution* and Margaret Martin's, 1939, *Merchants and Trade of the Connecticut River Valley 1750–1820.*

41. DW to JW, Oct. 9, 1812, in JBW.

42. JW to Leavitt & Burrall, New York, March 15, 1815, in JAO.

43. Such as William Johnson, who had emigrated from England along with the Watkinsons.

44. Jan. 1, 1817, Day Book, in JBW.

45. JW to WW, Dec. 1, 1817, in JAO.

46. JW to Jeremiah Lobdell & Co., New York, Dec. 12, 1817, in JAO.

47. JW to WW, Dec. 6, 1817, in JAO.

48. JW to WW, Dec. 23, 1817, in JAO.

49. JW to WW, Dec. 29, 1817, in JAO.

50. Vol. 1 in JAC.

51. Vol. 3 in JAC.

52. Ibid.

53. Day Book, in JBW.

54. Not only the method of accounting, which Watkinson used, but also the master-servant law and contracts (see chap. 5) that were being established for the factories were similar to the laws and customs that had regulated the relationship of captain and crew. Rediker viewed "mariners as key transitional figures in the movement from paternalistic forms of labor to the contested negotiations of wage work" (1988, 285).

55. Day Book, in JBW.

56. A valuable discussion of earlier forms of employment and the changes that were taking place in the early nineteenth century can be found in Steinfeld 1991.

57. William Crawford, the secretary of the Treasury, stated that "few examples have occurred of a distress so general and so severe, as that which has been exhibited in the United States in the 1819 recession" (Crawford, February 1820, quoted in Lebergott 1961, 293).

58. Sellers credits New England's fortunate escape to the restraint of its banks and the competition from European goods (1991, 138).

59. *Connecticut Courant,* June 22, 1819.

60. JW to Gilbert Brewster, June 5, 1819, in JAO.

61. Partnership agreement between David Watkinson and Ezra Clark June 21, 1819, in DWC.

CHAPTER FIVE: THE COLLINS COMPANY

1. SC Memo.
2. SC Memo, 14.
3. SC Memo, 2.
4. DC, Hartford, to Benjamin Smith, Middletown, June 20, 1825, in JBW.
5. SC Memo, 2.
6. SC Memo, 14.
7. Ibid.
8. In Bourdieu's useful term they inherited a "habitus," a deeply learned mode of acting and believing.
9. The cooperation that Wallace described among cotton mill owners in Rockdale was a far cry from the cutthroat competition of the axe business (1972, 21).
10. SC to William Wood, Feb. 4, 1869, Wood, William, papers, in Connecticut State Library.
11. SC to William Wood, Feb. 7, 1869, Wood, William, papers, in Connecticut State Library.
12. SC to DC, Sept. 9, 1830, in CCH.
13. Congregational Church records, in Connecticut State Library.
14. John Watkinson's machine-tool factory, Sanseer, was originally incorporated with Gilbert Brewster, the inventor of the machines, on the board of directors. Several years later, having amassed serious debts, he sold his interest to Watkinson, who took over his debts (in JBW).
15. Wittmer 1977, 28; SC Memo, 3; DW to Wm. Meeking, Nov. 16, 1831, in DWP.
16. See Gordon 1983; Gordon and Malone 1994; Hoke 1990.
17. William Wells was replaced as partner by his brother, John Freme Wells (Wittmer 1977, 34).
18. DW to Wm. Meeking, Nov. 16, 1831, in DWP.
19. A so-called wilderness, of course, that had been a home for Native Americans for centuries.
20. SC to Collins Company, Dec. 12, 1830, in CCA.
21. L. (name is indecipherable) & Co., Philadelphia, March 15, 1831, in CCH. Other axe manufacturers used these same names to describe their different types of axes.
22. See Dawley 1976; Faler 1981; and Prude 1983.
23. SC Memo, 8.
24. SC Memo, 12.
25. SC to DC, Aug. 12a, 1830, in CCH.
26. SC to DC, Aug. 12b, 1830, in CCH.
27. Ibid.
28. SC to DC, Aug. 27, 1830, in CCH.
29. SC to DC, Oct. 31, 1830, in CCA.
30. SC to DC, Nov. 4, 1830, in CCA.
31. SC to DC, Nov. 7, 1830, in CCA.
32. When such cases were brought to court, the lower courts tended to sympathize with the workers and to allow them to collect pay for the time they had already served. These judgments were overturned in the higher courts, which claimed that wages were

based solely on serving out the full time of a contract. These decisions were as much concerned with agricultural contracted labor as factory labor. (See Tomlins 1933.)

33. For example, two of the most respected and important judges, Lemuel Shaw and Joseph Story, were closely associated with Boston's elite "Brahmins." See Hall 1982 and Levy 1957.

34. An excellent source for the development of laws regulating the workplace is Christopher Tomlins, 1993, *Law, Labor, and Ideology in the Early American Republic.* An equally important book on law, which traces the ways in which customary and common-law regulation of resources was altered to meet the needs of manufacturers, is Horwitz, 1977, *The Transformation of American Law 1780–1860.*

35. SC to DC, Nov. 9, 1830, in CCA.

36. SC to DC, Sept. 10, 1830, in CCH.

37. SC to DC, Aug. 7, 1830, in CCH.

38. SC to DC, Aug. 16, 1830, in CCH.

39. SC to DC, Dec. 16, 1830, in CCH.

40. SC to DC, Aug. 12b, 1830, in CCH.

41. SC Memo, 5–6.

42. SC to DC, Aug. 12b, 1830, in CCH.

43. SC to DC, Sept. 9, 1830, in CCH.

44. Ibid.

45. SC to DC, Sept. 10, 1830, in CCH.

46. Ibid.

47. SC to DC, Dec. 13, 1830, in CCA.

48. SC Memo, 4; Wittmer 1977, 33.

49. SC to DC, Nov. 11, 1830, in CCA.

50. SC to DC, Nov. 12, 1830, in CCA.

51. SC to DC, Nov. 16, 1830, in CCA.

52. SC to DC, Dec. 12, 1830, in CCA.

53. Notice of 1832, in CCA.

54. SC to DC, Sept. 10, 1830, in CCH.

55. SC to DC, Feb. 23, 1833, in CCH.

56. SC to DC, March 27, 1835, in CCH.

57. SC Memo, 8.

58 In 1842 Judge Lemuel Shaw handed down what is referred to as a "capstone decision," which no longer considered associations per se as evidence of criminal conspiracy. They were criminal only if they acted unlawfully or if their goals were unlawful. This landmark decision, which appears favorable to labor, in no way inhibited the courts from finding associations guilty on one or the other of the above counts and from imposing far heavier penalties than before. See Tomlins 1993 and Newmyer 1987.

59. Legal historians regard these fines as mere slaps on the wrist and, compared with later penalties, that was certainly the case (e.g. Hattam 1992). Yet these historians seem unaware that for a worker even a day's pay frequently represented the difference between paying the rent or the grocer and being unable to. Despite these penalties, workers continued to create associations.

60. A large and interesting literature discusses republicanism at great length. See, for example: Appleby 1986; Banning 1986; Kerber 1985. Wilenz writes of "the process of ideological confrontation, negotiation, and redefinition" between employers and workers in which the many meanings of republicanism both held and changed as entrepreneurs used republicanism to defend industrial capitalism and artisans turned it into a

critique (1983, 38). What is also of interest is that workers in the United States argued their points of view in terms of the promises and goals of the Revolution (Tomlins 1993), while English workers debated in terms of ancient customs (Smail 1987).

61. SC Memo, 8.

62. SC Memo, 9.

63. SC Memo, 10.

64. SC Memo, 11.

65. SC to DC, Sept. 10, 1830, in CCH.

66. SC to DC, Dec. 16, 1830, in CCA.

67. SC to DC, Feb. 23, 1835, in CCH.

CHAPTER SIX: BREAKING COMMUNITY, BUILDING CLASS

1. SC Memo, 27. Battles over taxes were common to many factory towns. Another crucial source of friction between community and manufacturer was over the dams that flooded farmers' fields and destroyed traditional common fishing sites (see Kulik 1985 and Prude 1985). From the 1830s on, judges tended to interpret the law in favor of development, giving manufacturers privileged access to the use of water power, where earlier the rights of farmers and fishermen had limited industrial use to a few gristmills and sawmills servicing local villages (Horwitz 1977, 32–53).

2. This quote, which is undated, appears in a company publication of 1926: *One Hundred Years: A Brief Account of the Development of The Collins Company in the Manufacture of Axes, Machets and Edge Tools and in Commeration of Its 100th Anniversary.* Collinsville: The Collins Company.

3. The famous Waltham system of strictly supervising young female textile workers in company boarding houses is another example of paternalism in the early years of industrialization. For additional examples, see Coogan 1991, Murphy 1992, Nassaney and Abel 2000, and Prude 1983.

4. SC Memo, 12.

5. According to Trumbull 1886 and Woodward 1892, General Terry and James H. Wells were directors only through 1827. Woodward was himself a president of the bank, and it is his book that provides the interesting facts that both David and Robert Watkinson were directors in 1833 as was David's and Edward's father-in-law, Barzillai Hudson.

6. Biddle was successful in creating a serious financial disaster, but President Jackson, nonetheless, closed him down. See Hammond 1957 and Sellers 1991.

7. SC Memo, 13, 15.

8. The original partnership was named Collins & Co.; after incorporation, it became the Collins Manufacturing Company. In 1843, when it was authorized to make iron and steel as well as tools, it was renamed The Collins Company. In general, it will be referred to here at whatever period as the Collins Company, or simply the company.

9. Martin lists 23 incorporated manufacturing enterprises in Connecticut by 1834 (1939, 208–09). These were still relatively small companies, with capitalizations ranging between $100,000 and $200,000. When Roy states that the corporate form was rare in manufacturing before 1890, he is speaking of much larger corporations (1997, xiii). Despite their size these small Connecticut companies demonstrated structural changes and social impacts that were predictive of what would take place on a far greater scale at the turn of the century.

10. SC Memo, 13.

11. SC Memo, 19.

12. SC Memo, 19–20.

13. Along with most of the business community, Collins attributed the Panic of 1837 and the continuing economic depression to Van Buren's continuation of Jackson's efforts to separate the federal government from the banking interests. The opposing view blamed the banks for recklessly producing paper money with too little backing and the businessmen for greedy speculation in the years leading up to this inevitable crash (Sellers 1991).

14. Notice, 1838, included in SC Memo, after 22.

15. SC Memo, 43.

16. SC Memo, 24.

17. SC Memo, 24.

18. SC Memo, 24.

19. SC to Wm. Wood, March 23, 1868. Wood, William, papers, in Connecticut State Library.

20. "Samuel Collins...was unusual among nineteenth-century entrepreneurs in being willing and able to make the fullest possible use of the water-power resources available at the site of his work" (Gordon and Malone 1994, 89).

21. SC to DC, Feb. 23, 1835, in CCH.

22. Detailed studies of the axe-making technology of the Collins Company can be found in Hoke 1990, Gordon 1983, and Gordon and Malone 1994, all of whom note Collins's interest in and support for new methods and inventions. Root remained at the Collins Company until 1849, when he moved to Hartford to become superintendent of the Colt Armory and, eventually, its president. He married a Colt, a sister of Samuel Collins's wife.

23. Although England was the original source of ideas of industrial technology, American inventors soon rapidly surpassed the British. In British machine shops mechanics were taught skills in only a single branch of technology, whereas in American shops machinists could do everything and, as a result, were far more inventive and made better tools (Wallace 1972, 212–13). In addition, however, a different demand was at work in the United States, where labor was less abundant and more independent.

24. This topic is addressed fully in David Noble 1984. Anthony Wallace described this effect of technology in the textile mills: "The tendency in the 1830s and 1840s, then, was for the cotton mill machinery to become progressively more specialized and intricate, while the cotton mill operative became progressively more standardized and indifferently skilled" (Wallace 1972, 383). Gordon and Malone point out that the new forming machine at the Collins Company demanded different rather than fewer skills (1994, 358), but the general tendency at the Collins Company as elsewhere was to decrease the amount of training and skill that workers needed to carry on production. (See Collins's statement, "Axe-making has become so simplified" on page 12.)

25. Terms with Workmen, Collins and Company, in CCH.

26. SC Memo, 29.

27. SC Memo, 31.

28. In 1830, Dr. Arnold Knight, a physician in Sheffield, England, published his observations of affected men in the Sheffield General Infirmary (Knight 1830). Many of the men had worked in conditions like those in Collinsville, where the increased division of labor forced some men to work all day at grinding stones; there they continuously breathed the high concentration of stone dust in the air (Siskind 1988). Hoke 1990 also describes the serious health problems caused by the grinding machines at the Collins Company.

29. SC to DC, Nov. 8, 1830, in CCA.

30. SC Memo, 30.

31. A comparison of their responses to their working conditions with those of laborers in Sheffield as described by Knight reveals the importance of the labor market in influencing workers' behavior.

> Grinders' asthma is the name given by the Grinders themselves, to that form of consumption which prevails amongst the workmen, who are employed in grinding the different kinds of cutlery goods manufactured in Sheffield, and the neighbourhood. The name conveys but a very imperfect idea of the disease, since the grinders' asthma bears scarcely any resemblance to asthma, properly so called, except in those symptoms which are common to almost all affections of the chest. It is probable however that it has been so designated not only from the vague resemblance, but also from *a natural desire on the part of the grinders to conceal the fatal character of their complaint* by assigning to it the name of a disease, which does not necessarily interfere with the duration of life. (Knight 1830, 85, emphasis added)

Unlike Sheffield grinders, Connecticut Yankees in the 1840s were in a position to refuse this hazardous occupation and did not need to practice self-delusion.

32. SC Memo, 32.

33. See Tomlins 1993, chapter 10.

34. "Suits seeking to attribute responsibility for work injuries to employers and to compel them to pay substantial sums in compensation threatened a significant level of legal regulation of employers' capacity to exercise power over their employees. In the circumstances of the particular 'moment' at which this interference was mooted, circumstances of crisis in and challenge to the intensification of the accumulation process, the refusal of courts to admit the possibility of intervention established that the contested territory of production was a private sphere, occupied by the employer's disciplinary power and not by the state" (Tomlins 1993, 296).

35. See Kulik for a description of the impact on striking workers of the "stately houses" that "Pawtucket's newly rich" manufacturers had built among their more humble abodes (1979, 213).

36. This is not to suggest that workers had a clear view of a labor theory of value, but as Collins himself said, some of the Collins workers did, in fact, believe that he was getting rich at their expense. See his speech quoted this chapter.

37. SC Memo, 45.

38. SC Memo, 32.

39. SC Memo, 33.

40. SC Memo, 34.

41. Here he is forgetful or dishonest, as in his own memoir he mentioned that the company had shut down for two months in 1838.

42. SC Memo, 35.

43. SC Memo, 36.

44. SC Memo, 37.

45. SC Memo, 38.

46. SC Memo, 32.

47. SC Memo, 38.

48. In the field of American history debates have focused on whether capitalism was present from the time of early settlement or later; see Kulikoff 1989. In the study of European history debates concern capitalism's true origins. Clearly when and where

one locates the beginnings of capitalism depends on how it is defined—a topic of endless disputes and political passions. I am in accord with the numerous scholars who, following Marx, understand capitalism as a system in which those who control the means of production are able to purchase free labor and appropriate a portion of unpaid surplus value. This is what Stinchcombe describes for the crews employed in the eighteenth century long-distance trade of several European cities developing from "seeds recognizable several centuries earlier" (Stinchcombe 1995, 84–85); however, this definition is not applicable to the relatively small trading ships that made short runs from New England to the West Indies or along the coast of the United States (1995, 60). This definition of capitalism applies to what Brenner 1985 and Wood 1991 describe for the landless laborers employed on agricultural estates in fourteenth century northwestern Europe. In North America these defining relations of production became established for the first time in the United States within New England's early nineteenth century industrial factories.

49. This thought is indebted to Prude's succinct statement in the opening chapter of his study of industrialization in two Massachusetts towns.

A salient characteristic of postrevolutionary Dudley and Oxford—and a cause of considerable friction amid the changing/economic landscape of later years—was that affluent citizens enjoyed only limited leverage over the less wealthy... the rich did not fuse into a discrete, coercive class of creditors... and few creditors, whatever their economic position, were inclined to do more than badger recipients of their loans.... Nor did wealth typically yield the authority of an employer, for prior to 1810 no enterprise in either Dudley or Oxford required a large, full-time labor force.... In brief, there was no way—no continuing, established institutional structure—through which wealth was translated into domineering economic power. (1983, 12–13)

CHAPTER SEVEN: FOR THEIR OWN GOOD

1. Hartford's elite resembled Boston's on a smaller scale, and both became involved in similar types of charitable works. The two groups were also alike in focusing their philanthropic efforts exclusively on their own cities despite the fact that many of Hartford's businesses, like those of the Boston Associates, were beginning to operate on a national scale (Dalzell 1987, 129).

2. The simultaneous emulation and criticism of the British was an old tradition; see Bushman 1992, 193–96.

3. OW Journal, 3.

4. OW Journal, 4.

5. OW Journal, 4–5.

6. OW Journal, 92.

7. OW Journal, 99.

8. OW Journal, 14.

9. OW Journal, 28.

10. OW Journal, 57.

11. OW Journal, 16–17.

12. OW Journal, 41–42.

13. DW to Rev. Wm. Ward, March 3, 1820, in DWP.

14. OW Journal, 46.

15. Stock certificates and letter from Henry Ellsworth to DW, Feb. 25, 1836, in DWC.

16. See, for example, Keller 1968 and Sellers 1991.

17. As Johnson suggested in his remarkable *A Shopkeeper's Millennium* the social upheavals and religious outbreaks of this period were "generated in the problem of social class." He added: "Given that, it seems unwise to treat religion and class as separate and competing categories of explanation" (1978, 135).

18. DW, March 1, 1821 (the recipient's name was missing from this copy of the letter), in DWP.

19. DW to Wm. Meeking, Nov. 16, 1831, in DWP.

20. Rev. Wm. Ward to DW, March 6, 1830, in DWP.

21. Two excellent discussions of the connections between industrialization and upper-class promulgation of the temperance cause can be found in Johnson 1978 and Rumbarger 1989.

22. Terms with Workmen, Dec. 1, 1834, in CCH. Collins's regulations duplicated those of many other New England manufacturers; see, for example, Coogan's (1991) description of the temperance struggle in Adams, Mass., and Faler's (1974) description of it in Lynn, Mass.

However, basing their statement on Kathleen Bond's findings (Bond 1989a and 1989b), Beaudry, Cook, and Mrozowski point out that archaeological evidence of alcohol containers and patent medicine bottles, "all with extremely high alcohol content," has shown that similar efforts to curtail workers' use of alcohol in the Lowell boarding-houses were strikingly unsuccessful (1991, 169).

23. SC Memo, 18.

24. Their brothers, of course, had also drunk their share of spirits. In 1797, when Samuel Jr. estimated his "Supposed annual expences in the city of NYork," his first two items were "Boarding & Lodging 260, Porter & Brandy 39." These were the most expensive of his outlays on an annual budget of $540 (see page 32).

Richard described an evening at David's rooms with "brandy, apples and nuts and everything that [was] comfortable." RW to JW, Dec. 26, 1796, in RWL.

25. Capt. March to DW, Feb. 1, 1831, in DWP.

26. This section of the chapter owes a great deal to Rothman 1971.

27. In DWC.

28. DW to Wm. Meeking, July 11, 1827, in DWP.

29. Codicil 11, Watkinson 1858.

30. DW to Wm. Meeking, Nov. 16, 1831, in DWP.

31. Throughout the Northeast similar institutions were being constructed for orphans and other unfortunate or deviant youth, and all stressed the importance of obedience and regimentation (Rothman 1971, 228–29). A number of books on child rearing appeared in this period, recommending similar principles and practices to parents. One popular version was written by the Watkinson's friend Lydia Sigourney (Rothman, 218).

32. Rothman discusses at great length the beliefs underlying all of these nineteenth-century institutions, as does Foucault in far more complex ways. The discussion in this chapter derives from both, but it adds a consideration of why these discourses held such great appeal for the businessmen who chose to fund these and not other solutions to what they perceived as the problems of their times.

33. As Prude also observed: "It can scarcely be ignored that the notion of effecting reform through discipline linked manufactories to several other institutions emerging in this period." He listed penitentiaries, poorhouses, schools, and insane asylums and pointed out their "advocates" argued that "like mills" these were efforts directed at rectifying social ills (Prude 1983, 112).

34. It is not possible to read Watkinson's descriptions without thinking of Foucault's work, and in reference to *Discipline & Punish*.

35. DW to Rev. Wm. Ward, Jan. 23, 1827, in DWP.

36. The United States was the first nation to create prisons to do more than temporarily hold those convicted or accused. This dubious achievement was begun by the Quakers in Pennsylvania, where a different model of prison social structure was devised, an even more horrendous type in which prisoners were condemned to solitary confinement day and night. Their rehabilitation was to come from meditation to achieve divine understanding and guidance. Wethersfield was built on the New York State Auburn model, which followed the Quaker by a few years. See Orland 1975. DW to Wm. Meeking, Nov. 16, 1831, in DWP.

37. Estate of David B. Watkinson, May 18, 1843, in DWC. The letters from nephew to uncle had been open and informal, suggesting a close relationship. One was unwittingly very funny. David Blair described a wild scene in which the sophomores broke windows and smoked out the freshmen, and one student, who stabbed his tutor in three places, narrowly missed killing him. In the next sentence he wrote: "I very much regret that I did not come to Yale, when I first entered college…The discipline is so much better the standard is so much higher here" (David Blair Watkinson to DW, Oct. 3, 1843, in DWC).

38. WW to DW, Feb. 10, 1834, in DWC.

39. WW to DW, April 19, 1836, in DWC.

40. Ibid. Olivia was often called "Olive."

41. Jane Gill to DW, Nov. 21, 1837, in DWC.

42. WW to DW, Jan. 11, 1837, in DWC.

43. E. G. Hubbard to DW, Oct. 5, 1838, in DWC.

44. Her family was Anglican and descended from Irish landed gentry. The Watkinsons may well have held some prejudice against both categories of people.

45. WW to DW, July 12, 1838, in DWC.

46. Joseph Sanford Watkinson to DW, Nov. 10, 1841, in DWC.

47. Joseph Sanford Watkinson to DW, March 2, 1848, in DWC.

48. Jane Watkinson to DW, Dec. 23, 1845, in DWC.

49. Watkinson Family History, in WFP. This was a second marriage for Gill.

50. Edward Pessen also argued for the sincerity of the beliefs of wealthy philanthropists. "In advising the poor that individual social failure was caused by vice, intemperance, sloth, and ignorance…wealthy altruists said what they truly believed. In my judgment they voiced their deepest convictions" (1973, 277).

51. The practice of philanthropy as an implementation and demonstration of class power was clearly stated by Ignatieff: "Philanthropy is not simply a vocation, a moral choice; it is also an act of authority that creates a linkage of dependency and obligation between rich and poor of necessity, therefore, it is a political act, embarked upon not merely to fulfill personal needs, but also to address the needs of those who rule, and those who are ruled" (Ignatieff 1978, 153).

A discussion of the contribution of philanthropy to the construction of an upper-class identity in Boston can be found in Story 1980 and Hall 1982.

52. OW to Mrs. Wm. Meeking, Feb. 20, 1844, in DWP.

53. Robert Watkinson to DW, Aug. 11, 1845, in DWC.

54. OW to Wm. Meeking, Jan. 24, 1826, in DWP.

55. WW to DW, Aug. 21, 1840, in DWC.

56. Mrs. Elizabeth Watkinson to WW, care of DW, Hartford, Oct. 10, 1840, in DWC.

57. Mrs. Elizabeth Watkinson to OW, Feb. 13, 1841, in DWC.

58. Watkinson's fortune was comparable to that of some of the wealthiest donors to Harvard. "The average value of the estates was $620,000; the median value was $300,000. Both figures represented huge fortunes for pre-Civil War America" (Story 1980, 29).

59. Codicil 7, Watkinson 1858.

CONCLUSION: DISTANCING PRODUCTION

1. According to Smith-Rosenberg's analysis of two novels of this time, this relationship between New England and the West Indies, hidden in the account books and silenced in the letters, is revealed as a disturbing and contradictory element in the construction of what she terms "a Euro-American middle-class identity" (2000, 248).

2. A portion of a letter written by Samuel Watkinson Sr. asking his old friend Meeking about his workers back in Suffolk provides an example of this relationship. "It would be troubling you too much to inform me... after all my Old Workmen... whom I constantly employed during the last year I was in trade some of whom grown old in my employ it grieved me sorely to dismiss be pleased to give them a shilling each but to old Tom and Reynolds five shillings each (to remind them of us) and with all our best wishes for their welfare and if their country calls them forth to repel a French invasion may success attend them" (SW Sr. to Wm. Meeking, Aug. 21, 1798, SSA).

3. Roy 1997 convincingly demonstrates that corporations were not predictably, necessarily, or intrinsically more efficient than entrepreneurial partnerships, and owed their existence to the successful hegemony of the financial capitalist segment. Although Roy writes about the very large-scale corporations that appeared at the end of the nineteenth century, the Connecticut Valley in general and the Collins Company in particular were precocious. Although originally capitalized at a modest $100,000, by 1862 the company had reached a $1 million level.

4. See Dalzell 1987 and Story 1980.

5. Watkinson was one of the incorporators and trustees of Trinity College (originally called Washington College), a founder of the Connecticut Historical Society and the Watkinson Library, and a major subscriber to the Wadsworth Atheneum.

6. Perhaps this was due to his early years as part of a Dissenting congregation to whom the pretension and powers of the aristocratic Anglican faith were a mark of corruption.

7. Olivia was unusual in playing an important role in the organization and management of the Beneficent Society for Orphan Girls; nonetheless, David was far more involved than she in the directing of several philanthropic institutions.

8. DW to Lydia Sigourney, April 19, 1849, in Hoadly Collection, Box 6, Sigourney Correspondence, The Connecticut Historical Society.

9. According to Paul Goodman, "avarice" was considered "the greatest threat to character" in these early years of industrial capitalism (1966, 440).

10. The question of when the middle class emerged and what it was is clearly beyond the scope of this book. It is as much a definitional question as a factual one. Blumin (1989), *The Emergence of the Middle Class*, is a major source for this topic. Bushman (1992) traces the complex process through which "genteel culture" spread from European courts to republican America, from upper to middle class and below.

11. See Dalzell 1987 for the rise and demise as a ruling class of the Boston Associates. Also see Farrell (1993), who showed that descendants of the Associates held stock and directorships of various corporations well into the twentieth century. However,

Jaher (1995) seems justified in pointing out that contrary to Farrell's conclusion that this meant that they were still a ruling class, it was New York investors who were the controlling decision makers. See Beckert 2001 on the preeminence of New York's bourgeoisie and Roy 1997 on the formation of the nationally dominant corporate segment of the upper class.

12. See Sider and Smith's 1997 important discussion of differentiation.

13. See Nash's 1989 study of the effects of General Electric's decision to drastically reduce its workforce in Pittsfield, Massachusetts, where it had profited for some eighty years. See, also, Michael Moore's 1990 film about General Motors and the destruction of Flint, Michigan.

14. Paraphrasing Marx, Seed puts it: "Under free competition, the immanent laws of capitalist production confront the individual capitalist as a coercive force external to him" (1993, 27).

15. Muldrew offers an apt description of the potential results of such policies: "Especially now, when the political advocacy of the virtues of competition has become so pervasive, we must understand that the full realization of such values, without a concurrent emphasis on trust, sociability and the redistribution of wealth, would be the creation of a world of Hobbesian insecurity and debtor's prisons" (1998, 333).

16. See Palmer 1994 for a penetrating deconstruction of the Goodyear Tire and Rubber Company's public-relations materials and rewriting of history. Muldrew neatly summarizes: "thinking of the market as an 'invisible hand' is a self-imposed ethical myopia preventing us from finding our way" (1998, 11).

References

PRIMARY SOURCES
Archives
The Canton Historical Society, Canton, Connecticut
  MS E 19 A & B Collins, Samuel Watkinson: Letters; July 7, 1830–Dec. 28, 1830
  MS E 16 Collins Company, Industrial Relations. Copy of Notice written by Samuel Collins, 1832
The Connecticut Historical Society, Hartford
  Watkinson, David, 1778–1857; 1816–1852, 2 boxes, Letters to (Box 1, 1816–1843, Box 2, 1844–1852), including Journal kept by Samuel Watkinson Jr., 1795–1798
  Hoadly Coll. Box 6, Sig. Corr. Watkinson, David 1778–1857 to Sigourney, Lydia (Huntley), Mrs. Charles, 1791–1865, April 19, 1849
  Collins and Company, 1830–1921, 2 boxes. Correspondence and papers
  Ms 71554 Collins Company, 1826–1867, 1 vol. Memoranda
  Russell, Mary, 1797 Nov. 5—1801 April 5. Diary, Middletown, typewritten copy
Connecticut State Library, State Archives, Hartford
  RG69.35 Wood, William J. 1836–1885, papers
  974.63 M58W Watkinson, John Revel, Account Books of John Revel Watkinson, 1806–1835
Middlesex Historical Society Library, Middletown, Connecticut
  Elijah Hubbard Account Book for 1801–1806
National Archives, Washington, D.C.
  Record Group 36, Middletown shipping records
Olin Library, Special Collections & Archives, Wesleyan University, Middletown, Connecticut
  Watkinson, John R. & Co. Records 1796–1819
Suffolk Records, Bury St. Edmunds, England
  Transactions of the Congregational Church of Christ in Lavenham
The Watkinson Library, Trinity College, Hartford, Connecticut
  Watkinson Family Papers
  Genealogy
  Miscellaneous Watkinson Family Papers, 19c.
  Watkinson, David. Business and personal papers 1803–1855, including Watkinson, Olivia travel journal 1819, 1820
  Watkinson, John Revel. Business papers 1795–1833, correspondence 1799–1826, Day Book
  Watkinson, Richard. Financial papers 1796–1798: letterbook, cash book, and letters received

Watkinson, Samuel Jr. Personal and business papers 1795–1798, including journal and letterbook

Watkinson, Samuel Sr. Personal and business papers 1757–1815, including Samuel Watkinson's Last Book of Accounts 1790–1816; letterbook, financial document

Yale Shipping Collection, Sterling Library, Yale University, New Haven, Connecticut

Miscellaneous shipping records

Periodicals

Connecticut Courant, Hartford

Middlesex Gazette, Middletown, Connecticut

SECONDARY SOURCES

Agnew, Jean-Christophe. 1986. *Worlds Apart: The Market and the Theater in Anglo-American Thought, 1550–1750.* Cambridge: Cambridge University Press.

Albion, Robert. 1961 [c1939]. *The Rise of New York Port, 1815–1860.* Hamden, Conn.: Archon Books.

Appleby, Joyce. 1986. "Republicanism in Old and New Contexts." *William & Mary Quarterly* 43:20–34.

Bailyn, Bernard. 1984 [1955]. *The New England Merchants in the Seventeenth Century.* Cambridge, Mass.: Harvard University Press.

Banning, Lance. 1986. "Jeffersonian Ideology Revisited: Liberal and Classical Ideas in the New American Republic." *William & Mary Quarterly* 43:3–19.

Barnard, Henry. 1858. "Memoir of David Watkinson." In *The Will and Codicils of David Watkinson of Hartford Connecticut,* by David Watkinson, 87–89. Hartford: Case, Lockwood and Company.

Batterberry, Michael and Ariane. 1973. *On the Town in New York from 1776 to the Present.* New York: Scribner's.

Beaudry, Mary, Lauren Cook, and Stephen Mrozowski. 1991. "Artifacts and Active Voices: Material Culture as Social Discourse." In *The Archaeology of Inequality,* edited by R. McGuire and R. Paynter, 150–91. Oxford, UK: Basil Blackwood Ltd.

Beckert, Sven. 2001. *The Monied Metropolis: New York City and the Consolidation of the American Bourgeoisie, 1850–1896.* Cambridge: Cambridge University Press.

Blackbourn, David. 1991. "The German Bourgeoisie: An Introduction." In *The German Bourgeoisie: Essays on the Social History of the German Middle Class from the Late Eighteenth to the Early Twentieth Century,* edited by D. Blackbourn and R. Evans, 1–45. London: Routledge.

Block, Fred. 1990. *Postindustrial Possibilities: A Critique of Economic Discourse.* Berkeley: University of California Press.

Bluett, Mary. 2000. *Constant Turmoil: The Politics of Industrial Life in Nineteenth-Century New England.* Amherst: University of Massachusetts Press.

Blumin, Stuart. 1989. *The Emergence of the Middle Class: Social Experience in the American City, 1760–1900.* Cambridge: Cambridge University Press.

Bond, Kathleen. 1989a. "'that we may purify our corporation by discharging the offenders': The Documentary Record of Social Control in the Boott Boardinghouses." In

Interdisciplinary Investigations of the Boott Mills, Lowell, Massachusetts. Vol. III: *The Boarding House System as a Way of Life,* edited by M. C. Beaudry and S. A. Mrozowski, 23–36. Boston: Cultural Resources Management Study 21. U.S. Department of the Interior, National Park Service, North Atlantic Regional Office.

———. 1989b. "The Medicine, Alcohol, and Soda Vessels from the Boot Mills." In *Interdisciplinary Investigations of the Boott Mills, Lowell, Massachusetts.* Vol. III: *The Boarding House System as a Way of Life,* edited by M. C. Beaudry and S. A. Mrozowski, 121–40. Boston: Cultural Resources Management Study 21. U.S. Department of the Interior, National Park Service, North Atlantic Regional Office.

Brenner, Robert. 1985. "The Agrarian Roots of European Capitalism." In *The Brenner Debate: Agrarian Class Structure and Economic Development in Pre-Industrial Europe,* edited by T. H. Aston and C. H. E. Philpin, 213–327. Cambridge: Cambridge University Press.

Buel, Joy Day and Richard, Jr. 1984. *The Way of Duty: A Woman and Her Family in Revolutionary America.* New York: W. W. Norton & Company.

Bushman, Richard. 1992. *The Refinement of America: Persons, Houses, Cities.* New York: Knopf.

Chatfield, Michael. 1977 [1974]. *A History of Accounting Thought.* Huntington, N.Y.: R. E. Krieger Publishing Company.

Clark, Christopher. 1996. "The Consequences of the Market Revolution in the American North." In *The Market Revolution in America: Social, Political, and Religious Expressions, 1800–1880,* edited by M. Stokes and S. Conway, 23–42. Charlottesville: University Press of Virginia.

Clarke, Marian. 1966. *David Watkinson's Library.* Hartford: Trinity College Press.

Cole, Arthur. 1926. *The American Wool Manufacture.* Cambridge, Mass.: Harvard University Press.

Collins Company, The. 1926. *One Hundred Years: A Brief Account of the Development of The Collins Company in the Manufacture of Axes, Machets and Edge Tools and in Commemeration of Its 100th Anniversary.* Collinsville: The Collins Company.

Comaroff, John and Jean. 1992. *Ethnography and the Historical Imagination.* Boulder, Col.: Westview Press.

Coogan, Timothy. 1991. "Mill Workers and Their World: Adams, Massachusetts, 1820s–1850s." In *Working in the Blackstone River Valley: Exploring the Heritage of Industrialization,* edited by D. Reynolds and M. Myers, 89–108. Rhode Island Labor History Society.

Cott, Nancy. 1977. *The Bonds of Womanhood: "Woman's Sphere" in New England, 1780–1835.* New Haven: Yale University Press.

Cross, Barbara. 1958. *Horace Bushnell: Minister to a Changing America.* Chicago: University of Chicago Press.

Cross, Whitney. 1950. *The Burned-Over District: A Social and Intellectual History of Enthusiastic Religion in Western New York, 1800–1859.* Ithaca: Cornell University Press.

Dalzell, Robert, Jr. 1987. *Enterprising Elite: The Boston Associates and the World They Made.* Cambridge, Mass.: Harvard University Press.

Daniels, Bruce. 1988. *The Fragmentation of New England: Comparative Perspectives on Economic, Political, and Social Divisions in the Eighteenth Century.* New York: Greenwood Press.

Davidoff, Leonore and Catherine Hall. 1987. *Family Fortunes: Men and Women of the English Middle Class, 1780–1850.* Chicago: University of Chicago Press.

Dawley, Alan. 1976. *Class and Community: The Industrial Revolution in Lynn.* Cambridge, Mass.: Harvard University Press.

Dickinson, H. T. 1985. *British Radicalism and the French Revolution.* Oxford: Basil Blackwell Inc.

Ditz, Toby. 1994. "Shipwrecked; or Masculinity Imperiled: Mercantile Representations of Failure and the Gendered Self in Eighteenth-Century Philadelphia." *Journal of American History* 81:51–80.

———. 2000. "Secret Selves, Credible Personas: The Problematics of Trust and Public Display in the Writing of Eighteenth-Century Philadelphia Merchants." In *Possible Pasts: Becoming Colonial in Early America,* edited by R. St. George, 219–42. Ithaca: Cornell University Press.

Doerflinger, Thomas. 1986. *A Vigorous Spirit of Enterprise: Merchants and Economic Development in Revolutionary Philadelphia.* Chapel Hill: University of North Carolina Press.

Dublin, Thomas. 1979. *Women at Work: The Transformation of Work and Community in Lowell, Massachusetts, 1826–1860.* New York: Columbia University Press.

Dudden, Faye. 1983. *Serving Women: Household Service in Nineteenth-Century America.* Middletown, Conn.: Wesleyan University Press.

Duffy, Michael. 1997. "The French Revolution and British Attitudes to the West Indian Colonies." In *A Turbulent Time: the French Revolution and the Greater Caribbean,* edited by D. Gaspar and D. Geggus, 78–101. Bloomington: Indiana University Press.

Faler, Paul. 1974. "Cultural Aspects of the Industrial Revolution: Lynn, Massachusetts, Shoemakers and Industrial Morality, 1826–1860." *Labor History* 15:367–94.

———. 1981. *Mechanics and Manufacturers in the Early Industrial Revolution: Lynn, Massachusetts, 1780–1860.* Albany: State University of New York Press.

Farrell, Betty. 1993. *Elite Families: Class and Power in Nineteenth-Century Boston.* Albany: State University of New York Press.

Field, David Dudley. 1819. *A Statistical Account of the County of Middlesex in Connecticut.* Middletown: Connecticut Academy of Arts and Sciences.

Foucault, Michel. 1979. *Discipline and Punish: The Birth of the Prison.* Translated by Alan Sheridan. New York: Vintage Books.

Friedman, Gerald. 1991. "The Decline of Paternalism and the Making of the Employer Class: France, 1870–1914." In *Masters and Managers: Historical and Comparative Perspectives on American Employers,* edited by S. Jacoby, 153–72. New York: Columbia University Press.

Gaddis, Eugene. 1985. "Foremost upon This Continent." *Connecticut History* 26:99–114.

Garrioch, David. 1996. *The Formation of the Parisian Bourgeoisie, 1690–1830.* Cambridge, Mass.: Harvard University Press.

Geary, Dick. 1991. "The Industrial Bourgeoisie and Labour Relations in Germany 1871–1933." In *The German Bourgeoisie: Essays on the Social History of the German*

Middle Class from the Late Eighteenth to the Early Twentieth Century, edited by D. Blackbourn and R. Evans, 140–61. London: Routledge.

Gilbert, Ann (Taylor). 1876 [1874]. *Autobiography and Other Memorials of Mrs. Gilbert (formerly Ann Taylor)*, edited by J. Gilbert. London: Henry S. King.

Gilje, Paul. 1997. "The Rise of Capitalism in the Early Republic." In *Wages of Independence: Capitalism in the Early American Republic*, edited by P. Gilje, 1–22. Madison, Wisc.: Madison House.

Goodman, Paul. 1966. "Ethics and Enterprise: The Values of the Boston Elite, 1800–1860." *American Quarterly* 18:437–51.

Gordon, Robert. 1983. "Material Evidence of Development of Metal-Working Technology at the Collins Axe Factory." *Journal of the Society for Industrial Archaeology* 9:19–28.

Gordon, Robert and Patrick Malone. 1994. *The Texture of Industry: An Archaeological View of the Industrialization of North America*. New York: Oxford University Press.

Grant, Ellsworth. n.d. *The Miracle of Connecticut*. Hartford: The Connecticut Historical Society.

Gray, Brenda. 1978. "The Mercantile Community of Middletown, Connecticut 1780–1820." Honors thesis, Wesleyan University.

Hall, Peter Dobkin. 1972. "Family Structure and Economic Organization: Massachusetts Merchants, 1700–1850." In *Family and Kin in Urban Communities 1700–1930*, edited by T. Haraven, 38–61. New York: Franklin Watts.

———. 1981. *Middletown: Streets, Commerce and People, 1650–1981*. Middletown, Conn.: Wesleyan University.

———. 1982. *The Organization of American Culture, 1700–1900: Private Institutions, Elites, and the Origins of American Nationality*. New York: New York University Press.

Hammond, Bray. 1957. *Banks and Politics in America from the Revolution to the Civil War*. Princeton, N.J.: Princeton University Press.

Hattam, Victoria. 1992. "Courts and the Question of Class." In *Labor Law in America: Historical and Critical Essays*, edited by C. Tomlins and A. King, 44–70. Baltimore, Md.: John Hopkins University Press.

Hazen, Azel. 1920. *A Brief History of the First Church of Christ in Middletown, Connecticut for Two Centures and a Half*. Middletown, Conn.

Heard, Nigel. 1970. *Wool, East Anglia's Golden Fleece*. Lavenham, Suffolk: Terence Dalton Ltd.

Henretta, James. 1991. *The Origins of American Capitalism: Collected Essays*. Boston: Northeastern University Press.

Hoke, Donald. 1990. *Ingenious Yankees*. New York: Columbia University Press.

Horwitz, Morton. 1977. *The Transformation of American Law 1780–1860*. Cambridge, Mass.: Harvard University Press.

Ignatieff, Michael. 1978. *A Just Measure of Pain: The Penetentiary in the Industrial Revolution, 1750–1850*. New York: Pantheon Books

Jaher, Frederic. 1995. "Review of Farrell, Betty, *Elite Families: Class and Power in Nineteenth-Century Boston*." *Journal of Interdisciplinary History* 26:141–42.

Jeremy, David. 1981. *Transatlantic Industrial Revolution: The Diffusion of Textile Technologies between Britain and America, 1790–1830*. Cambridge, Mass.: MIT Press.

Johnson, Paul. 1978. *A Shopkeeper's Millennium: Society and Revivals in Rochester, New York, 1815–1837.* New York: Hill and Wang.

———. 1993. "The Market Revolution." In *Encyclopedia of American Social History,* 545–60. New York: Scribner's.

Jones, Colin. 1983. "Introduction." In *Britain and Revolutionary France: Conflict, Subversion and Propaganda,* edited by C. Jones, 4–26. University of Exeter Press.

Kalb, Don. 1997. *Expanding Class: Power and Everyday Politics in Industrial Communities, the Netherlands, 1850–1959.* Durham: Duke University Press.

Kalb, Don, Hans Marks, and Herman Tak. 1996. "Historical Anthropology and Anthropological History: Two Distinct Programs." *Focaal* 26/27: 5–13.

Keller, Charles. 1968 [1942]. *The Second Great Awakening in Connecticut.* Hamden, Conn.: Archon Books.

Kerber, Linda. 1985. "The Republican Ideology of the Revolutionary Generation." *American Quarterly* 37:474–95.

Knight, Arnold. 1830. "On the Grinders' Asthma." *North of England Medical and Surgical Journal* 1:85–91, 167–79.

Koditschek, Theodore. 1990. *Class Formation and Urban-Industrial Society: Bradford, 1750–1850.* Cambridge: Cambridge University Press.

Kulik, Gary. 1979. "Patterns of Resistance to Capitalism: Pawtucket Village and the Strike of 1824." *In American Workingclass Culture: Explorations in American Labor and Social History,* edited by M. Cantor, 209–40. Westport, Conn.

———. 1985. "Dams, Fish, and Farmers." In *The Countryside in the Age of Capitalist Transformation: Essays in the Social History of Rural America,* edited by S. Hahn and J. Prude, 25–50. Chapel Hill: University of North Carolina Press.

Kulikoff, Allan. 1989. "The Transition to Capitalism in Rural America." *William & Mary Quarterly* 46:120–44.

Lebergott, Stanley. 1961. "The Pattern of Employment since 1800." In *American Economic History,* edited by S. E. Harris, 281–310. New York: McGraw-Hill.

Lee, Susan and Peter Passell. 1979. *A New Economic View of American History.* New York: W. W. Norton & Co.

Levy, Leonard. 1957. *The Law of the Commonwealth and Chief Justice Shaw.* Cambridge, Mass.: Harvard University Press.

Mann, Bruce. 1987. *Neighbors and Strangers: Law and Community in Early Connecticut.* Chapel Hill: University of North Carolina Press.

Martin, Margaret. 1939. *Merchants and Trade of the Connecticut River Valley, 1750–1820.* Northampton, Mass.: Department of History of Smith College.

McCusker, John and Russell Menard. 1985. *The Economy of British America, 1607–1789.* Chapel Hill: University of North Carolina Press.

McGaw, Judith. 1987. *Most Wonderful Machine: Mechanization and Social Change in Berkshire Paper Making, 1801–1885.* Princeton: Princeton University Press.

Merrill, Michael. 1977. "Cash Is Good to Eat: Self-Sufficiency and Exchange in the Rural Economy of the United States." *Radical History Review* no. 3 (winter):42–71.

Moore, Michael. 1990. "Roger and Me." A Dog Eat Dog Production. Burbank: Warner Home Video.

Muldrew, Craig. 1998. *The Economy of Obligation: The Culture of Credit and Social Relations in Early Modern England.* London: Macmillan.

Murphy, Teresa. 1992. *Ten Hours' Labor: Religion, Reform, and Gender in Early New England.* Ithaca: Cornell University Press.

Nash, Gary. 1979. *The Urban Crucible.* Cambridge, Mass.: Harvard University Press.

Nash, June. 1989. *From Tank Town to High Tech: The Clash of Community and Industrial Cycles.* Albany: State University of New York Press.

———. 1995. "Crisis in World Capitalism." *Meanings of Work,* edited by F. Gamst, 1–45. Albany: State University of New York Press.

Nassaney, Michael and Marjorie Abel. 2000. "Urban Spaces, Labor Organization, and Social Control: Lessons from New England's Nineteenth-Century Cutlery Industry." In *Lines That Divide: Historical Archaeologies of Race, Class and Gender,* edited by S. Mrozowski, J. Delle, and R. Paynter, 239–75. Knoxville: University of Tennessee Press.

National Trust, The. 1975. *The Guildhall, Lavenham, Suffolk.* Dorset: National Trust.

Nevins, Allan. 1923. "(Introduction) Travellers of the First Period, 1789–1825: Utilitarian Inquiry." In *American Social History as Recorded by British Travellers,* edited by A. Nevins, 3–6. New York: Henry Holt and Company.

Newby, Howard, et al. 1978. *Property, Paternalism and Power: Class and Control in Rural England.* London: Hutchinson.

Newmyer, R. Kent. 1987. "Harvard Law School, New England Legal Culture, and the Antebellum Origins of American Jurisprudence." *Journal of American History* 74:814–35.

Noble, David. 1984. *Forces of Production: A Social History of Industrial Automation.* New York: Knopf.

O'Brien, Jay and William Roseberry. 1991. "Introduction." In *Golden Ages, Dark Ages: Imagining the Past in Anthropology and History,* edited by J. O'Brien and W. Roseberry, 1–18. Berkeley: University of California Press.

Orland, Leonard. 1975. *Prisons: House of Darkness.* New York: The Free Press.

Pacioli, Luca. 1924 [1494]. *An Original Translation of the Treatise on Double-Entry Bookkeeping by Frater Lucas Pacioloi.* Translated by Pietro Crivelli. London: The Institute of book-keepers Ltd.

Palmer, Bryan. 1984. "Social Formation and Class Formation in North America, 1800–1900." In *Proletarianization and Family History,* edited by D. Levine, 229–309. Orlando, Fla.: Academic Press, Inc.

———. 1994. *Goodyear Invades the Backcountry: The Corporate Takeover of a Rural Town.* New York: Monthly Review Press.

Pessen, Edward. 1973. *Riches, Class and Power Before the Civil War.* Lexington, Mass.: D. C. Heath.

Porter, Glenn and Harold Livesay. 1971. *Merchants and Manufacturers: Studies in the Changing Structure of Nineteenth-Century Marketing.* Baltimore: Johns Hopkins Press.

Price, Jacob. 1974. "Economic Function and the Growth of American Port Towns in the Eighteenth Century." *Perspectives in American History* 8:123–86.

Prude, Jonathan. 1983. *The Coming of Industrial Order: Town and Factory Life in Rural Massachusetts, 1810–1860.* Cambridge: Cambridge University Press.

———. 1985. "Town-Factory Conflicts in Antebellum Rural Massachusetts." In *The Countryside in the Age of Capitalist Transformation: Essays in the Social History of Rural America,* edited by S. Hahn and J. Prude, 71–102. Chapel Hill: University of North Carolina Press.

Rediker, Marcus. 1988. "The Anglo-American Seaman as Collective Worker." In *Work and Labor in Early America,* edited by S. Innes, 252–86. Chapel Hill: University of North Carolina Press.

Rothenberg, Winifred. 1992. *From Market-Places to a Market Economy: The Transformation of Rural Massachusetts, 1750–1850.* Chicago: University of Chicago Press.

Rothman, David. 1971. *The Discovery of the Asylum: Social Order and Disorder in the New Republic.* Boston: Little, Brown & Company.

Roy, William. 1997. *Socializing Capital: The Rise of the Large Industrial Corporation in America.* Princeton, N.J.: Princeton University Press.

Rumbarger, John. 1989. *Profits, Power and Prohibition: Alcohol Reform and the Industrializing of America 1800–1930.* Albany: State University of New York Press.

Saladino, Gaspare. 1964. "The Economic Revolution in Late Eighteenth Century Connecticut." Ph.D. dissertation, University of Wisconsin.

Seed, John. 1993. "Capital and Class Formation in Early Industrial England." *Social History* 18:17–30.

Sellers, Charles. 1991. *The Market Revolution: Jacksonian America, 1815–1846.* New York: Oxford University Press.

———. 1996. "Capitalism and Democracy in American Historical Mythology." In *The Market Revolution in America: Social, Political, and Religious Expressions, 1800–1880,* edited by M. Stokes and S. Conway, 311–29. Charlottesville: University Press of Virginia.

Shepherd, James and Gary Walton. 1972. *Shipping, Maritime Trade, and the Economic Development of Colonial North America.* Cambridge: Cambridge University Press.

Sider, Gerald. 1996. "Anthropology and History: Opening Points for a New Synthesis." *Focaal* 26/27:127–33.

Sider, Gerald and Gavin Smith. 1997. "Introduction." In *Between History and Histories: The Making of Silences and Commemorations,* edited by G. Sider and G. Smith, 3–28. Toronto: University of Toronto Press.

Siskind, Janet. 1988. "An Axe to Grind: Class and Health in a 19th-Century Factory." *Medical Anthropology Quarterly* 2:199–214.

Smail, John. 1987. "New Languages for Labour and Capital: The Transformation of Discourse in the Early Years of the Industrial Revolution." *Social History* 12:49–71.

Smith-Rosenberg, Carol. 1985. *Disorderly Conduct: Visions of Gender in Victorian America.* New York: Knopf.

———. 2000. "Black Gothic: The Shadowy Origins of the American Bourgeoisie." In *Possible Pasts: Becoming Colonial in Early America,* edited by R. St. George, 243–69. Ithaca: Cornell University Press.

St. George, Robert. 1985. "Artifacts of Regional Consciousness in the Connecticut River Valley, 1700–1780." In *The Great River: Art and Society of the Connecticut Valley, 1635–1820,* edited by W. Hosley Jr. and G. Ward, 29–39. Hartford: Wadsworth Atheneum.

Steinberg, Marc. 1999. *Fighting Words: Working-Class Formation, Collective Action, and Discourse in Early Nineteenth-Century England*. Ithaca: Cornell University Press.

Steinfeld, Robert. 1991. *The Invention of Free Labor: The Employment Relation in English and American Law and Culture, 1350–1870*. Chapel Hill: University of North Carolina Press.

Stinchcombe, Arthur. 1995. *Sugar Island Slavery in the Age of Enlightenment: The Political Economy of the Caribbean World*. Princeton, N.J.: Princeton University Press.

Story, Ronald. 1980. *The Forging of an Aristocracy: Harvard and the Boston Upper Class 1800–1870*. Middletown, Conn.: Wesleyan University Press.

Strathern, Marilyn. 1982. "The Place of Kinship: Kin, Class and Village Status in Elmdon, Essex." *Belonging: Identity and Social Organization in British Rural Cultures*, edited by A. Cohen, 247–77. Manchester: Manchester University Press.

Thompson, Edward P. 1966 [1963]. *The Making of the English Working Class*. New York: Vintage Books.

———. 1978. "Eighteenth-Century English Society: Class Struggle without Class?" *Social History* 3:133–65.

Tilly, Charles. 1995. *Popular Contention in Great Britain 1768–1834*. Cambridge, Mass.: Harvard University Press.

Tomlins, Christopher. 1993. *Law, Labor, and Ideology in the Early American Republic*. Cambridge: Cambridge University Press.

Trumbull, J. Hammond. 1886. *The Memorial History of Hartford County, 1663–1884*. Boston: E. L. Osgood.

Twomey, Richard. 1989 [1974]. *Jacobins and Jeffersonians: Anglo-American Radicalism in the United States, 1790–1820*. New York: Garland Press.

United States Treasury Department. 1969 [1833]. *Documents Relative to the Manufacturers in the United States Collected and Transmitted to the House of Representatives, Vol. 1*. New York: A. M. Kelley.

Uselding, Paul. 1974. "Elisha K. Root, Forging and the 'American System.'" *Technology and Culture* 15:543–68.

Wallace, Anthony. 1972. *Rockdale: The Growth of an American Village in the Early Industrial Revolution*. New York: W. W. Norton & Company.

Watkinson, David. 1858. *The Will and Codicils of David Watkinson of Hartford Connecticut*. Hartford: Case, Lockwood and Company.

Wilenz, Sean. 1983. "Artisan Republican Festivals and the Rise of Class Conflict in New York City, 1788–1837." In *Working-Class America: Essays on Labor, Community, and American Society*, edited by M. Frisch and D. Walkowitz, 37–77. Urbana, Ill., University of Illinois Press.

———. 1984. *Chants Democratic: New York City & the Rise of the American Working Class, 1788–1850*. New York: Oxford University Press.

Williams, Raymond. 1977. *Marxism and Literature*. New York: Oxford University Press.

Winjum, James. 1972. *The Role of Accounting in the Economic Development of England: 1500–1750*. Urbana: University at Urbana-Champaign, Center for International Education and Research in Accounting.

Wittmer, Paul. 1977. "Early History of the Collins Company." In *Bicentennial Lectures, 1976,* 21–50. Canton, Conn.: 1976 Canton Bicentennial Commission.

Wolf, Eric. 1999. *Envisioning Power: Ideologies of Dominance and Crisis.* Berkeley: University of California Press.

Wood, Ellen Meiksins. 1991. *The Pristine Culture of Capitalism: A Historical Essay on Old Regimes and Modern States.* London: Verso.

Woodward, Patrick. 1892. *One Hundred Years of the Hartford Bank.* Hartford: Lockwood and Brainard.

Young, Jennifer. 1979. "John Revell Watkinson: 1772–1836: A Study in Early Industrial Development, Middletown, Connecticut." Honors thesis, Wesleyan University.

Index